Hot Stones & Funny Bones

Teens Helping Teens Cope with Stress & Anger

Brian Luke Seaward, Ph.D.
with Linda K. Bartlett, M.A.

HCI
TEENS™

Health Communications, Inc.
Deerfield Beach, Florida

www.hci-online.com

P9-EMQ-078

Library of Congress Cataloging-in-Publication Data

Seaward, Brian Luke.
  Hot stones & funny bones : teens helping teens cope with stress & anger
/ Brian Luke Seaward with Linda Bartlett.
    p. cm.
  Summary: Provides an inside look at ways in which teens cope with their
stress and anger, such as keeping a journal, meditating, or having a good
laugh, and includes advice for parents and other teens.
  ISBN 0-7573-0036-7 (tp)
  1. Stress in adolescence—Juvenile literature. 2. Stress management for
teenagers—Juvenile literature. 3. Anger in adolescence—Juvenile literature.
[1. Stress (Psychology) 2. Stress management. 3. Anger.] I. Title: Hot stones
and funny bones. II. Bartlett, Linda (Linda K.) III. Title.

BF724.3.S86 S43 2002
158.1'0835—dc21   2002068836

©2002 Brian Luke Seaward
ISBN 0-7573-0036-7 (trade paper)

Publisher: Health Communications, Inc.
            3201 S.W. 15th Street
            Deerfield Beach, FL 33442-8190

All inside photos by Brian Luke Seaward and Linda K. Bartlett
Cover and inside book design by Lawna Patterson Oldfield

For my niece and nephew,
Ashley and Ian Wall

and for
Holly Bartlett

Also by Brian Luke Seaward, Ph.D.

Health of the Human Spirit

The Art of Calm: Relaxation Through the Five Senses

*Stressed Is Desserts Spelled Backward: Rising Above Life's
Challenges with Humor, Hope, Courage and Love*

*Stand Like Mountain, Flow Like Water:
Reflections on Stress and Human Spirituality*

*Table for Two, Please: Morsels of Inspiration
over the Noon Hour*

Health and Wellness Journal Workbook

Managing Stress: A Creative Journal

*Managing Stress: Principles and Strategies
for Health and Well-Being*

Contents

Part III: Final Comments from Teens

One Thousand Thank-Yous!

This book was a huge undertaking. It would never have seen the light of day if not for the help of hundreds of people.

First and foremost, I extend my deepest gratitude to Linda Bartlett, who never once flinched when I told her I needed to find forty kids to interview for a book on teens and stress. Nor did she flinch when I handed her countless chapters for feedback. Linda, without you, this book would not have been possible. Many, many thanks!

Thanks always to my close friend and colleague, Mary Jane Mees, who gave priceless feedback on both the interview questions and each chapter throughout the entire writing process.

My deepest gratitude to all the wonderful teenagers, coast to coast, who offered to bare their souls through their interviews. It was such a delight to meet and spend time with each and every one of you. You guys are the best! Special thanks to the teens who submitted poetry, artwork and photos as well. Thanks, too, to the parents of all the kids who were interviewed, for granting permission to have your son or daughter be a part of this project!

I would particularly like to thank my friends and colleagues across the country who helped recruit sons, daughters, neighbors and any teenager they thought could give this book a national flavor, especially Mike Clow in Chicago, Lorelei Schlafhausen in Maryland, Joanne Hill-West in North Carolina, Mary Hall in Chapel Hill, Bonnie and Lee Knuti in Denver, Gail Wall in Vermont, Connie Dake in St. Louis, Karen Abbott in Maine, Mary Linda Landauer in Columbus, Steve Siders in Oregon and Joan Cantwell in Illinois.

A special thank-you to my assistant, Marlene Yates, who spent countless hours transcribing all the interviews (and got quite an education in the process!).

A hearty thank-you to the folks at Sunset Middle School in Longmont, Colorado, including Mike Gradoz, Dawn Macy, Shelly Jones, Karen Eggert and all the wonderful front-office staff, who made me feel at home whenever I walked in the front door. A special hug goes to Laura Sarff, who invited her students to contribute their art to the book—thanks, Laura, they're awesome! Kudos also go to Chris Rugg and Lisa Duffy at Silver Creek High School. Special appreciation to all the speakers in Health Quest, including co-facilitators Michelle Bowman and Cathy Baudar, Lana Leanord for the life story activities, and Susan Harvey for her crisis kit.

Thanks also to the staff at Niwot High School, including Don Haddad, Ella Padilla, Katherine Petri and Holly Asmuth, who were so generous in accommodating space for so many of the Colorado interviews.

A big hug goes to Suzanne Smith at Health Communications, Inc., who encouraged me to publish this book at HCI. Special thanks to Peter Vegso, who recognizes the importance of addressing the needs of teenagers. As always, thanks to Christine Belleris, Lisa Drucker, Susan Tobias and all the people at Health Communications, Inc., who nurtured this book from a dream to a reality.

To Randy Glasbergen, David Cohen and Jennifer Berman. Thanks for sharing your wonderful and priceless cartoons. They are fantastic! A wink and a smile to Raegan Carmona at Universal Press Syndicate and Jim Cavett at King Features Syndicate, as well.

The jokes in chapter 11, as well as the piece in "What Parents Really Teach," were sent to us by teens from around the country. If these are your creations, please let us know and we will give you credit in the next printing.

And a final thanks to Sandy Brooks, who planted the seed for this book in the summer of 2001 at the New Hampshire Celebrates Wellness conference. Sandy, when I told you I would try to find a book for teens about stress and anger, I had no idea I was going to write it. Thanks!

Preface

The poet Carl Sandburg once said, "Time is the coin of our lives. We must take care of how we spend it." How have you spent your life this past week? Have you been suffering from a migraine headache or an upset stomach? Have you been anxious about an upcoming exam, or worse yet, your grades? Have you been replaying the fight you had with your "former" friend over and over in your mind? Is it what your friend said to you that is keeping you up late at night, or is it what you *didn't* say?

If time is truly the coin of your life, have you spent your time well this past week? Are you well? Are you healthy? More importantly, are you happy?

Chances are, if you are reading these pages, the answer is "NO." If it makes you feel any better, please know that you are not alone! You are one of a multitude of stress-engulfed teens searching for relief.

Such a search has led many of my students to participate in a pilot project called Health Quest: A Stress-Management Seminar, in which health and wellness professionals volunteer to share their knowledge, strategies and techniques. That is how we met Dr. Brian Luke Seaward and how he came to interview my students and teens across the country about the many issues surrounding anger and stress management. Within the covers of this book are a collection of insights and ideas that he has shared with students in Health Quest.

If you have the opportunity to join others on a quest for health and wellness, do yourself a favor and join such a support group. In the meantime, this book is for you.

Ms. Linda K. Bartlett
eighth-grade teacher, Sunset Middle School,
Longmont, Colorado

The Cast of
Hot Stones & Funny Bones

In the fall of 2001 and spring of 2002, more than one hundred teens from across the country—Maine to California, Miami to Seattle—were interviewed for this book. Many more teens contributed poems and artwork. About half of the teens interviewed were from the Denver metro area; however, most every teen had recently moved to Colorado from elsewhere (including, to name a few states, Michigan, Illinois, California, Texas and Arizona). What you're not going to see when you read this book are the individual faces, voices, personalities and enthusiasm that textured each teen's comments. Many of the Colorado students are graduates of Ms. Bartlett's Health Quest class. The majority of interviews were conducted in person, and many more were conducted over the phone. Several teens e-mailed their friends, and soon letters and e-mails poured in from all corners of the country. All teens interviewed had the permission of their parents. All interviewees were sent a packet with an introductory letter, a consent form and a list of possible questions. Everyone interviewed was encouraged, but not obligated, to answer all the questions. Teens had the option to change their names and locations for any or all of their answers, giving them complete anonymity;

however, few did. (On occasion, names were changed to protect the teens or their parents.) Some parents, after reading the questions, chose not to have their children take part in the project. Several teens, parents, and middle- and high-school teachers were invited to read sample chapters to give feedback. Their comments and suggestions were invaluable and used extensively throughout the book. Thanks, everyone!

Introduction

Anger is like a hot stone. When you pick it up to hold or throw at someone, you get burned.

ANCIENT PROVERB

Howdy! If you picked up this book because you feel stressed, you're in good company. Everybody is stressed these days! Kids your age seem to have more than their share of it. Let's face it, it's not easy being a teenager in this world. You're definitely not a child, but in the eyes of your parents, you're not quite an adult.

While many adults may tell you that the teenage years are some of the best years of your life, these years often feel like limbo for many young adults. You're trying your best to fit in and be accepted at school, while also trying to make sense of the adult world you're about to step into. Not only that, you're learning more about who you really are, while also trying to please parents, teachers, coaches and everyone else who places demands on you. Let's face it, the teenage years can be very frustrating!

There is an old proverb that states, "Anger is like a hot stone. When you pick it up to hold or throw at someone, you get burned." If you were to talk to teens across the country, you'd find out pretty quickly that there are countless kids getting burned. Perhaps you have a friend who is really frustrated with some issues; perhaps you become frustrated yourself at times.

Suicide, anorexia, school violence, depression, drugs, alcoholism and racism are just some of the issues facing kids today. And while it's never been easy being a teenager, it's becoming more and more difficult to navigate the waters before adulthood.

As hard as the teen years may be, they don't have to be pure hell. There are many effective ways to cope with stress—ways that really work. One of the best is to have a good sense of humor (even if you think you don't have one!), which is where the funny bone comes in. There are other great ways, too, which is why this book was written.

Good stress management is common sense, but common sense isn't too common when people are freaking out. You may already know some of the things in this book, and that's great. Use this book as a reminder. There may also be some new things you never thought of before. Like a spread of food at a delicious smorgasbord, try the ones that look appealing and give them a shot. And remember, good stress management skills are good life skills at any age—but to have them serve you well, you need to practice them.

It's time to reclaim the teen years as some of the best years of your life. So put down any hot stones you may be carrying, flex your funny bone and let's go.

Part I

Telling It Like It Really Is

It's Not Easy Being a Teenager Today

My biggest stressor is school and the direction of my life, where I am going and who I am, because I'm not certain about this stuff.

JASON M., 14

Artwork by Eduardo Ramirez, Erin Tolooee and Matt VonLoh

Homework. Parents. Hormones. Stress! Clean T-shirts. Driver's ed. Facial hair. Stress! Menstrual cramps. Girl-friends. Boyfriends. Stress! Cell phones. School dances. Parent's divorce. Stress! GPA. Stepparents. Best friends. Dating. College applications. Body image. Double stress! Acne. Parent's marriage. Varsity basketball game. Stress, stress and stress! And this is all before fifth period! Whew! Add to this list the looming cloud of the Columbine massacre, school lock-downs, anthrax scares and September 11, as well as the rapid pace of technological development and teens who are lit-erally wired, and it becomes very clear that today's teens, the Millennium Generation, are living in a time of tremendous stress and tension. It has never been easy being a teenager, but with each passing year, it seems to grow increasingly difficult. Everybody has stress these days! And teens your age seem to have more than their share of it. Perhaps you've noticed.

By all accounts, the teen years seem like an endless transi-tion time from childhood to adulthood—with all the respon-sibilities and few, if any, of the freedoms. More than at any other period in your life, the teen years are an intense time of identity building—a time when you are constantly trying to figure out who you are, what you like and dislike, where your life is headed, what you want to be when you grow up, and what really makes you happy. There are all kinds of pressures coming at you: the workload from teachers, expectations from parents, expectations from your friends, the subtle yet powerful influence of the media, and God only knows what else. Throw some hormones into the mix, and the teen years become a powder keg of anxiety.

This book is a guide to help you navigate the often-turbulent waters of the teen years. Between the covers of this book are many ideas and strategies to help you make some sense of what's going on and actually enjoy this part of your life rather than dread it. Perhaps more important than the strategies are the thoughts and wisdom of teens from all over the country who have shared their insights. As one teen said, "I don't know if suggestions can help deal with stress, but the biggest help with this book is knowing that other teenagers are going through the same thing I am. That's where this book will help."

This book is divided into three parts. The first part, Telling It Like It Really Is, highlights some of the real issues that face teens today, from relationships and peer pressure to anger. The second part, The Best Ways to Cope with Stress, focuses on effective ways to cope with stress and anger. The third part, Final Comments from Teens, includes thoughts and reflections on various topics, including advice to peers and parents, concerns on the global environment, and pearls of wisdom learned along the way.

Honoring the proverb "To know and not to do, is not to know," this book's goals are to help you gain clarity on the issues that push you off balance while giving you skills and techniques to gain a sense of inner peace. So, in an effort to avoid information overload, each chapter is punctuated with passages called Thoughts, Reflections and Action Plan. These passages contain insights and questions to help you process the information better and build a successful strategy to minimize the stress in your life. So please, give yourself permission to write in the book to get the most out of it. Ample space is provided. Even if you don't feel like writing, browse through these sections to see if you really got the message.

Wonder, Wish, Become

It's hard to be a teenager today
Living in a world full of strangers
Not even knowing yourself
Wondering constantly
Will I fit in? You ask yourself
Can I look like that? You wish you could
And in the years ahead,
When all the answers find their way to you
There will still be questions
Should I have fit in? You ask yourself
Did I really look like that? You know you did
What will I become, you will always wonder.

Haila Ashley, 16

Identifying Your Stressors

Like many teens, Jennifer works hard at her schoolwork to earn good grades. She says that school is her biggest stressor, but if you talk to her for a few moments, you'd learn that her parents are divorced and there is also stress at home. On top of all this, her best friend was killed in a car accident last week. Jennifer is a bundle of stress. Her grief includes sorrow as well as anger. Her older brother, Ryan, is no stranger to stress, either. In addition to school, he's got varsity basketball and is juggling a part-time job. Welcome to the teen years!

It might seem to older people like the only responsibility facing teens is getting your homework done, but there are a zillion other things coming at you, from bomb scares and standardized tests to school dances and college application deadlines. Perhaps equally important to school grades is the circle of friends you have—or don't have. If these were the only problems, it might not be so bad, but as you might have guessed, there are deeper issues, including body image, cancer, bulimia, suicide, racism, alcoholism, sexual abuse and depression.

So let's take a look at what some issues are today and count yourself lucky if you cannot relate to them all.

Academic Stressors

Grades! School would be so much better without homework, quizzes, tests and report cards, wouldn't it? Perhaps in a fantasy world! Unfortunately, this is how things have been done for decades, so it might be best to go along with the system for now. If you have stress from schoolwork, take comfort in the fact that you are not alone.

Lacey, 14, Colorado: "Stressors? Homework! Being in the IB program, I get a lot of it. IB stands for the international baccalaureate, and basically, it's an advanced program so all of your main courses—English, math, science and foreign languages— go at a faster rate. By the time you get to your junior and senior year, you can earn college credit. (It's spread among all of your classes rather than just two or three.) Basically, it's accelerated learning. As a freshman, there is pressure to think about college because in some cases they look at your freshman GPA (even your eighth-grade GPA). If you're not at least at a proficient level, most colleges will put you at the back of their list."

David, 15, Illinois: "Homework is probably the really big thing right now. I'll get between two hours and three hours of homework on any given school night. On average, it's probably about two. On the weekend, it's probably about three hours. My school is very competitive academically, and there is pressure from my parents because they know I do really good in school, so I have to work to keep my grades up for them."

Alana, 16, Colorado: "I went from a private school where I had thirty kids in my eighth-grade class to a public school with six hundred kids in the freshman class. It was like a huge shock! There are so many more people here. It was good and bad in a lot of ways. All my friends changed. I had a girlfriend who I was best friends with since first grade, and now we aren't really friends anymore. Things happen like that. The teachers are a lot different. The classes are different. Just the amount of people and how everything is done are shocking. They give you a lot more homework, and expectations are a lot higher."

Reprinted by permission of David Cohen

Eric, 16, Arizona: "Homework. That's a big one, mainly because you have to get it all done to get a good grade. My parents really expect me to excel in school so that really motivates me to do a good job on my homework. It kind of stresses me out sometimes when I have a deadline, like two days for an essay or a school project."

Anjulie, 14, Colorado: "For me, school is the biggest stressor, especially the transition from middle school to high school. What I find stressful is trying to live normally, becoming an adult and acting responsible, but I guess my responsibility is just to be fourteen. I have other issues, including parents and everything else they bring upon kids. They try to cram as much knowledge as they can into you right now before you graduate and leave. It kind of bums me out, because I feel like I have to change so fast. It is like being torn between two worlds, being a kid and being an adult."

Thoughts and Reflections

Is schoolwork a stressor for you? What is it about schoolwork that frustrates you? Is it the amount of work, the difficulty of work or the lack of help from teachers?

_____

_____

_____

_____

A large part of stress management is good time-management skills, not making more time in the day (after all, it's only twenty-four hours), but using your time efficiently. First, try to identify four ways that time slips away (these are called time robbers, such as watching television).

a. _____

b. _____

c. _____

d. _____

Next, please identify four ways you can use your time more efficiently (like a designated time and place to study, etc.).

a. _____

b. _____

c. _____

d. _____

Schoolwork can be a stressor for everybody. Can you think of three ways to effectively cope with homework and school projects? One technique might be to use TV as a reward after all your homework is done. Can you come up with three more ideas?

a. _____

b. _____

c. _____

Acceptance Issues

The jocks, the cheerleaders, the IQs, the nerds and computer geeks, the skaters, the preppies, the outcasts, and let us not forget "the populars." No matter where you live, where you go to school, or with whom you hung out in grade school, in middle school and high school you are going to come face to face with the social class structure of the teen years. Let there be no doubt: This process can be brutal. Even if you're beautiful or handsome and your parents have lots of money, there are no guarantees. It's brutal! The good news is that by the time you're a senior in high school, there is a little less importance placed on this aspect.

At some level, no matter who you are, everyone's looking for acceptance and approval. In this case, it's acceptance to be liked by new friends and peers. Even among those who won't admit it, everyone would love to be considered popular. Appearance is about 80 percent of acceptance, but there are other factors in this complex equation. The most difficult factor and the wild card in the deck is the teen ego. Look out! Like an episode of *Survivor,* you could be voted off the island.

It would be impossible to like and be liked by everybody, but we can accept people for who they are without branding them as untouchables. The stress of being lonely is devastating.

Soma, 14, New York: "My whole life has been stressful because of all the verbal abuse that I get from other kids. You know, like being made fun of. I've had to deal with it my whole life. I'm a little overweight; that's probably why. That kind of stresses me out a lot. I try not to let it, but it always gets to me when people make comments to me or about me. Well, that's why I get made fun of the most. That, and because I do things my own way. I do what I like instead of what everyone else does. I wear the clothes I like. I listen to the music I like, and for some reason, that seems to bother some people. I don't know what their problem is, but they seem to have one with me. There are different groups in high school. They all mesh together somehow, I guess. The group I hang out with are not dorks, but they are people who are judged by their appearance, and so they have negative things said to them, like verbal abuse. It's kind of over now, but I used to get really, really depressed. I see a shrink and take Zoloft and Ritalin.

I've been sad most of my life because I didn't have any friends, but I'm good now."

Thoughts and Reflections

Acceptance by one's peers is perhaps the biggest concern teens have these days (even if they don't admit it). Acceptance includes issues ranging from the style of your hair and clothes to the music you listen to and the friends you have. Why do you think acceptance causes so much stress?

_____

_____

_____

_____

_____

_____

Between acne and hormones, everyone has days when they feel like the ugly duckling. (Remember the rest of the story? Every duckling grows up to be a beautiful swan!) List three times each week or three places you go where you feel accepted for who you are.

a. _____

_____

_____

b. _____

_____

_____

c. _____

_____

_____

Artwork by Jessica Podel

Kirby, 14, Colorado: "What stresses me out are mostly social issues in school because everybody pretty much stereotypes everybody else in high school. I don't think there is a single high school in the country where everybody gets along. There is a lot of social pressure on you to be what everybody else wants you to be. There are the cheerleaders, jocks and the smart kids. You just get a label put on you, and that's the end of it. I just pretty much try to make friends with different people, and I try not to be stereotypical and decide that I'm not going to talk to somebody because they are with that group or whatever. I've been trying to get away from that, and I've noticed that if you don't try to stereotype people, you won't get stereotyped as much. They won't look at you and decide you are with one particular group because you are hanging out with so many different people."

Thoughts and Reflections

What groups or cliques are at your school? What group do you associate with? Are you the kind of person who travels or floats from group to group? Do you judge or stereotype people who are not in your group?

_____

_____

_____

_____

Jon, 13, Colorado: "I get blamed for many things in school, just about anything wrong that happens. When there are problems with my friends, they always bring up my name. I think it's because I'm a skateboarder. The way teachers and principals act toward us is stressful. It just seems like they watch out for us all the time, as if we are going to do something bad at every moment."

Thoughts and Reflections

Acceptance from your peers is one matter; acceptance from your teachers and principal is another. There is a very good chance that your principal may not even know who you are, but your teachers sure do. How is your level of acceptance by adults in your life?

_____

_____

_____

_____

Problems on the Home Front

For some teens, school isn't a prison. It's an escape from prison! Time at school offers a break from some serious issues at home. In some cases, the home, which is supposed to be a safe haven, feels anything but safe, or perhaps simply it's in a state of constant flux. Part of entering the teen years is becoming more aware of a dysfunctional home life. These issues are not typically discussed with friends in the halls, bathrooms or locker rooms, often because of embarrassment or simply being overwhelmed. It could be that you learn your parents are getting divorced, or perhaps you come from a single-parent home. It could be that one or both parents have a drinking problem or an extremely bad temper. Regardless of the problem, school becomes a refuge.

Peter, 15, California: "My dad and I don't have a really good relationship, so we always fight about many things, which is an everyday occurrence. We really don't talk anymore. We just kind of lost our whole relationship. So I have to watch what I do around my house. I'm the only child, which is also a stressor because my parents place so many expectations on me. They focus entirely on me. Sometimes that can be annoying. My mom says that my dad and I are exactly alike, and if you put two things together that are exactly alike, they kind of repel each other. So everything that I don't like about him, I'm becoming. It's troubling to think that when I become a dad, I'll probably be like him. He has a lot of anger problems, and he does a lot of things that I don't really approve of him doing, like drinking. That kind of makes us not associate with each other. It's tough to be in the same house and not talking. I'm rarely home anymore. I just hang out with my friends or go to work or something. I don't really see him."

Thoughts and Reflections

Problems on the home front typically involve parents. How strong is your relationship with your father? Your mother? If it's not good, is it salvageable? Who in your family do you turn to when your relationship with your mom or dad is tense?

_____

_____

_____

_____

Lance, 17, Kansas: "I came back to school as a junior after being away for a year in drug rehab. While I was away, I missed all that time in school. There are ways in Paradise Cove to make up the schoolwork. Instead, I read books. When my mom came to get me, I hugged her and started crying. My family flew all the way from Nebraska to Western Samoa in the South Pacific—that's where Paradise Cove is, and believe me, it's no paradise. My mom said, 'Look who else I brought.' There was my sister, and that was a real treat for me. My sister and I were real close growing up. We just hugged and cried for a while. I hadn't seen them for more than a year, and that was a difficult adjustment. We had only corresponded through letters, and then a full year later, here they were, back in my life again. A lot can happen in a year's time. I learned my brother tried to commit suicide. My grandpa died while I was away in rehab. My grandpa was closer to me than my dad (my parents are divorced), and that broke me up. I cried for about two days over that, because I couldn't leave to get back to his funeral. I didn't even write to him while I was there, because I just wanted to come back and start fresh with him. Unfortunately, I was never given the opportunity."

Thoughts and Reflections

Chances are that you have not missed a year of your life on a South Pacific island like Lance, but in the rush of everyday life, there may be stressors because you don't have strong bonds with your family. Do you feel disconnected from anyone?

_____

_____

_____

_____

Anne, 13, California: "My parents got divorced when I was six. People often ask me, 'What do you do when you get home from school?' I just say that I do homework. They ask, 'Who do you live with?' and I say that I live with my dad all the time. He gets home at seven or eight at night. I don't switch off staying with my mom, like some kids do. I make dinner every night, and they think that is really weird. It's crazy to think about how much time I spend home alone. The thing that stresses me is that I had to learn to cook when I was six, and that's a real hardship for me. It's hard to live a normal life. It's weird to hang around with girls who have the best relationship with their moms. I don't have the best relationship with my mom, but my dad and I get along well. I think that as long as I have one good relationship, that works. My mom lives a few towns over, so I see her every once in a while."

Thoughts and Reflections

Some teens assume various roles and responsibilities when family dynamics change because of divorce, or perhaps when one parent travels frequently on business. Can you relate to this, and if so, how does it create stress in your life?

_____

_____

_____

_____

_____

_____

_____

Rob, 14, California: "My dad left my mom when I was two years old, so I don't really know him. Then my mom became very sick, so my grandfather raised me for a couple of years. I went back to live with my mom when she remarried, but my step-dad was physically abusive to me. At age eight, Social Services sent me to live with my grandfather where I lived for three more years. Then my mom died when I was nine. My grandfather developed some type of cancer, so I relocated again to live with my aunt, because it would have been more stressful for me to live with my grandfather when he was sick. So my life has been rather stressful because of all the different times I've moved. It's just kind of hard moving to a different community, and each time, it gets harder and harder. I've always felt like a visitor wherever I go. My father is still alive. I recently got a birthday card from him, and I actually have his telephone number, but I haven't called him yet."

Thoughts and Reflections

In the blink of an eye, your home situation can change. A parent dies, the remaining parent remarries, and you can feel like a stranger in your own home, if indeed it is your own home. If you care to share any thoughts about this, please take a moment to reflect. Also, how do you cope with this situation without feeling like a victim? How do you empower yourself?

_____

_____

_____

_____

_____

Gabrielle, 14, New York: "My biggest stressor has been my parents' divorce. It's been almost two years. It was just after my eleventh birthday. The divorce was awful. It was terrible! It took me a really long time to deal with it. I took part in this support group with some other teenagers whose parents were getting divorced at that time. I went through all the different phases, like denial—I couldn't believe it was going to happen. I kept thinking that my parents were going to get back together, because at first they told us they were just separated. Instead, they were really getting divorced. Then I was angry, because I felt they lied to me by getting my hopes up and letting me think they were getting back together. It took me a long time to get over the divorce, and still, to this day, it frustrates me.

"It started out so complicated with this weird living arrangement. I was with my mom on Mondays, Tuesdays and Wednesdays and with my dad Wednesday afternoons, Thursdays and

Fridays. Then they would switch to see who got me for the weekends. I was always changing houses. It was insane. So basically I said to them, 'I can't do this anymore.' Now, I'm on a one-week-with-him, one-week-with-her basis. Mom says that she thinks it would be best if I just stayed entirely with one parent, and she wants it to be her, of course. She feels that we should have a more permanent place. It would be easier for me and my sister to grow up and learn in a stable environment. I like the one-week-on, one-week-off arrangement, because I can't be without my mom for more than one week, and I can't be without my dad for more than a week. I like it the way it is now."

Thoughts and Reflections

There is a saying that nearly every family in America is dysfunctional, meaning that no family is perfect and some family member has a problem that affects everyone else. So if you can relate to this, consider yourself in good company. We may not have control of the cards we are dealt in life, but we do have control of our feelings. With more than half of marriages ending in divorce, many children are often left packing their bags every weekend and moving to another house. If you are in this situation, how does it make you feel?

_____

_____

_____

Do a little daydreaming and write about how you would like your family situation to look.

_____

_____

_____

Phuong, 14, Colorado: "I came to the United States when I was seven, and I didn't know any English. My dad fought in the Vietnam War. He was a POW for eight years. After he was freed, he was allowed to come over here. He was sponsored by the United States government because he fought with the United States. I liked coming here. I learned new things that I would never have learned if I were in Vietnam. Oh gosh, I got to know so many people, and when you are the new kid and you don't speak English, you have tons of friends. Everyone wants to be your friend, because you're different and you're strange to them. But . . . that's where I feel like I'm different from everyone else, because in my family, I translate for my mom. I'm the only one who speaks good enough English to translate for her.

"My dad works a split shift. We're not poor, but we're not living in luxury either. Right now my mom doesn't have a job because her shoulders are injured. If she raises her arm, it causes her severe pain. Much of my stress is cultural, but I feel like I have more responsibility and more stress than a normal teenager does. I've received straight A's since middle school, and the thing my parents tell me is that I have to be good because I represent the Vietnamese people. Some folks say that Vietnamese people are not very smart. I want to grow up and be successful and not have the same struggles as my parents. I work hard in school to get good grades. If I get a bad grade I won't go to college, and I won't get a good job. So little things become very big stressors for me."

Thoughts and Reflections

It's one thing to have your parents be immigrants. It's quite another to be one yourself. The expression "culture shock" doesn't even begin to explain all the stress that goes on behind the front door of your home. Are your parents immigrants? Are you an immigrant? Are you experiencing culture shock coming to America? Is your best friend suffering from the stressful shock of changing cultures, whether it's country to country, or just county to county?

_____

_____

_____

_____

After-School Stressors

What do you do outside of school hours? Do you play sports, surf the Internet, or just raid the fridge during commercials? If your hours outside school aren't occupied with making money in a part-time job, are you bored with life? Or freaking out with way too many extracurricular activities? The key to life is to find a sense of balance between too little and too much mental stimulation, so your threshold of excitement is satisfied. This goal of balance is a lifelong process. Getting a good handle on it now prepares you for a more balanced life down the road. Learning to entertain yourself can be stressful.

Aaron, 13, Colorado: "I would say what is most stressful for me is my hectic schedule. I have all sorts of after-school enrichments, Monday through Friday, with a small break on Wednesday. I have music programs with different instruments, I have church programs, and I have martial arts. I also get stressed out by standards; not just my parents', but all the ones I know I should be meeting at this level of school. Just trying to meet what I expect of myself is hard at times, but it's something I should keep track of. My personal ambitions are something I also really stress myself out about. I want to make it to law school and Yale. It's something that I've wanted since fifth grade, and so I've been reading books on the subject."

Thoughts and Reflections

How do you fill your after-school hours? Do these activities help you cope with the stress of school, or add to it? What goals have you created from your extracurricular activities?

_____

_____

_____

_____

By now, you have probably heard the expression, "All work and no play makes Jack (or Jill) a dull person." Do you live a balanced life between schoolwork and recreational activities? What activities do you do outside of school that validate you as a person (not just a student)?

_____

_____

_____

_____

Amanda, 17, Colorado: "The biggest issues would have to be my environment. The place I live, the people I live with, my friends and most definitely school. A surprisingly big stressor is the small, boring town where I live. I moved here from the city last year as a sophomore. Everything here is different. The way people dress, act, think (a lot of them are born and raised with small-town mentalities), and even the way they speak is different. Living in a small town makes finding something new and fun on the weekends practically impossible. Worrying about getting good grades is a huge stressor. If I don't, I may not be able to get into some of the colleges I want or do the things I want to do in life. What I accomplish now will, most likely, have a big impact on what will become of my future. There are other things that stress me out, like money and appearance and superficial things, but those are the ones with the biggest impact."

Thoughts and Reflections

What is your life like outside of school? Are you bored with life, or are you barely keeping pace with all your nonschool activities? If you feel like you have too much going on, it's time for some time management. Good time-management skills do not mean cramming as much as you can into twenty-four hours. Instead, the idea is to edit things to a reasonable level. If you are maxed out with things to do, what can you delete to achieve that sense of balance? If you are bored, what can you do to be satisfied?

_____

_____

_____

_____

_____

_____

Coping with Parents

Listen to the next conversation you have with your friends: Most likely the topic of parents comes up within the first five minutes. Parents aren't a stressor for every teen, but it sure seems like it sometimes. In fact, nearly every teen interviewed for this book mentioned their parents as a source of tension. Some parents are controlling and others are too lenient, yet most parents want the best for their child. Stress from the parent/teen relationship begins with expectations.

Heather, 16, Vermont: "One of the hardest things to do as a teenager is to please your parents. They want us to do everything their way, and you'd like to please them. But that doesn't always happen because I am my own person. I want to do things my way some of the time. As teenagers, we have to deal with peer pressure, which means pleasing not only our parents, but friends, teachers and even ourselves. We have to deal with harassment and finding where we fit in at school and in life."

Thoughts and Reflections

Do you find yourself in the trap of always trying to please your parents? How does this make you feel? How do you address these feelings? Do you ever sit down and talk about it with your parents?

_____

_____

_____

_____

Cindy, 14, California: "What gets me stressed? Schoolwork, outside activities, sex, and my relationships with my parents, friends and teachers. Want to hear more? Getting emotional about things. Relationships—whether or not I can be comfortable with this guy or that guy; if I do what they like, or if they are okay with the way I am. Will my parents like him? Relationships are so hard. My mom was sexually abused as a child, and my mom is really dominant at home. My dad is really quiet. It's like reverse psychology. Parents think that if they keep their children in, they are less likely to get into trouble. In a way, that can be true. But on the other hand, the kid is going to want to know what various things are about. So parents can't stop them. I think controlling parents create rebels."

Thoughts and Reflections

How well do you know your parents' backgrounds? They may not talk about it, but if they do, how have their life experiences affected you and your stress levels?

_____

_____

_____

_____

Michelle, 15, Colorado: "I think stress is anything you put against yourself as either self-motivating or basically 'sinking' yourself. Stress can be good, or it can be bad. It can even be normal stress, and the reasons vary every day. And let's not forget parents, because they expect you to be their baby, you know. They say, 'Oh, I want you tell me everything that is going on in your life. I want to help you in every decision.' Yet they tell you

you're an adult while they still want you to tell them everything. It's so hard, because you don't know what to tell them and what not to tell them. To be honest, any situation can make you stressed these days."

Thoughts and Reflections

Are your parents a cause of stress in your life? If they are, you are not alone. At best, parental relationships are hard. At their worst, they can be downright impossible. What kind of pressures do you feel from your parents?

_____

_____

_____

_____

_____

How is your relationship with your parents? Do you get along better with one than the other? What about stepparents? What is that relationship like?

_____

_____

_____

_____

_____

Peer Pressure

As you journey from childhood to adulthood, many opportunities will come your way. Some will be good and fun. Others will be dangerous. Most likely, your parents have already tried to warn you about this. They speak from experience, because they have been through it all before. But if you're like most teens, there is a trust issue between you and your parents, and this tends to lessen their credibility. Peer pressure is a huge stressor for teens. The need to feel accepted by friends is constantly weighed against the possible health risks and legal issues involved in an activity. Good personal boundaries are essential to dealing with peer pressure, but even having good boundaries doesn't take the stress of peer pressure away.

Morgan, 13, Tennessee: "It's hard not getting into trouble at school because of all the influences of friends. Everybody gets into trouble. It's the cool thing to get in trouble, but my parents say, 'No, you don't have to do that.' For instance, everybody is always smoking at school! There is pressure, and I've had plenty of chances to do that, but I don't. Boys are also very stressful, and there is pressure from them, too. People get so caught up in the 'he said, she said' stuff. Everything gets mixed up and people get mad, because so-and-so went out with so-and-so's boyfriend. People get mad about that and start fights. Today, two guys got into a fight over a girl. They both like her and want to go out with her. It's stupid!"

Brittany, 14, Illinois: "The biggest issues that stress me out as a teenager are sex and peer pressure. The reason I have a lot of stress is because sometimes I want to impress my friends, to be well liked by them, but they try to make me do things I would not normally do if I wasn't with them. So I do things anyway to impress them and be accepted. Most of the time I feel pretty bad after it's done, because I realize that, being caught up in the pressure, I cannot think for myself. I'm just another face in the crowd."

Pam, 16, Virginia: "I think school is a huge issue. There is a big effect on teenagers from the pressure of getting good grades, and of course, the expectation of going to college and the pressure that parents put on their kids to get good grades. There is also peer pressure to do drugs."

Thoughts and Reflections

Take a moment and honestly ask yourself if you ever feel pressure to do things with your friends that you wouldn't do by yourself. What does peer pressure mean to you? Is it having someone else influence you to do something you might not normally do, or is it a feeling inside of not being well-liked if you don't go along with the crowd?

_____

_____

_____

_____

Have you ever talked to your parents about peer pressure? Ask your parents for some help dealing with this issue.

_____

_____

_____

_____

Prejudice and Racial Problems

The human mind likes to place things in categories, and in the very early years, this is how learning takes place. You learn the difference between a horse and a cow, hot and cold, sweet and salty. As teens enter middle school, the ego turns these pattern recognition games into stereotyping. This sows the seeds for prejudice. The ego is quickly threatened by differences. However, the truth is, if we all looked alike, spoke alike, ate alike and dressed alike, we would be bored out of our minds. Cultural diversity is more than just eating a burrito, wearing a nose ring or listening to rap music. It is appreciating our differences as well as our common human heritage. Stress arises when people forget how boring life would be if everything was the same and instead start pointing out our differences, particularly when the prejudice is aimed at you.

Artwork by Noland Pickerell

Maria, 14, Colorado: "I get stressed sometimes because Americans sometimes try to antagonize Mexicans. When we go to lunch in the cafeteria, the teachers only see what we (the Mexicans) are doing, but never the Americans. The teachers always seem to take the Anglo side. I get kind of angry because, to me, that is racist. Sometimes the Americans try to speak Spanish so the Mexicans get angry, I think. Other times I hear the Americans say, 'Oh, this is America, so you have to speak English.' But I come from a Mexican family; both of my parents were born in Mexico. I was born in Los Angeles. We moved to Colorado five years ago. My dad speaks some English, but my mom doesn't speak any. Americans can be racist. Like if we are in a line to get food at a deli or something, the Anglos behind the counter always choose the Americans first. I think they shouldn't worry about the color and the difference between the Mexicans and the Americans. They should treat everyone the same."

Alonso, 18, California: "At some point you realize that life isn't fair. No matter how hard you try, you're gonna get stepped on, or worse, just ignored like you're not even there. This whole thing about tolerance is just an act, just lip service."

Mariko, 14, Colorado: "There is a stereotype about being Asian. The Asians are supposedly smarter than everyone else. It may seem hard to believe, but this is stressful because there is a lot of pressure. Education is a big deal in Japan; it's very cultural. I think if you were to take a look at it, you would realize that we work really hard at it."

Thoughts and Reflections

Do you feel racial prejudice from other teens in school? How does it make you feel?

_____

_____

_____

Do you harbor any feelings of prejudice (racial or otherwise) to others? Why do you suppose that is?

_____

_____

_____

How do the feelings you have differ from those of your parents, or are your attitudes about people from other races really your parents' attitudes?

_____

_____

_____

Depression and Suicide

Depression was once thought to be a serious health concern for only adults, but the number of teens on antidepressants today is overwhelming. Teen suicide is even worse! How do you know if you're depressed? Some people compare the feeling of being depressed to walking slowly underwater. Nothing seems funny; nothing even seems interesting. Food tastes bland.

Appetites drop off, or in some cases, food becomes a means to cope with stress. Colors seem muted, only the sad songs on the radio are appealing, and all you want to do is sleep. Everybody gets down in the dumps now and then; this is actually natural. But if you find yourself down in the dumps every day for several weeks, then it's time to get some help. Depression may indeed be a chemical imbalance in the brain (low levels of serotonin), and there are many reasons why this can happen. It could be the foods you eat. It could be a lack of acceptance in school. It could be factors related to family issues, or it could simply be from watching too much headline news. Chances are good that someone you know suffers from depression. It's that common. It starts with a day or two of feeling down in the dumps, perhaps a headache that won't go away or some other sign from your body that something just isn't right.

Gina, 14, Arizona: "I sometimes get headaches from stress; the bigger the problem, the more intense the headache. When I was depressed, stress used to make it a whole lot worse, and I would cry for hours because I was so stressed out. I have been depressed for almost my whole life. I never told my parents. I always thought it would go away. I kept telling myself that it's nothing, it's nothing, but it got worse and worse. It was terrible having that feeling. You are always asking yourself, 'What's wrong with me? What's wrong with me?' But you never can answer that question. It's really hard to deal with depression, and you are afraid to tell your parents because you think they are going to get mad or yell at you for not telling them sooner. Some parents don't know what to do, and most parents don't know how to deal with it. But for other kids, I just want to let them know that they will be able to get through it. Suicide or even hurting yourself (self-mutilation) is not the way out. I did attempt suicide many times. I just didn't see any point in living, and it was terrible. But I never could go through with it. I felt too bad for my family and my friends. Luckily, I started going to therapy, and they told me I had a chemical imbalance that could be fixed over time. I'm on medication now, and I am doing a lot better, but I still get headaches."

Peter, 15, California: "Kids in school can be really cruel. People are always making fun of me. I get called a faggot every day, or just a piece of *!#$ or something like that. My dad sometimes calls me a loser, too! I've never tried drinking, because my dad drinks too much. I'm afraid of becoming an alcoholic like he is. If my dad drinks, and his dad died from that, I'm probably going to become an alcoholic, and that can really mess you up and screw you over. It happened to my uncles. They had to go to jail because of alcohol. It's not the best thing to admire in your family. My dad beat me up once, not bad, but I told him my friends and I would beat the #$&! out of him if he ever touched me again. All this teasing and stuff made me feel like there was nothing good about myself, so I couldn't even see why I was here. I decided to take myself out. So one day when my parents were at work, I got home from school and I loaded a gun. (We have guns in the house.) I sat there and held it to my head, but I obviously didn't do anything since I'm still here. I just couldn't go through with it. I was too afraid, and I didn't see why I was doing that or why other people did it. I thought to myself, *If I actually do this, I'll prove that I am a loser.* The other thing that stopped me was that I told my friend I was thinking about doing it. He called his mom, and she called my parents and they came running home. My mom was really sad, but I didn't hear my dad really say anything about it."

Rain

It's one of those days when you just want to cry
Fall on the ground and scream you could die
The sky seems dark all around your head
Would it be better if you were dead?
Your tears fall like raindrops into your soul
Your world has begun to spin out of control
What you need is too far out of reach
There are so many lessons in pain you could teach
When you think about tomorrow, it's another lousy day
Sure you want a hint of happiness, but it doesn't work to pray
Maybe you can find what you are looking for
But one good thing would leave you wanting more
Why is your life so bad?
Why are you always sad?
Why must it be this way?
Does this rain have to stay?

Trisha Roiniotis

Thoughts and Reflections

If you have ever had a serious thought about suicide, know that you are not alone. Feelings of depression often lead to thoughts of suicide. Many things can lead to feelings of depression, from sexual and physical abuse to the foods we eat and the way we are treated by our peers at school. The first step in dealing with feelings of depression is to identify any possible symptoms you may be feeling. As best you can, make a list of factors that make you feel like you may be suffering from depression (feeling sad or blue, tired or fatigued, grumpy, overeating, poor appetite, sleepless nights headaches, backaches, upset stomach, poor concentration skills, feel like crying, low self-esteem, poor self-confidence and hopelessness).

a. _____

b. _____

c. _____

d. _____

The next step is to talk to someone about it, even if you feel this is the last thing you want to do. Logic would indicate that your parents would be the best place to start, but perhaps not. With your list in hand (see above), name three people (teachers, counselors, minister) whom you could turn to at a time like this, and then make a goal to meet with one of them.

a. _____

b. _____

c. _____

Having good friends to support you is one of the best ways to cope with the blues. You don't need a zillion friends, just one or two to help you get over the hump. Who are two friends whom you can trust with your innermost feelings? If you don't have a close friend, is there an adult you could turn to?

a. _____

b. _____

Friends: The Good, the Bad and the Ugly

Friends! You can't live without them. Sometimes it seems that you can't live with them. It helps to know that they, too, are going through the hormone thing, the parental thing, the dating thing, but jeez, it sure would be nice if they could be a little more stable when you need them to be there, right? Above all else, friends are THE most important thing in a teen's life. When things are good, they're great, and when they're bad, they're awful. Friends are such an important part of the stress equation, we have a whole chapter devoted to it, but here is a little preview:

Lacey, 14, Colorado: "Friends are great, but they can also be stressors. Friends are stressful because at this age people go through friends so fast. It's like one week you have a best friend who you hang out with all the time, and then you realize that you don't have a lot in common and they'll get mad at you or you'll get mad at them. You block each other out, and there are a lot of hurt feelings and all sorts of stuff. People are moving way too fast toward relationships and being sexually active. It can hurt."

Brent, 16, California: "What stresses me out is how people get mad at the stupidest things and totally blow things out of proportion. That really makes me mad. I might have said something that was totally meant one way, but they took it a different way. Like the time I asked a friend for help with a situation, and she blew up and said, 'All you do is ask me for advice. It's like you are using me for advice.' I said, 'Excuse me! I thought friends were supposed to help friends,' so I just walked away."

Aden, 14, Colorado: "Friends are a really big issue. What they expect of you and how you have to act around them is really tough. It's hard to be who they want you to be. Friends place certain expectations on you to act or feel a certain way. For me, they expect me to be there for them, and I try as hard as I can, but I don't do everything they want me to do. Then they get mad at me. My girlfriends always expect me to be a nice person and always have something nice to say. And if I'm not nice to them or if I'm mad, they wonder why or wonder what's wrong with me. I always have to be the same happy person. I have to be nice all the time."

Thoughts and Reflections

Friends can be your greatest joy and your biggest headache. How many friends do you have?

_____

_____

If you were asked to group your friends, (close friends, best friends, "sisters," lunch crowd, sports teammates), how would you do it?

_____

_____

_____

Planning to Go to College?

About the time you become a high-school sophomore, you begin to hear a question from parents and family members that goes like this: "Have you given thought to where you might like to go to college?" We are not even going to talk about the cost of going to college. That topic is depressing and merits a whole book in itself!

Going to college has become an accepted part of not only the American educational process, but the growing-up process as well. Until now (school vouchers notwithstanding), you pretty much went to the school you were assigned. With college, however, you have some choice. And with freedom of choice comes the responsibility to not only get good grades to be accepted, but to find schools you're really interested in, download the applications off the Internet and start writing those college application essays.

Kyle, 18, Tennessee: "The stress as a senior is different than the stress of being in middle school. Now my stress comes from not having enough time to do what I really want to do. I have a job and, of course, schoolwork, and I play soccer. I'm working on getting my college applications and deciding where to go, where to apply. There definitely is some pressure about going to college. But right now, I just feel like I don't have the time to do everything. At school, teachers tell you that it's really important to get these applications done (the essay is the hardest part) and turn them in by the deadline! Then they pile on lots of schoolwork as if you've got nothing else in the world to do."

Asia, 17, Colorado: "Right now, school is really stressing me out, just trying to keep my grades up. My dad went to an Ivy League school. He was valedictorian. I have a 3.8 GPA, so I have to make sure I stay really focused on my schoolwork and balance that with my social life, cheerleading and my friends. I just got back from California, where my dad and I looked at six different schools all along the coast. I even had one interview. Right now, I have until January. Then I need to figure out who I'm going to ask for my teacher recommendations and stuff. The whole college thing is very stressful."

Thoughts and Reflections

College has become an American tradition, and the expectations to go to college begin well before high school. If you are a junior or senior, you have probably given this some thought. Is there pressure from your parents to go to college? What stress do you feel about going to college?

_____

_____

_____

_____

Information seeking is a coping technique for dealing with stress, particularly the fear of the unknown. You may not know what you want to major in when you get to college (don't worry, many college seniors have no idea either), but if you think that going to college is in your future, start making a list of where you might like to spend the next four years of your life. Talk with friends, parents and your teachers. Every college and university has a Web site, so try surfing the Internet and see what you learn.

When you visit a college campus, try to meet with some professors or college students to see what they think of the place. Try to find a school that is a good match for not only your academic interests, but also your personal interests.

It's a Guy Thing!

Of course there's stress being a guy.
Take acne. You know you are supposed to have
a perfectly clear face, but who does?
And guys are supposed to be macho
and kind of thin and athletic.

CHRIS L., 14

Artwork by Svetlana Vladimir and Emily Shirk

L et's face it guys, it may not be easy being a teen these days, but in certain ways it's a whole lot harder being a male teen! There are hundreds of messages from society to be manly and macho, but at the same time, there are messages to be sensitive, caring and understanding. What's a guy to do? The last thing you want is to reveal too much about yourself by showing your true feelings, for fear of looking vulnerable to other guys. Yet this is exactly what the girls say they really want to see: a guy who's caring and sensitive. So in today's world, being a guy means either being a great actor or walking through life with a poker face. Either way, this image invites problems and possibly years of therapy down the road.

There was a time when a man's role in life was fairly well established. Back when television programs were in black and white, the man of the house was the provider, the breadwinner and the one who cooked meat on the barbecue. The woman raised the kids, cooked the rest of the meals and kept the house clean. Then came the feminist movement, and all the rules changed. Now women have more freedom in career choices, but no one really cooks anymore. Everyone just orders out or eats out, day-care professionals are raising the kids, and nearly everyone's on Ritalin, Prozac or Zoloft. And they still call this the American Dream.

All problems in life cannot be blamed on the male gender, but sometimes it sure seems that way. Most school violence is attributed to guys. More often than not, it's the guys who get in trouble at school for picking fights, roughhousing and all the other less-becoming behaviors attributed to the male gender.

This chapter takes a look at some of the aspects and issues of being a guy in the new millennium. It doesn't provide answers so much as give a snapshot of what it's like surviving as a teenage guy in these turbulent times.

Role Models and Heroes

There was a time long ago when young boys only knew their fathers, grandfathers and perhaps brothers as role models, people they looked up to and admired, perhaps even emulated. Much has changed in the past twenty-five years. Today there is about a 50 percent chance your parents are divorced, and your contact with your father is not as frequent as it might be otherwise. This social dynamic often leaves a hole in the fabric of male mentoring. Not having a good male role model is often cited for problems with today's youth.

There was also a time long ago when every young boy had a hero, someone of world renown who defied the odds of adversity and came back a winner. Abraham Lincoln, Jackie Robinson or Neil Armstrong come to mind. Today, American teens are sorely lacking in heroes. Instead we have celebrities, talented people and sports figures who earn their fifteen minutes of fame only to collapse under the pressures of their own stardom. It's a well-known fact that having a good role model, as well as a hero or two, helps contribute to your self-esteem. We all need a mentor to look up to and help guide us on our journey. Good heroes are hard to find today. Instead, we seem to have a lot of antiheroes (people who are celebrated for their bad qualities or morals; Luke Skywalker is a hero, Anakin Skywalker is an antihero).

Keegan, 14, Colorado: "I think having a role model for young boys is definitely a good thing because some kids are growing up in households that may not have a father, or they live with a step-father who is not a good role model. I believe having good role models can help you become a good person. They would stop you from doing certain things that hurt others, like teasing, which is not nice. People can get hurt, and I wouldn't want to be teased either. I think male role models are a good thing. If I had to pick a hero, I would choose my brother. He has really helped me, and he has always been there for me. I think guys tend to have better relationships with brothers than parents because we can be more comfortable with them. My brother lets me hang out with his friends, he takes me out to eat and to the reservoir, and he takes me to football games."

Lance, 17, Kansas: "Role models? I didn't really have any growing up. I had no one I wanted to emulate. I didn't really grow up with a father figure. I didn't know what it meant to be a man. I looked up quite a bit to the guy who actually got me into drugs. We met at church. He was a spiritual mentor as much as he was a friend. He was older than I was. He was someone I could look up to. That may have been part of why I was so easily swayed into drugs, because I looked up to this guy. For me, he was kind of a hero. One day he said, 'Hey, these are drugs, they're cool.' So I thought, *Hey, if he likes them, I should, too, I guess.* Big mistake!"

Dave, 14, Illinois: "I would say my dad is my hero. He has a big influence on my life, and I live in his house. We talk and have fun the majority of the time. We do a lot of things together, like every Christmas we put up a train track because he has done that since he was a little kid, and so now I do it with him. We'll go hunting together. Whenever possible, he tries to come to any sports I'm involved in. And if he isn't doing anything, and I'm not doing anything, we'll play a little sports outside. We'll throw the football around."

Brandon, 13, Maryland: "I don't know if you will understand this, and I know she is not a guy, but my mom is my hero because she is always doing good stuff for me and my stepdad. She is always trying to make life easier for me. I think my mom is the best person I know. I also want to say that my dad is one of the best friends I could ever have."

Jackson, 14, Nebraska: "I don't have many heroes. There is one, Rodney Mullen; he's a skater. I do look up to my parents. I know they'll push me sometimes to do things, and I'll look like I don't really care about them, but I always look up to them for advice because I know they care and they are only trying to help me."

Harris, 14, Colorado: "I really don't have any heroes. There are probably actors and singers, and TV and sports stars that some people look up to. Some of them are good, and some are not. Some baseball and football players get in trouble and do weird stuff, and that's not good. Some movie stars can look good on the outside but are bad on the inside. In general, I suppose they all try to be good people, but I wouldn't call them role models or heroes."

Joe, 13, Colorado: "I would probably say my grandpa is my hero. I look up to him because he is pretty strict and came from a tough childhood and a very poor family in Mexico and became a doctor. I think he's kind of a role model. I don't think I have any role models from TV or anything like that because I can't talk to them."

Kyle, 18, Tennessee: "Do I have any heroes or role models? Not really! I like Landon Donovan (a soccer player) because he's really young, but I wouldn't call him a hero. He's only nineteen.

He plays in the National Soccer League. It's pretty amazing that someone who is only nineteen can be that successful."

Kyle, 15, Colorado: "The drummer from the group Mudvayne. He's a very good drummer, and I always like to practice to him. I've met the other guys in the band but not him. They say he's like a little hermit crab. I met the band on the Pledge of Allegiance tour. I got there really early so I could meet him. When all three other members walked up to me, I hoped I could talk to him, but the guy I wanted to meet just ran inside. I was told, 'He's a little hermit crab. He won't talk to anybody.' So that was kind of disappointing because he was actually the only one in the band I wanted to talk to. I don't really have that many role models."

Thoughts and Reflections

Do you have a role model or hero? List three people who you look up to and admire, and describe why.

a. _____

b. _____

c. _____

Expressing Your Emotions

Love and Passion

There is a feeling that strikes the heart of all people.
It is a strong emotion that makes people express the true person they are.
This feeling is brought out by what you deeply show toward one another.

The way you caress them and look at them with a deep
 broadness in your eyes.
This certain feeling can either be painful or joyful in a sense
 that you cannot let go from the direction your heart leads
 you.
It is a spell that can only be broken when the ship of your
 emotions sets another course of destination.
It is hard to explain the elements that make up this equation.
It is the first sight, first smell, first taste and sound of your
 want for them.
Every time you fall into the trap, you have two ways out.
One is to follow the dreams that you feel and live, or deny
 the act as if it were tricked upon you.
The feeling is strong and powerful, as it owns its very own
 source and empire among all beating hearts over the universe.
It is the building block for a man and woman, to add levels of
 feeling and tranquility as they go along.
So when you get struck by this certain feeling of love and
 passion, think of these words, for they may keep you aware
 of the direction your heart points.

Noah Rhodes, 16

Sentiment

Seas of secret sentiment
Hidden in the mist
Heaven never did lament
Our wishes to exist
An angel falls across the rain
And takes away the sky

Tears away like cellophane
And never to rely
Who are we?
Lurking silently behind our secret walls
SENTIMENT

Jason McKee, 15

The last thing in the world a guy wants is for anyone to attack his masculinity. After all, as a teen, this is the core of your identity and what separates you from being a girl. Hearing the words "fag," "pussy," "wimp" and "fairy" make any guy cringe. So it stands to reason that the hardest part of being a guy is knowing what emotions to express and when best to express them. You want to come across as caring, but not too caring (that might be construed as feminine). You want to come across as assertive, but not aggressive because that will earn you a trip to the principal's office and possibly get you thrown out of school. Somewhere between machoism and sensitivity there has to be a balance. Here is how one teen stated it: "I realize that I care about others' feelings more than I let on. I think that I have more of a sensitive side than most guys would want to admit, but this is by no means a bad thing. I also realize that I have a great distaste for violence against another human being. I strongly believe that violence is a way for guys who don't know how to deal with their feelings properly to relieve themselves of this perceived negative."

Perhaps the biggest issue regarding fully expressing one's emotions, especially the emotions of fear and love, is trust. To really confide in your buddies, or even your parents for that matter, you have to trust they are going to totally accept you.

Situations in which your girlfriend breaks up with you, your parents decide to end their marriage or someone close dies are not trivial matters. Talking to your guy friends, girlfriends, friends who are girls and parents is one way. Another way (although it's not common) is writing down your thoughts (essays, poems) or creating song lyrics. The end of this chapter has some more poems that speak from the heart and soul.

Kyle, 15, Colorado: "Do I show my feelings? Sure, I do. I've cried in front of my friends. Sure, I've done that. I probably wouldn't do it in front of one hundred people because I'm really a shy person. But I do show my emotions. I've shown them to my girlfriend. I've shown them to my parents. I've shown them to a lot of people. If guys can't show that, then they're kind of insecure about everything they do. They're once again worrying about what people are going to say about them. If someone makes fun of me for crying, I'm just going to deal with it. I'll just say, 'Screw you. I'm glad you feel better about yourself now.'"

Keegan, 14, Colorado: "I think it's definitely okay to show your emotions. I think it should be okay for guys to show their emotions anywhere. I think it is morally wrong to make fun of someone who is hurting. Heck, if you want to cry, cry! Did you see the firemen and the policemen crying on TV on September eleventh? It gave permission for every guy to cry. So it's okay to cry! Some guys hold it in and wait until they're by themselves so they can cry alone. I say, 'Just let it out.'"

Jackson, 13, Colorado: "If guys show their emotions (like crying or something like that) they usually get made fun of, unless it's about something really bad. That's why guys don't do it."

Sean, 18, Michigan: "It's great if guys can express their emotions well. It's healthy, and everyone—whether they're male, female, young or old—should have a keen sense of their emotions and shouldn't be afraid to express those to others. On the other hand, I do feel that disclosing too much or expressing too many emotions can be unhealthy, mainly for relationships you're in, not particularly for yourself. Also, if you cry constantly and you're always upset, that isn't healthy for anyone or anything."

Joe, 13, Colorado: "I think it's impossible to talk about your feelings with other guys because they might think of you as a sissy. You know what I mean? Now women, they can do that a lot better with themselves, even with somebody they've known for two days, because they tell each other their life stories. Guys just don't do that. Guys are kind of doing their own thing."

Chris, 14, Colorado: "It's okay to show anger and frustration, but not fear or sorrow. There are times I feel like I want to cry, kind of, but not in front of my friends. Guys just don't want to make other guys think they are vulnerable, because once that happens, they take advantage of you and pick on you."

David, 14, Illinois: "I don't like showing my emotions in front of people. There are a few close friends I know and who have known me for a really long time and are real close to me, and I'm real close to them. I don't mind showing my emotions in front of them. So if I'm around people I know, I show my emotions more, but if I'm not really close to them, I don't show my emotions."

Pablo, 13, Colorado: "You know what I think it is? I think guys just want to keep their macho look. They feel they will be laughed at if they show their emotions. Usually, if they get hurt, they'll keep it to themselves. Now, when guys are home alone they let out their emotions, and they might even cry."

Ryan, 16, Florida: "It's okay for me to show my emotions to some people, like with my mom. It's all right to show her my emotions. And sometimes it's all right to show my emotions to my dad, but he doesn't really understand it very well. With good friends it's okay, but it's not okay at school. I try to let out my good emotions, but my sad emotions I keep to myself a little bit."

Thoughts and Reflections

Describe two ways that you feel best express your emotions.

a. _____

b. _____

Stranger

For just a moment, a stranger
Rests her head upon my shoulder
Am I to push her away?
Am I supposed to scold her?
I've spent so many years
In yearning for this touch
I've honestly wanted to die
Because it hurt so much
And whenever I reached for love
Whatever "stronger force above"
Chose to throw me right back down
And when I smiled at you, you frowned
So though this touch is out of place
It feels to me like love's embrace

Jason McKee, 15

Understanding Girls

For the most part, boys and girls get along rather well until the hormones start kicking in. Once puberty hits, all the rules change. In fact, it takes years just to figure out what the rules really are. No one ever said understanding the opposite sex was easy, and there is no guarantee you'll have this puzzle solved by high-school graduation (sorry guys, even your dads are still working on this one!). If it's any consolation, the girls say they don't understand you either. Some girls want attention, some want affection, and some just want to be left alone. What's a guy to do? You can spend great hours on the phone or the Internet and still be as confused as ever. But hang in there guys, don't give up, because eventually the right girl (woman?) is going to come along and make it all worthwhile.

Rob, 14, California: "What stresses me out? Among other things, besides friends and parents, if you're a guy, it's girls, girls, girls!"

Tom, 15, Colorado: "Girls most definitely stress me out. Sometimes you see a girl you're attracted to, and you're not sure if you should ask her out or ask her to the dance because you're not sure what she's going to say—you know, all that stuff. I liked a girl back in Illinois and she liked me back, but we didn't officially go out. At this age, I'm not really sure what qualifies as 'going out.' I'm just as confused about it as I probably ever will be. I suppose going out is just a way to get to know a person better. Like, you want to just focus on that person for a while and get to know them. And if it works out, that's great and you keep going and you build your relationship on that. If it doesn't, you don't get too involved at the time."

Phillip, 16, New York: "I don't get it. They try to be so grown-up, it can be annoying. All they talk about are clothes, fashion and makeup; some girls practically drown in makeup."

Jesse, 18, Colorado: "Girls are as confusing as hell at this age. I'm giving up. I'm going for older women. I can't take high-school girls any more. They act like they are interested in you, or they'll be interested in you for a while, and then it will start to fall apart. One day they'll come out of the blue and say, 'I don't like you anymore.' Then you say, 'Why?' And they reply, 'I don't know.' Take this last girl I went out with. After two days she dumped me because she was getting crap from people for seeing me. People I didn't even really know. So she broke up with me. She still acted like she liked me. Then she started acting kind of bitchy and mean about things, and it's just been going downhill ever since. We were good friends before. It seems like just when I get something going it gets shut down. I have bad luck with women."

Joe, 13, Colorado: "Girls are definitely a stressor, mostly because guys are trying hard to impress them, and it's a losing battle. Most guys I know are trying hard to impress them, so they goof off in school, get bad grades in their classes and that kind of crap. Doesn't make sense to me! As for me, I just try to stay away from girls. They're trouble! They cost money, especially the popular ones. They want you to buy them things or give them money to go shopping. Girls are expensive."

Tim, 13, Illinois: "Girls can be tiresome. Last year, for example, one girl liked me a lot, and all throughout the year she'd give me candy and send me roses and stuff. It was really annoying. She knew I didn't like her, and I tried to stay away but that didn't help. So she'd bring flowers to the school. I would just give them back to her, because I didn't want her to waste her money."

"The real girls I know aren't as cool as
Cybergirls, mom. Real girls don't talk to me!"

©Reprinted with special permission of King Features Syndicate.

Eric, 15, Colorado: "Well, in defense of girls, they have their time of the month, and then they are really testy. You just want to not mess with them at that point in time. My advice is to stay away, give them some room and be careful of what you say. By far, girls have more stress than guys do because they are really emotional, and sometimes their emotions get carried away in times of stress."

Take My Hand

Take my hand and come along
Do not fear the coming dawn

It's all right. I see it in your eyes
The rain will fall and I will hold you
Finally I will have told you
Everything, and we will watch the skies.
Wide awake, I'm in my bed
The world banging in my head
It wasn't real, I should be dead
I don't want this at all
And though I hold you, oh, so dear
You're always far and never near
And the only reason you are here
Is to watch me fall.

Jason McKee, 15

Expectations of Being a Guy

Like everything else, certain expectations are included with being a guy. Aside from being well-behaved, doing the chores around the house and possibly earning some money for college, other subtle pressures and expectations loom overhead. These expectations come from society, adults, parents and other guys.

David, 14, Illinois: "It's not really a big thing for me, but for other people, it's like the 'look.' Guys worry about how they look and what they're wearing. For me, I still kind of dress in what everybody else is wearing, but I don't go to the limits to look as up-to-date as possible. If the 'look' changes, I don't go out right away and buy a whole new wardrobe like other kids do. I'm not into fashion that much, but I'm into it enough that I don't look *out there*."

Aaron, 13, Colorado: "In my case, my parents set high expectations. They keep very high standards for me based on what happened to my older brother, who's in college now. They hold really high standards and expectations that sometimes I don't agree with, but I know in the long run it will be worth it. My family's got a long line of overachievers. My brother got a perfect score on his SATs. He came really close to a presidential scholarship. He made it to the semifinals and got a national merit scholarship. There are also cultural expectations. My father's family dates back more than two hundred years to China, before they immigrated to Malaysia. Then, when my dad was fourteen, he moved to New Zealand in the exchange program. He studied engineering there and also got his master's in engineering. Then he moved to California, where he met my mom, who was from Korea. She had decided to leave home and start a new life in California. They have passed on a legacy of academic excellence, and at times, that's pressure."

Adam, 17, Connecticut: "I always thought you were a man when you turned eighteen, but I think there is definitely an expectation to be a man before then. Not just how you look or if you shave (I can only grow a football mustache—eleven hairs on each side), but financially and all that. It's tough to step out on your own."

Jesse, 18, Colorado: "There are certain expectations from society regarding teenagers. Like most adults, when you're walking around town, some people you don't even know give you these weird looks. They expect guys to be perfect, but we're not. I think they forget their teenage years and what they tried to get away with. We're not stupid! We know most of you guys did most of the same stuff that we're doing, if not more, especially back in the sixties!"

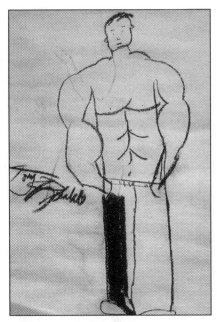

Artwork by Tony Robledo

Brad, 17, Oregon: "Even though times have changed some, I think there is still this expectation that, as the guy, you have to have the better job than your girlfriend or your wife—you've got to be the major breadwinner. I know guys who moved home after college just to save money. They're twenty-five, and they're still living at home."

Thoughts and Reflections

What expectations make it hard to be a guy?

a. _____

b. _____

c. _____

Coping with Bullies

Bullies have been around since the day Cain killed his brother Abel. Kids have been picking on other kids ever since. Bullying can be as simple as tossing snide comments toward unsuspecting individuals to shoving someone in his locker for not handing over his lunch money. The worst-case scenario is what happened at Columbine High School and other schools across the country where violence erupted, turning schools into mass casualty sites. So far as we know, scientists have not located the "bully" gene in DNA, and most likely they never will. Ask any teen about bullies in school and they will tell you that bullies are jerks, insecure people who pick on others to make themselves feel good. These people should be avoided and ignored, and that seems to be the consensus on how best to deal with them. The sad truth is that kids labeled as bullies are most likely the kids neglected by their parents. Deep inside they are lonely, and some have no real friends.

Chris, 16, Vermont: "At school, I tend to stick with people I feel comfortable around and who I'm not having problems with. I don't get along with the school bullies, so I avoid them. There are all kinds of groups in school: the geniuses, the preppies, the jocks, the regular guys like me and, of course, the bullies. I'm in the everything group."

Rob, 14, California: "The whole violence thing is just hard to explain. There's no logic to it. There's no reason for these guys to do what they do. Some people say the reason they act this way is fear or envy or stuff like that, but I don't buy it. I don't know what it is, but if I had to make an educated guess, I don't think that's it. If you ask me, the gene pool needs a better lifeguard. The way I deal with these jerks is I try to ignore them."

Tom, 15, Colorado: "I know a couple of kids who aren't so much bullies as they are jerks. They're in my science class. They're smart alecks. They like to play jokes on people, but sometimes it can really hurt. If they're picking on someone, I'll say, 'Hey, guys, lay off.' Then sometimes I'll just say, 'Whatever, just get away from us.' Sometimes they might stop. It just depends on what kind of a mood they're in that day. Other times, I'll confront them and say, 'Shut up,' or yell at 'em, but it's not like I'm going to punch them or anything. From what I can tell, in high school the bullying is more psychological, more egotistical."

Thoughts and Reflections

How do you cope with the other guys in school who act like bullies, idiots or just plain jerks?

_____

_____

_____

Sexual Maturity

There is a joke in Hollywood, and it goes like this: Years ago teens would go to the movies and watch adults having sex; now adults go to the movies and watch teens having sex.

All it takes is a quick surf through the television channels to see that sex is a big part of programming. Hollywood sends a mixed message, at best, about freedom and responsibility. At some point in their teens, guys are faced with the issue of sexual maturity, and there is no shortage of mixed messages from all sides. Parents, teachers and ministers tell you to wait, while the media, from television shows to commercials, send a message that it's okay to "explore." There is still a double standard among girls and guys: Girls are supposed to be virgins, and guys are supposed to be experienced. So they don't look foolish, guys talk about doing it, even though all they're doing is just talking. Insecure feelings about sexuality and talking to compensate for it are as old as time itself.

Philip, 15, California: "There is talk about sex in school, but I don't really pay attention, 'cause my dad is really strict about that kind of stuff. He won't let me date until I'm sixteen. He says, 'Don't get a girl pregnant, or I'll kill you.' I think if that ever did happen, my dad would beat me up. Guys talk about things like this at school, but pretty much they are just joking around."

Eric, 15, Colorado: "Well, in my opinion, there is never real love at age fifteen. I think there are just conquests. Guys are just curious and trying not to look embarrassed. If guys are talking about sex, most are just lying and trying to be cool. I don't know how that makes you cool, but that's what they do. But they are trying to do that by telling you that they slept with someone last weekend or last night, and they are going to do it again tomorrow night. I don't really care. They don't go into detail about it so I don't know. I would assume that they use precautions, but I don't know. Guys don't really talk about that."

Harris, 15, Colorado: "I think guys talk more about sex than actually do anything. They want to feel like they're the cooler person by talking about it. I just let that go. I feel like whatever way you want to feel, go ahead, I don't care."

Keegan, 14, Colorado: "I think the popular media puts a lot of pressure on girlfriends and boyfriends. The message they give is, 'Oh, I made out when we went to the movies, or I bet I've had more girlfriends than you.' Or, 'Oh, you're still a virgin?' They act totally obnoxious. It's big pressure. I just think it's stupid, because you're not showing how great you are by making out with a girl. Kids having sex at a young age is not a good choice. If you have a girlfriend and you have sex with her and she gets pregnant, you are going to have to provide for the baby, or your parents are going to make you provide for the baby. The best thing is to either wait until you are married or until you are out of college, so that you are on track with your life and have a good job. I had a friend who had a baby at eighteen and had to get married. He had to quit school and support the baby. He said to me, 'Don't have sex until you are out of college and you at least know what you want to do with your life.'"

Blake, 14, Oregon: "Some guys just talk big so people think they are cool or macho. They talk a lot just to be cool. I heard in some high schools that jocks have a competition to see how many girls they can actually sleep with. I think that when people have sex at a young age and start blabbing about it, it doesn't put pressure on them, but it puts pressure on the girl. If the parents find out, it's just going to be hectic, like, 'You had sex. You shouldn't have sex right now, and you're grounded and can never leave the house.' People might scowl because you were this nice, good person, and you had sex. All of a sudden people are saying, 'You're not good. You're just a girl who likes to go out and have sex with everyone.'"

Eric, 14, Illinois: "There's some peer pressure that is really hard to resist. For me, drugs are not an issue, but girls and sex and all

"I've had to reprogram my voice recognition
software six times—I hate puberty!"

Reprinted by permission of Randy Glasbergen. ©Randy Glasbergen,
www.glasbergen.com

that kind of stuff are kind of hard for me. Maybe not actual sex,
but what you want to do when you're alone with a girl. I feel
there is certain pressure regarding this. But you have to live with
the decisions you make. I made a promise in my church not to
have sex 'til I was married."

Odds and Ends

Tim, 13, Colorado: "Guys have sleepovers, but not the same
way as girls do. It's kind of like what girls do, but we talk for
long periods of time, and we have pillow fights and play video
games. We wake up and eat ice cream and drink sodas. And when
your friends are asleep, if you have more than one person, you
put shaving cream on their noses or wrap their feet with toilet
paper. This has never happened to me because I make sure I am
always the last one to go to sleep."

Charles, 15, Virginia: "For me, sports are an escape from reality. I like playing tennis. When I play tennis, I don't think about anything else. Sports are good that way. They kind of make me feel invincible. I also like acting, and if I could play anybody, I would play James Bond."

Wild Hearts

Emotion comes strong,
And often sweet.
Feelings bring passion,
Maybe even deceit.

Life should be treasured,
Like the gold in the box.
If it has some value,
The opportunity knocks.

One thing is always true,
How the heart beats.
Fire runs through the veins,
When the pulses run through the sheets.

Anger and happiness,
Can always prevail.
Even if the occurrence is small,
Or taken through the mail.

Strength proves to be true,
Similar to the beasts of the wild.
The hearts continue to beat,
Never ever being mild.

Noah Rhodes, 16

N'Spice: Secrets of
the Sisterhood

*Guys, don't assume that when we take
two aspirin a day for several days that we
have PMS. It may just be you!*

EVERY TEENAGE GIRL!

About twelve teenage girls are sitting around a coffee table. Two are comfortably crammed in the same easy chair, and everyone else is close enough they could practically whisper. What starts as a quiet discussion quickly becomes lively. Soon, someone begins to giggle, and the laughter becomes contagious. Immediately the rest start giggling as well. Within an hour's time many topics are discussed, from teenage boys (if we could only understand them), clothes (we can never get enough), fathers (we hang on every word they say), movies (what is the best chick flick?), older sisters, food, depression (who isn't depressed?), music (Sheryl Crow has a new album out), suicide (horrible!), magazines (we are never going to look this good!), mothers, shopping, dating and what-ifs. The conversation moves gracefully from topic to topic, punctuated with giggles, serious heartfelt comments, casual glances, serious questions, long sighs, frequent smiles, more laughter and an occasional tear. To teenage girls there is nothing mysterious about who they are. Teenage girls are empowered!

On this day, like most every day when teen girls get together, there is no hidden agenda to their conversation. Girls talk about this stuff all the time. In fact, that's what teenage girls love to do—talk. This is no secret. When two or more gals are gathered in this timeless group, it's called "the sisterhood," and there is great strength in numbers. There is also compassion, humor and curiosity. The sisterhood begins forming in middle school and goes clear up to grandmas playing church bingo on Tuesday nights. Guys should be so lucky!

Kirby: "*Legends of the Fall* is the best chick flick. I'm gonna make a list. Where's a pen? Give me your favorite estrogen entertainment suggestions."

Stacy: "That's the one with Brad Pitt. He has long hair. He is so cute!"

Kirby: "Chick flicks are movies that girls love, and guys don't understand the point."

Anjulie: "Last week I asked my dad to bring home a chick flick from the video store and instead he brought home *Die Hard II*. He said it had more guns in it."

Lacey: "Guys are like that. The more things get blown up, the better."

Caitlin: "Guys have a really strange sense of humor sometimes."

Beth: "And guys don't understand PMS. They think whenever you take two aspirin, it's that time of the month. They haven't a clue it might actually be them who gives you a headache."

Laura: "I find guys who talk about PMS degrading!"

Danielle: "Me, too!"(Everyone nods.)

Trisha: "Let's get back to movies: No one ever talks about cute guys in Disney animation, but I think Peter Pan is hot!" (Everyone laughs!)

Kirby: "How about Dimetri in *Anastasia*?" (More laughter.)

Tiffany: "I cried during *The Green Mile*. Did anyone see that? It was so good."

Katherine: "Did anybody see *Girl Interrupted*? I don't know one girl who's not dealing with depression."

Caitlin: "I think we should address suicide, too! It is so prevalent today."

Kirby: "Any more favorite chick flicks?"

Anjulie: "Please put *The Mists of Avalon* on the list. Did anyone see *The Mists of Avalon*?"
Trisha: "I read the book. It was great!"
Leslie: "Let's talk about the prom."

The following insights about life from the vantage point of teenage girls aren't really secrets (it's just the guys who think so). In this chapter, teenage girls openly discuss their thoughts and feelings on stress-related issues so that their "sisters" can feel empowered and guys can finally get a clue to understanding their female counterparts.

Secret #1: Thoughts on Acceptance and Identity

Aside from the obvious stress from parents, friends and school, one of the greatest stressors is a teenage girl's appearance. It's not just about looking to make a great impression, but a subtle cultural influence to look a certain way: the beautiful look. Usually, the way to look (served up daily through Hollywood television and movies, supermarket magazines, and Barbie dolls) is thin, beautiful and sexy. The problem is that the media makes it seem like everyone does (or should) look glamorous. The truth is that less than 1 percent of the population has this "look." By the time a girl reaches her teen years, she is brainwashed to think she's supposed to look like this. Something is terribly wrong with this picture! Layered on top of the look is the identity that goes with the look (do you want to look more like Britney Spears, Cameron Diaz, Jennifer Lopez or Halle Berry?). Teen girls will do just about anything to acquire this impossible look—from starving themselves to breast implants—always at a cost to their health. Luckily, some teenage girls can see through the illusion.

Alana, 14, Colorado: "There is definitely pressure (subtle and obvious) to look a certain way. Girl movie stars and singers like Jennifer Lopez or Britney Spears wear these little tiny outfits. So the average girl thinks, 'Wow! She looks good, she has wealth, she has friends and she has the perfect life. If I look like her, I'll get to be like her.' How realistic do you think that is? How shallow is this, really? You've got to live your life and not have your whole world revolve around how you look. I like to look good, but I don't let my life revolve around how I'm going to look every day."

Artwork by Jacqueline Jimenez and Keith Martin

Chelsea, 16, Ohio: "Television can send a really bad message to kids. There are models and members of pop groups who all seem to be this 'perfect' person. You see them everywhere. It makes you feel really insignificant about who you are and what you look like. Girls think there's pressure and they need to look like that. No one really pressures them; they just put the pressure on themselves. It comes down to this: Girls want boys to be impressed with them. When I was in middle school it hit hard, but I'm better now. Yet, sometimes, I still have my days when I feel very insignificant compared to Britney Spears or anybody like that because they have all the publicity and everything that everyone sometimes wants. I used to feel really bad about the way I looked. But I'm starting to accept myself more, even though I still have my issues sometimes. It's weight mostly—I was really stressed out about that because I weigh more than a lot of my friends, but I'm also five inches taller than most of them. But still, I always wanted to be a certain weight that I probably will never be. I accept myself for the way that I am. I've just gotten to the point that if I'm not impressed with someone's personality they're just not worth the time."

Lacey, 14, Colorado: "Right now, I don't know any girls who are anorexic, but there are some friends I worry about. I don't know if it's a high metabolism or something wrong, but they look like they are one day away from danger. Oprah did a show about girls who are anorexic and bulimic. There was a girl who was eight or nine, and she felt fat. She saw herself in the mirror and thought she was so fat. She got into the habit of eating paper because she thought it would make her full. This girl was only eight years old! I think a lot of the anorexic and bulimic things are associated with low self-esteem. I think that if you involve yourself with people who will boost your self-esteem, you can overcome it."

NON SEQUITUR ©*Wiley Miller.* **Distributed by** *UNIVERSAL PRESS SYNDICATE.* **Reprinted with permission. All rights reserved.**

Kaitlyn, 14, Colorado: "I decided not to buy into the image thing. I think it's shallow. There are some girls who say, 'I'm too fat, and I don't wear the right clothes and I have to wear brand-name preppy clothes.' I wear Wal-Mart clothes. I just go with whatever looks cute. If I like it, I'll wear it. I've gotten to the point where I don't really care what people think, having to wear this or having to look like that. I just wear whatever makes me feel good about myself. I have pink hair—it's a statement to be different."

Thoughts and Reflections

Everyone wants to look appealing and look his or her best. This is natural, but do you find yourself getting caught up in the whole acceptance identity thing?

_____

_____

_____

_____

_____

Do certain brand-name labels boost your self-esteem? Which ones? Why does wearing certain clothes with specific labels change your feelings about yourself? Have you ever stopped to think about how people are influenced by marketing?

_____

_____

_____

_____

_____

Secret #2: Thoughts on Decoding the Male Mystery

Teenage girls are very observant. You study your fathers and brothers and take note of their behavior. You do the same with your friends' dads and brothers. You're looking for clues on how to understand men. But when you do the same with guys, whether it's at school, church functions or social events, more often than not you shake your head in disbelief (there are major inconsistencies in their behavior). Perhaps not all guys but the vast majority of them. Here are some thoughts on the teenage male gender.

Anne, 15, California: "Guys are so hard to describe. They talk to you differently than girls do. Guys may hang around girls, but they don't really talk to them. They just sit there and acknowledge you, but they don't talk to you much. Then there are some guys who flirt constantly, and you begin to question their sincerity, you know, their personalities. It's hard to describe how frustrated guys can make you. You ask them, 'How is your day?' and all they want to talk about is some hot girl instead. By and large, guys can be extremely immature. The guys who hang around lots of girls are much more mature. The guys who hate girls are just goof-offs. Guys should realize they need to treat girls like sisters, or better. They need to take a class once a week (maybe a two-hour class) on how to treat girls, how to talk to girls and how to be nice to girls because they simply don't know."

Alana, 14, Colorado: "Guys are stressful! It's hard to figure out what to do in a lot of situations, because you'll see some guy and you might begin to really like him, but it's hard to figure out how he feels toward you. I think a lot of girls sit there and wonder, 'Does he like me or not?' A lot of stress comes from wondering how the other person feels and wanting to know what he really feels about something, or what he really did in some situation. It's this big guessing game. You can find out months later that someone thought you were attractive, but he didn't approach you and someone else comes along."

Lacey, 14, Colorado: "I tend to hang out with guys a lot more than I do with girls, but you have to really know how to put up with guys. Guys are a lot different from girls; girls really want to stick with their own group until the time they are thirteen or fourteen, and so they have a tendency to push you out. Some girls are just too snotty for me. All they talk about is their looks and, of course, guys, guys, guys. Guys just have a different personality about them. You can joke a lot more with guys and not hurt their feelings as much as you can with girls."

Cassandra, 18, Maryland: "Guys can be a stressor sometimes because they like to play games, and some guys still act like they are in middle school. They want to act cool, but I find some of them very disrespectful, and they get upset if you don't feel the same way. That's why the majority of my friends and I turn to older guys, maybe a year or two older, because the guys my age or younger just aren't interesting, and it doesn't tend to work out too well."

CALVIN AND HOBBES ©*Watterson. Reprinted with permission of UNIVERSAL PRESS SYNDICATE. All rights reserved.*

Beth, 16, Hawaii: "I think what girls want most is to have a guy friend who treats them like their girlfriend would, who can talk to them about girl stuff and listen, because sometimes you just get sick of just talking to girls. So it's cool to talk to a guy about girl things. Let me tell you, though, finding a guy like this is rare. Most guys are too into their masculine macho stuff."

Thoughts and Reflections

Male friends (not boyfriends, but guys who are like brothers) are very important. Do you have any guy friends who are just friends you can talk to?

_____

_____

_____

_____

It's no secret that girls think guys are immature, but in defense of guys, not all guys are jerks. If you want to get some insight on the male perspective, try talking to your dad or a male teacher. Remember, approach the subject carefully and be ready for the fact that he might be defensive (this is common among guys). Good luck!

If you are being treated rudely by a guy, do you let him know that his behavior is inappropriate? If not, try this: Tell him nicely but firmly that his words are offensive or inappropriate, and until he can be more polite, you choose not to talk with him.

Secret #3: Thoughts on Shopping— Retail Therapy

Long ago, before the days of strip malls and Imax theaters, long before Diet Coke and the Internet, even before the pyramids were built, people were labeled as "hunters and gatherers." Although nobody today was around to watch them back then, it is speculated that the men did the hunting and the women did the gathering. What exactly did the women gather?

Berries, nuts, herbs, ornamental objects and all kinds of stuff to make the cave look nicer and life in general a little easier. Things may look like they have changed, but old habits die hard, perhaps because we are genetically hardwired to hunt and gather. Today, men play sports (some still hunt), and the women still gather stuff, only today it's called shopping.

Kirby, 14, Colorado: "Shopping is to women what sports are to guys. Women love to shop. I don't know why, it's just fun. Maybe not all girls like to go shopping, but I do. It gives us a sense of power. I'm not sure why that is, but to be able to go around and buy stuff is fun. I always go with my friends. Somehow it makes really good conversation; I have had some of the best fun of my life shopping with my friends at the mall. Sometimes I don't even buy anything. If I do buy something, it's usually clothes, jewelry or music. Not all girls like shopping. It's not something that should be stereotyped, but most girls do like shopping. Personally, it makes me feel pretty."

Tiffany, 17, California: "I like shopping, but I don't always buy things. I shop for clothes with my baby-sitting money and sometimes buy gifts for other people. Mainly I go to the mall to hang out with my friends. It's more of a social thing, really. Sometimes I go shopping with my mom and that's fun, too, a girl's thing. I am really close with my mom. It's something we do to bring us closer together."

Thoughts and Reflections

Shopping can be empowering, if for no other reason than you get a chance to bond with your friends, discussing likes and dislikes about clothes, jewelry, makeup and even home decorations. Do you find shopping fun? Why or why not?

_____

_____

_____

_____

Whether you realize it or not, your mom is a member of the sisterhood, too. Believe it or not, your mom has done just about everything you have ever thought about doing. She may not tell you this, but when she's ready, she will. What activities do you do, or what things can you do with your mom to strengthen this relationship?

_____

_____

_____

_____

Secret #4: Thoughts on Depression and Suicide

It's no secret that many teenage girls today are suffering from depression, yet there are many girls who try to keep their feelings a secret. They cover their arms and wrists where they have cut themselves. They purge the contents of their stomachs when they think no one is looking. Many have contemplated suicide. If this is something you have ever thought about, please don't keep it a secret.

Claire, 14, New York: "I started thinking about suicide when I was in the seventh grade and actually tried it. When I was in the seventh grade, I hung out with a bunch of friends, and that's all they thought about. They were the 'fake stress' kind of girls, and they would cry every day. They would pick really stupid reasons that weren't good reasons to get mad or cry. It was mostly the 'everything is wrong in my life' attitude I got from them that made me want to commit suicide. Back then, when I was with people for a certain time, I used to be a follower, and I would model their personalities. It wasn't good! (Peer pressure is more than just sex, drugs and alcohol.) Now that I'm in the eighth grade, I've changed friends, and things are much better. There is definitely a connection between depression and suicide. A lot of girls I know are taking drugs for depression."

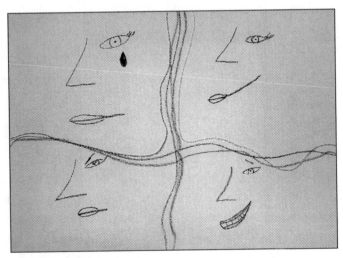

Artwork by Caitlyn Cardenas

Lisa, 16, Illinois: "Not only have I thought about it, I went one step further last year. I don't even know why. I wasn't happy. I was almost there. I had a knife ready, and I was going to cut my wrist, but then I closed my eyes and saw myself lying in a puddle of blood. I opened my eyes and saw my little brother looking at me in disbelief. It was then that I decided not to go through with it and put the knife down. I talked to my friend about my attempt, and my sister and I talked about it for a long time, too. Then she told my mom, and my mom talked to me about it."

Caitlin, 14, Colorado: "Yes, suicide has crossed my mind. I think suicide crosses everyone's mind these days. As a teenager, you're going through so many different things at one time. It's overwhelming, and sometimes you just don't know how to cope with it all. I think everybody has had this thought running through their mind, perhaps not seriously, but it would be foolish to think that only a small percentage of kids think about taking their life. People need to talk about this more because it's a big problem."

Thoughts and Reflections

Depression is a HUGE concern these days for teenage girls (and guys, too!). It's true that the pressures of being a teen can be overwhelming, but depression doesn't just come on like a tornado. It builds up slowly with little thoughts that eat away at the foundation of your self-esteem. Thoughts like "I am fat" or "I am ugly." These thoughts (called self-talk) run through our minds constantly. Self-talk (like a radio station in your head) can be positive as well as negative. What are some things you can say to yourself to shift the focus from a negative conversation to a more positive one? An example is, "I am loveable." Think of an affirming phrase to say to yourself and write it down in a place where you can see it often each day.

_____

_____

Dealing with depression is rarely something that can be solved alone. Getting help is not a sign of weakness; it's a sign of strength. Seeking help with feelings of depression takes courage. If you have any suspicion you might be suffering from depression, now is the time to get help. Make a promise to call or see someone today.

Secret #5: Thoughts on Girlfriends

As a teenage girl, you are well aware just how important your girlfriends are. A best friend is more than a friend; she's like a sister (even if you already have a sister). You can confide EVERYTHING in her! Sometimes, girls form really tight friendships—so tight the girls become nearly inseparable. But becoming that close can lead to competitiveness, even jealousy, when both become attracted to the same guy. Sometimes the smallest thing can become a wedge in the friendship and drive you apart. Some people can hold grudges (the Revenge Hot Stone!), and they hold grudges for a long time. Friends who were once sisters soon become bitter rivals, adding more stress to an already stressful life. Thank goodness for the sisterhood, which can be strong enough to overcome the squabbles in the "family."

Beth, 16, Hawaii: "I don't know how it is for guys, but girls like the closeness of relationships. They will hook themselves to each other and expect that nothing will ever go wrong between them. But things go wrong all the time, or the girls just grow apart.

Girls consider their friends to be like family, or put another way, an escape from family. Girlfriends are a safe haven."

Winter, 14, Maryland: "I had a really good friend, but she and I aren't doing too well right now. She doesn't want to talk to me because of a guy. She had this crush on a guy for two days. He didn't like her all that much, and he kind of avoided her and started hanging out with me. Then she got extremely defensive. I said, 'He's a friend. I can't tell a friend to leave me alone.'"

Michelle, 14, Colorado: "Girlfriends are great, but not without their problems. We have sort of this pyramid. We each talk about each other behind our backs. We don't tell each other, and it all comes together sometimes and it's sad. Then there are more problems when guys enter the picture because they have a lot of anger-management problems usually."

Thoughts and Reflections

How do your girlfriends differ from your guy friends? In your opinion, what makes these friendships so special?

_____

_____

_____

_____

Are you holding a grudge against a former friend? (A grudge is a Hot Stone, and we will talk more about this in the next chapter.) Ask yourself why you are still harboring these feelings.

_____

_____

_____

_____

Chick Flicks
("Estrogen Entertainment")

By the end of the hour, Kirby had compiled a good list. Everyone sitting around the coffee table agreed that each of these movies will definitely stir the heart. So girls, if you're looking for a good movie on your next sleepover, try one of these!

Legends of the Fall *The Saint*
Ever After *Enemy at the Gate*
Sliding Doors *The Shawshank Redemption*
The Joy Luck Club *Stand by Me*
Down to You *The Green Mile*

Pretty in Pink
Pretty Woman
Erin Brockovich
The Princess Bride
You've Got Mail
Sleepless in Seattle
Sweet November
Now and Then
Love Stinks
The Mists of Avalon
The Color Purple
Gigi
Don Juan DeMarco
Pearl Harbor

Gone with the Wind
Carousel
The Sound of Music
Anastasia
The Little Mermaid
Ice Age
Monsters, Inc.
Titanic
Romancing the Stone
Chocolat
Out of Africa
Return to Me
Girl, Interrupted

Holding Hot Stones: How NOT to Deal with Stress

I am labeled as a depressive.
When I get angry, I cut myself.
I know it's strange, but it serves as
a way to relive the pain.

JENNIFER P., 15

Artwork by Erin Tolooee

On August 10, 2001, Mt. Etna erupted and spewed hot lava down the side of the mountain, causing panic and pandemonium among nearby Italian villagers. But a volcano doesn't need to erupt for us to see that these are explosive times. In the same year, more than twenty teens nationwide were charged with violent behavior in their schools. Several hundred teens attempted suicide and untold thousands (girls and guys) cut themselves in acts of self-mutilation. Have you noticed there are oodles of angry people in the world today? Road rage, sports rage, airplane rage, all kinds of rage. And it's getting out of hand. It's almost like there is a flu virus, and almost everybody is infected with it. There are many metaphors about anger. Today, the image of Hot Stones seems to be the most descriptive: Unresolved anger is like a Hot Stone; if you hold it too long, you get burned!

Anger itself is not a bad emotion. It just becomes bad when we hang on to it for days, weeks, months or even years. Some people hang on to anger for decades, and they always get burned in the process. There are many ways anger surfaces: impatience, resentment, frustration, annoyance, envy, jealousy, guilt, hatred, indignation, arrogance, hostility and rage. When you take this into account, you begin to see why there is so much anger in the world.

Unlike talking about your favorite actor, musician or athlete, anger has never been a polite topic of conversation. In fact, like the topic of sex, it's considered taboo and often avoided. Most people don't really think about it, including young adults like yourself. Yet when asked directly, teens say they have lots of anger. In fact, when teens really open up and start talking, you realize a lot of kids are really ticked off. This chapter highlights some of the thoughts and feelings many teens experience, and it ends with a description of four types of Hot Stones to avoid at all costs.

Teens' Thoughts on Anger

Did you ever stop to think about anger? Why do you get angry? Why *do* your friends get upset or frustrated? Why do your parents go ballistic? Okay, even though it might seem like your parents are mad at you, you should realize that much of their frustration starts when they arrive at work, and it follows them home, just like your frustrations from school follow you home. Perhaps you've noticed that the aftertaste of anger can last a long time. Some teens don't even know what makes them upset. They're just angry! Feelings of frustration seem to follow them like a permanent black cloud, but learning to let go of anger begins with just identifying how you're feeling and why you're feeling that way.

Michelle, 14, Colorado: "Sometimes it's just something that nags at you, and other times it's a feeling, like steam building inside of you. It just builds and builds, and you don't want to talk about it. Then one day, it feels like it's going to explode, and all you want to do is cry. There are other times when you stuff it down, and the anger stays inside for a while. Then, days or weeks later, something reminds you of it, and that makes you angry all over again. There are some times when the feelings of rage are just too big, and when somebody says something, tempers flare right away like there's no stopping the reaction; it just goes off!"

Peter, 16, Florida: "I don't think specific situations or even certain people can make you feel angry. It's how you can make yourself feel. Basically, anything that has to deal with stress can make you angry because it's affecting how you think. I guess anger can be anything that fixates your thoughts about one thing. Anger is anything that makes you lean toward the negative. You can have anger toward yourself to do better, but that's more like negative anger. It could make you do positive things, like in sports, but for most people, anger is destructive. It's hard to put into words; does this make sense?"

Reprinted with special permission of North American Syndicate.

Soma, 14, New York: "I get annoyed really easily, but I don't get mad with my friends very easily. They would have to do something really big, like something I had asked them not to do. That's basically all that would make me really angry. Sometimes teenagers can dish out a lot of verbal abuse. That makes me mad. When that happens, I usually come out and say something back. That makes me feel better, even though it's probably not the right thing to do, but it makes me feel better and makes me feel like they're not over-powering me. I think maybe that's all it is; they just want to feel better about themselves by feeling superior to me. If I don't say something back, then it's just like proving to them that they are better than me. There is some aspect of being assertive when you're angry. In other words, you don't let people walk all over you or pounce on your face. You basically stand up for your rights. Being assertive helps me stand up for what I believe."

Keegan, 14, Colorado: "Sometimes you feel like you breathe in all the world's anger, hatred, violence and everyone who has made fun of you, and you hold it inside, and then one day, it all comes out like a volcano erupting. Sometimes you hurt your family when you do it. Sometimes you hurt your friends. You don't mean to; it's just that you don't know any other way to get it out. You finally reached the top. Sometimes that happens with me; I get too angry. I just reach the top, but later I apologize for how mean I was. It's like there is a good side to you, and you know, a bad side to you. When you get angry, more of the bad side starts to come out, but there is a little bit of the good side left in there, controlling everything. But sometimes you find that you're dishing back out what people are dishing to you tenfold."

Thoughts and Reflections

What does the word anger mean to you? Describe what you feel like when you get angry.

_____

_____

_____

_____

_____

Anger includes many other emotions. In what ways do you feel anger surface during the course of a normal day?

_____

_____

_____

_____

Do you feel that you are influenced by the violence you see on television and in movies, or perhaps even the music you listen to? Why or why not?

_____

_____

_____

_____

There is an expression that says, "Pick your battles." It means you cannot fight everything that makes you mad—you'll go crazy. Instead, make your choices. (Another saying says, "Choose what mountain you want to die on.") There is an expression that asks, "Do you want to be right, or do you want to be happy?" You cannot change everything. What battles can you let go—rather than being right and proving it—and just be happy?

_____

_____

_____

_____

Things That Push Your Hot Stone Buttons

As the world races into the twenty-first century, there is no shortage of things over which to get frustrated. While your parents are dealing with traffic, paying bills, urban sprawl and tax audits, most likely you are dealing with annoying brothers and/or sisters, friends who cannot be trusted, demanding parents, teachers who show favoritism toward other students, coaches who give mixed messages about schoolwork and team loyalty, popular kids who flaunt their wealthy lifestyles, or you are being told to act mature but being treated like a child. What promotes frustration and anger in teens? Here are some insights.

Heather, 16, Vermont: "There is never a week that goes by in which I don't feel angry at least one of the days. I am a short-tempered person. Many things, big and little, can easily upset me. One thing that really gets me pissed is when people purposely try to upset me because they know that I am short-tempered and they think it's funny to see me go off. No one should feel angry, and it sucks being short-tempered. No matter how much I try to change, it's hard. Some of the bad ways include the feeling of wanting to break something, or hit something or someone. I haven't hit anyone or broke anything, but the thought of it isn't pleasant. I sometimes take my anger out on the wrong people, like my brother or parents, and I say hurtful things and inappropriate words. One thing I do when I am angry is cry—that seems to make me feel better a lot of the times."

Anne, 14, Texas: "How do I feel when I get angry? Mentally, I just push things out of my mind and forget about them, but sometimes the feelings return to create an inner boiling in my stomach and a ringing in my ears. My sister lives in India right now, and right before she left, I got angry with her. For the rest of the week, I hated her. All I could say to her was, 'Get away from me!' and I totally chewed her out. I felt really bad after that, because she isn't going to be back for four months. I feel real guilty. I took my anger out more than I should have."

Brittany, 15, Illinois: "Yes, I feel angry quite often, and the reason why I am angry is because I feel as if no one appreciates what I do. Sometimes I go out of my way to please people. I like to make people happy, so I clean the house, or I cook a meal or I do something special for someone, and no one even notices. Then I get mad and I say to myself, 'I took my time to help you, and you don't even notice.' Then I ask myself, 'What's the point?' I guess inconsiderate people really make me mad."

Chelsea, 16, Ohio: "I try to never feel angry, but I do. More often than not, my anger is just frustration. What frustrates me the most are my teachers, because I'm in a really hard school, and they expect a lot out of me. It gets really frustrating. It feels overwhelming sometimes. Often I want to scream, but I'd rather not. There are other things I do to make myself feel better. I like to read a lot. That helps. And I listen to music or talk to my friends. That's my favorite thing to do—talk to my friends."

Pablo, 14, Colorado: "A lot of things make me angry, like teachers. They're on your back all the time, saying, 'Do this; do that.' And if you don't, they just get mad at you. They get mad at you because they know you can do the work, but you just don't do it. I can understand that, but it really gets you mad, and then they yell even more."

Jamie, 18, Colorado: "I would probably say what makes me angry is the level of immaturity among my peers. I see so many immature kids in high school. I just want to say, 'Grow up!' I want to say to them, 'You're going to be leaving high school in about a year or two, and you're still out there throwing eggs on Halloween.' I get stressed walking around seeing people not respect each other. They don't even respect themselves. They just do foolish things that hurt other people. I think money comes into play in this town—arrogance is a form of anger—and it angers me when people think about only themselves or think they're better than others because they have more money."

Chris, 16, Vermont: "I get pissed when I am always being told what to do, which, of course, sucks. I also get angry when my brother goes into my room and touches my stuff, like when he messes around with it or breaks it, or uses it without permission, or loses it. Sometimes I work hard on something, and he destroys it. I also get mad when I am not able to do something, like if I really want to do something with my friends. I think being angry is a way of letting out your frustrations. Everybody feels angry."

Alice, 14, Colorado: "Little things get me upset. Like when you are trying to do something (homework) and you don't understand it. I'm a very impatient person, so if I'm explaining something or talking to someone and they don't understand or don't get what I'm saying, I get kind of angry. I also get angry at how the world is right now, specifically terrorism, and how the world is turning out to be. It angers me how thousands of people are dying because of terrorism, and it gets me mad because these are innocent people. It also gets me upset and angry because the world didn't seem so violent a long time ago. Now it's at a point where money, power and wealth are the focus of terrorism. I

Artwork by Katherine Smith

know that money isn't the path to true happiness; it's only temporary pleasures."

Pam, 15, Virginia: "Yeah, I feel angry a whole lot. It's mostly my parents who make me angry because I'm not exactly the best student. My sister is a good student and a good child. I'm the rebel of the family when it comes to getting in trouble. So I get angry at my parents because it seems like they're always on my back about getting good grades, being more like my sister and being more involved. It makes me angry, because when I do something good it really doesn't get recognized. They say, 'Oh, good job.' Whatever. And when my sister does something, anything, it's like, 'Oh, my God,' as if it's the biggest thing in the world. I could say there's no competition, but believe me, it's competition. She's older. I feel like I want to hit something or rip posters off my wall or something to vent my anger. I have to do something when I'm angry. I don't know, maybe yell and scream, even though I feel like I can't in the house. So instead I put on music or play my guitar or write something."

Chris, 14, Colorado: "What gets me angry the most is schoolwork and my little sister, who just annoys me. I'll try to go home after school and sleep because I'm really stressed from getting up so early for hockey practice, and she'll come home at 3 P.M. and start yelling and screaming and turning on the PlayStation. My feelings of frustration get bottled up in my chest area. Sometimes I throw pillows, other times I swear a fair amount—but in my parents' opinion, I swear way too much."

Thoughts and Reflections

If you were asked to identify three things that push your buttons, what would they be?

a. _____

b. _____

c. _____

Now that you have listed these, ask yourself how long these buttons have been pushed. Do you hold your anger for a long time? If so, why?

_____

_____

_____

Please! Don't Touch These Hot Stones!

Believe it or not, there are several cultures around the world that deal with anger well. Unfortunately, Americans are not included in this group. As a matter of fact, we are among the worst. People have a strange habit of grabbing Hot Stones and holding on to them. You would think that getting burned once would help you remember, but memories run as short as tempers, and a lot of teens are getting burned repeatedly.

Hot Stone anger behaviors start early in childhood, but the habits seem to become carved in stone during the teen years. Adults who study the topic of anger have discovered four distinct styles of behavior common among all people. Everybody exhibits behaviors from each of these categories, but one style of mismanaged anger tends to dominate more than the other three. Remember that these mismanaged-anger styles don't have to be permanent (you can drop the Hot Stones anytime!). By taking the time to recognize various traits and behaviors you see in yourself, you can begin to identify things you do or say that actually promote stress and anger rather than decrease and resolve it. Then you can learn to modify and change these actions so that mismanaged anger can become well-managed anger.

First and foremost, unresolved anger is a control issue. Either you are trying to control yourself (and doing a bad job of it), or you're trying hard to control someone else, usually through intimidation. Either way, this type of control is an illusion because, instead of gaining control, you end up giving your power away: You let others control your feelings or you lower yourself to their level. This is where the real burn from Hot Stones occurs.

Here are the four Hot Stones you want to avoid holding because of the ensuing damage: the Silent but Deadly Hot Stone, the Volcanic Hot Stone, the Razor Hot Stone and the

Revenge Hot Stone. Unlike the first Harry Potter story *(The Sorcerer's Stone)*, these stones are bad news all the way around. Please read through each description and the teen comments to see which of these four most accurately depicts your mismanaged-anger style.

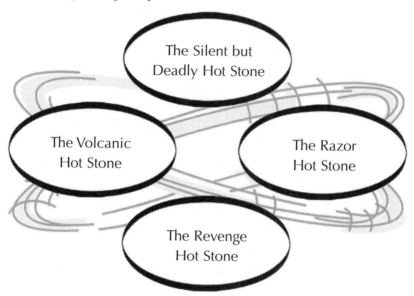

Diagram 4.1: The Four Hot Stones of Anger
You Don't Want to Touch or Hold

The Silent but Deadly Hot Stone

Some people never seem to get angry. Perhaps, as kids, their parents told them repeatedly, "Don't ever get mad" or "Don't ever talk back to me," and so they never do. Maybe *you* know people like this. Maybe you are this kind of person. It's one thing to hold a Hot Stone and get burned. For teens who don't show their anger, it's as if they actually swallow these Hot Stones just to get rid of any trace of anger. It may look like these teens never show a trace of frustration (just a happy face), but what is silence at first soon becomes a health problem. In essence, *the body becomes the battlefield for the war games of the mind.* What are some examples of these health problems? Unresolved anger shows up as migraine headaches, tension headaches, TMJ (grinding your teeth at night), digestive problems and several other related illnesses that might not show up for several years. Holding or swallowing this Hot Stone is to attempt to control your anger by not showing it, but eventually feelings of anger, whether impatience, guilt, envy or frustration, will show up as an illness, begging for attention.

Jackson, 14, Nebraska: "Sometimes I'll try not to show my feelings of anger. I'll just keep it bottled up inside me so no one has to worry about anything. I like to keep other people out of it as much as possible. I don't want them to worry, so I usually keep problems to myself. Mainly what pushes my buttons are my parents and their expectations. How I express my anger depends on where I am and what I'm doing. Usually, if I'm angry at school, I don't really do anything. I keep it bottled up. I'll just kind of hang my head. I don't initiate conversations. I try and stay to myself."

Jason, 15, Colorado: "I'm not really an angry person. I can get frustrated at times, but I just sort of let it go. Maybe I don't show anger and I don't let it out, and I guess that can be bad. I'm just not an angry person. Angry music can help a lot, and anger art and violent video games also help relieve my tension. A lot of people think it's a bad thing and that it will lead to violent behavior, but I think it's a good way for me to deal with anger."

Stacy, 17, Texas: "I was raised to be polite, which I am, but that means not having a temper, or not showing it if you do. I know I stuff my feelings away, but this is how women are raised or else they get labeled as troublemakers or worse. I have to wear a night brace to stop my teeth from grinding, and my dentist shared with me that this is stress-related."

Harris, 15, Colorado: "I feel angry every once in a while, and I may take it out on my friend. He kind of gets me angry sometimes. He gets angry very easily, but he doesn't hold it in like some people. He always lets it go, so that kind of helps me when I need to release my anger. He just listens and doesn't really say anything back. We do the same thing for each other. We know each other very well. I kind of clench my teeth and get tense. I just have to think about it in my head. I start talking to myself and figuring it out in my head to see why I am angry."

Thoughts and Reflections

Are you the kind of person who doesn't show anger? It may be that you simply deal with your frustrations well, but perhaps not? Do you hide your anger so you will feel more accepted by others?

_____

_____

_____

_____

_____

Do a quick check on your physical health. Can you think of any health concerns that might be related to stuffing your anger feelings, such as migraines, digestive problems or TMJ?

_____

_____

_____

Do songs with angry lyrics make you feel less angry, or do they really validate/reinforce your anger by adding fuel to the fire? Pull out some of your CDs and take a look at the lyrics. Is it the melody that you really like, or is it the lyrics? Sometimes what you focus your attention on expands in your mind. Do these song lyrics expand or contract your anger? Do the lyrics calm your emotions, or are you just adding fuel to the fire?

_____

_____

_____

_____

The Volcanic Hot Stone

When some teens get mad, they are like a volcano ready to erupt. It may take a while for the hot lava and volcanic stones to shoot up, but when they do, look out and run for cover. Like a volcano, these people seem to have steam coming out of their ears and nostrils. They often use swear words, they may hit something or someone, or they might "flip the bird" at the slightest provocation. Unlike the teens who swallow their Hot Stones and never show any anger, these teens show it often. Sudden outbursts of anger may cause bodily harm (to yourself or others), and there are always bad consequences. People who exhibit the explosive behavior tend to make the news headlines (Columbine High School being the prime example). Road rage, sports rage and recess rage are examples of explosive anger.

Amanda, 17, Colorado: "I don't deal with anger very well. I guess I should try to stay calm and try to think rationally about whatever it is that has me upset. Instead, I get kind of violent, not just physically, but mentally, too. I never hurt anyone physically; it's more like punching holes in my wall to relieve stress. If it is a person who has me angry, I'll generally find the one thing that I could say to hurt them the most and say it. Oh yeah, I'm a nice girl."

Sean, 18, Michigan: "There are many times when I feel anger. I mean, who doesn't feel angry from time to time? Anger is a natural human trait. Many times it's inescapable. Most of the time what angers me is impatience, whether it's driving in my car or sitting in front of the computer, or even with an annoying friend. Impatience leads to frustration, and obviously, frustration will lead to anger. And that anger might turn in to yelling obscenities at the car in front of me, using finger gestures, punching walls, and hurting people emotionally and/or physically. All those actions I just described aren't very desirable for either party, giving or receiving. In most cases, when people lash out in anger, it will just make the situation worse. For example, I mentioned that computers will often anger me, sometimes they just won't work, and there isn't any obvious reason. Recently, my computer was not cooperating at all, and it crashed. At that point, in frustration, I lashed out and punched a hole through my closet door. Now this just made the situation really bad, because I now live in an apartment with a roommate and we have to pay for any damage when our lease is up, so my roommate wasn't real pleased with me and neither was I. When people get angry, and I don't think this is a surprise to anyone, they don't think in a logical manner. Hell, people don't think at all when they're angry, and I am no exception."

Monica, 14, New Jersey: "I don't really get angry. I think that I get a little upset, but I don't really get angry. If I get angry, it's big. I've only been angry a few times in my life, because it's not worth it. When I get angry, I get very violent. I'm not the best of people when I get angry. I kick people when I get mad. I guess I don't realize my strength, so I have been known to get violent over the years, although I didn't punch anybody out. I don't like being angry because it isn't good for you."

Steven, 17, Oregon: "I get a lot of anger from my dad, because he has a lot of anger. I don't like to take it out on people like he does, though. If I'm really mad, and people do something really stupid, I get even more mad, which is a common thing. I don't know why, but I always punch things in my house. We have a Ping-Pong table downstairs, and it's folded in half. I guess I punch it because we don't have a punching bag, and because I don't want something stupid to happen like Columbine. I don't want to do anything like that because I don't see a point in it, so I just kind of deal with it in my own way. I yell in my room because I don't know any other way to deal with my rage. I'm taking these antidepressants now. They told me when I first started taking them it would make me a little more upset for the first couple weeks because my brain chemicals are messed up. I've been really mad lately at a lot of things that are going on, and the way my life is going in general. I take it out on people."

Eric, 16, Arizona: "Yeah, I do feel angry sometimes, such as when a situation with friends happens, and they totally blow it out of proportion. I'm the victim of that, and it makes me really angry. I feel like throwing something as far as I can. Or, you know, I go into my room and punch my pillow and really feel the anger, and then I can go back to some kind of normal living for the rest of the day. I don't get mad often. It really depends on what kind of day I'm having. One day, nothing might happen and I'll be perfect, and I won't get angry. But something could be terribly wrong the next day, and I'll be really angry. Usually, my feelings of rage just last that day, however if it was something really big, it might last for a couple of days."

Eric, 14, Illinois: "Well, for me, it happened early on, swearing that is. Instead of me punching or hitting things, I'll just go up into my room and swear. When I'm angry, that's a way I can get it out of my mind. I'm finding that's not too successful anymore, because eventually, you know, I find myself getting tired of it. Eventually, I get so used to it that it doesn't do anything for me. Like the other day, I was mad so I went upstairs to my room ranting and raving. So I'm sitting up there for an hour swearing at myself, and I finally realized, hey, I'm not getting any better. I've got to find some other way to deal with these feelings. I'm probably the most stressed-out person you'll ever meet. Whenever I get angry, I get really angry!"

Thoughts and Reflections

Is your temper like a volcano? Do you not only hold Volcanic Stones, but also throw them? Do you have any friends who exhibit this style of mismanaged anger? How about your parents?

_____

_____

_____

Oftentimes, people who hold Volcanic Stones use various expressions to describe their anger. Can you think of three expressions people used to describe explosive anger? (Here's a hint: "I was so mad, I could blow my top" or "I was so mad, I could spit bullets.")

a. _____

b. _____

c. _____

The Razor Hot Stone

The Razor Stone is not only hot, it's sharp. First it burns, then it cuts deep. Not only is there frustration associated with this stone, but there is guilt, too—*guilt from feeling angry*. The kind of person who holds this Hot Stone feels so bad about feeling guilty that they engage in some behavior to make them feel better, like excessive eating, sleeping, exercise or even shopping. Many eating disorders, such as anorexia and bulimia, fall into this category. With teens today, however, the classic example of holding the Razor Stone is someone who does self-mutilation (also known as cutters). It could be sexual abuse, it could be your parents' divorce, or it could be just about any experience that makes you want to grip this Hot Stone rather than drop it. The Razor Stone has a long shadow called depression. *Depression is anger turned inward.* Whatever Razor Stone behavior people use has an addictive quality to it, making it really hard to stop, which is why this Hot Stone is so dangerous.

Darcy, 18, North Carolina: "I get so angry and not at just big things. It's gotten so bad that I get angry if my shoe comes untied. It's really weird because I used to be such an easygoing person, although that attitude got me in a lot of problems, too. I just didn't care, and when I didn't care, I didn't value myself or do good things for myself. It was all about drugs and sex and drinking, and did that cute guy think I'm a hottie? My feelings of anger got so bad they drove me to attempt suicide. Now I am walking down a never-ending path to recovery. However, every now and again I relapse (as I call it). The hatred just takes over and consumes my body sometimes; it's like I am not Darcy anymore."

Gabrielle, 14, New York: "I use cutting to distract myself. I used to cut myself because I wanted to die because I was so frustrated with my parents. I wanted to say, 'Look what you're doing to me. You're getting divorced. You're ripping my life apart. You're changing my whole world. So look what I'm going to do to make you feel so bad.' I was in a really bad headspace then because I felt so terrible. Then cutting became a habit, an addiction. Just like people get addicted to drugs, cutters get addicted to cutting. I'm breaking the habit now, though. It's hard to do. It's almost as hard as quitting smoking. When life gets so overwhelming, you can focus on the pain. Cutting gives you something else to think about. In the moment, it feels good in a weird way, but afterward you have this awful feeling of resentment, thinking, 'I really shouldn't have done that.' Then something new happens, and you do it again. It's really hard to quit doing it because I say to myself, 'I've got to find something else to do.' I'm wishing I could just give it up, but it's not easy."

Gina, 15, New Jersey: "I'm really introverted. I tend to hold my anger feelings inside. Even though I might like to go up to people and say something or read them the riot act (I get frustrated with people who are rude and inconsiderate), I don't go up to people and say, 'You're not acting right.' I used to put pain on myself (I was a cutter). When I was depressed, I used to hurt myself. I used to cut my wrists as a means to let anger and sadness out. It made me feel better. Now I know this is not an option; it only makes things worse."

Thoughts and Reflections

We all have ways to lessen our emotional pain. Some of us eat ice cream; others listen to music. Still others inflict damage to themselves (cutting). How do you escape the pain that results from anger (both positively and negatively)?

_____

_____

_____

_____

Are you a cutter (someone who practices self-mutilation)? Have you sought help for this? This behavior can be deadly and needs attention immediately. Who can you turn to for help?

_____

_____

_____

Have you ever made the association (link) between the things you do and the emotions they soothe? Are there any routines you have that you think might lean toward addictive behaviors? If so, what are they?

_____

_____

_____

_____

The Revenge Hot Stone

The motto of the person who holds the Revenge Stone is, "Don't get mad; get even." Some people try to get more than even; they try to get one up. This kind of person seeks revenge by getting even in a passive-aggressive way. In other words, these people are nice to you, but the minute you turn your back, they start hurling the Revenge Stone. For others *the Revenge Hot Stone is the "grudge stone." Once again, the holders of this stone may hit his or her target, but get burned badly in the process.* The most common behaviors of people who hold this Hot Stone include backstabbing (cutting people down behind their backs), sarcasm (a word that actually means to tear flesh!), or some other form of sabotage. This type of mismanaged anger backfires. As the expression goes, he who seeks revenge should dig two graves. People who hold and throw the Revenge Stone not only get burned, they lose the respect and trust of their friends.

Caitlin, 14, Colorado: "Sure, I get angry at some people. I just get mad at people—the backstabbers. It's this indescribable feeling; I tense up all my muscles, and I get stressed out. It really bothers me when people spread rumors and especially when they lie. Lying is a big thing; I can't deal with lying. I used to have a friend who lied about everything, trying to make herself look better, but it was causing her to lose friends. I find that a lot of girls do this."

Abby, 14, Colorado: "What gets me mad is gossip about a bunch of different things. Gossip is when people say stuff that maybe isn't true, and then it gets bigger and bigger, and more things sup- posedly happen. It makes me angry. People end up not knowing the real story. It's not just the girls who gossip; guys do it, too. I find that as we get older, people start manipulating others deviously. I think this is because we are older and more stuff happens."

Morgan, 13, Tennessee: "My friends make me angry often. I don't really have many true friends who I can rely on because some of them go behind my back. Then my other friends come back and tell me about it, and then I get into this big old argument. It happens all the time. You have to watch everything you say. Today I had a conflict at practice with one of my friends. I made it a point to talk to her today, and we got things worked out. We might talk again, but we won't be good friends anymore. There's a lot of backstabbing. She's known for talking about people and saying she didn't. People do that all the time."

Thoughts and Reflections

Everybody has tried to control somebody else at one time or another. Teens try to influence their parents. Parents (as we all know) certainly try to control their kids. Teachers try to control the classroom (but that's their job). Some people can be very manipulative. Often, we try to control or manipulate our friends, sometimes directly, other times less obviously but more deceptively. The teens who hold the Revenge Stone do this all the time. Are you someone who tries to control others? Are you someone who talks behind other people's backs?

_____

_____

_____

_____

_____

It's easy to criticize others, but it's hard to take an honest look at ourselves. Observe your own behavior for the next few days and see how many times you use underhanded behaviors such as sarcasm, not returning phone calls, showing up late to meet friends, etc.

Burning

Burning anger deep down inside
Aching hunger alone in my mind
When will it stop?
When did it begin?
The fighting pain from somewhere within
Make it stop
Make it go away
I can't survive one more day.
Stranded in this world full of impossible demands
Everywhere I turn I'm left with empty hands.
I table the anger by going inside
I can't keep control. I'm lost inside my mind.

Pam Bushey

Suggested Reading List

Lerner, Harriet. *The Dance of Anger.* New York: HarperCollins, 1997.

Middelton-Moz, Jane. *Boiling Point.* Deerfield Beach, Fla.: Health Communications, Inc., 1999.

Warren, Neil Clark. *Make Anger Your Ally.* Colorado Springs, Colo.: Focus on the Family Publishing, 1998.

Part II

The Best Ways to Cope with Stress

Dropping Hot Stones: Good Ways to Deal with Anger

*To cope well with anger, I will either
just go sit in my room and listen to music, or
I'll go up to my room and play my guitar.
Either way, it helps me let off steam.*

DAVID C., 14

In Spite Of

The beckoning which comes
From beyond, rises to
Occasional outcast, but leaves
Behind the confusion of mystery

The drawing in, no one
Loses pity or wastes reason,
The comfort of covenant
In time will be hastened

To deviate from guidelines set
To eliminate the destruction, here
We rise, here we stand, lost in
Quarry, memories suppress the anger
Shared by this vulnerable body
But lost is the experience
Of unknowing, unwilling to
Return what was, yet
Will never be again
Trapped in uncertainty,
Patience is traded for
Anxiousness, set forth from
The deterrence of coveting
Resurrected by lack of interest

Beauty is lost, but found again
Uncertain of how long this
Beauty will once again
Fall in spite of the remorseful
Anger that has blanketed the masses.

Sean Dupuis, 18

The week Marty turned seventeen, his father was diagnosed
with pancreatic cancer. Within a month of his diagnosis,
Marty's dad was gone. The shock was devastating for the
whole family, but Marty took it especially hard. For those left
behind, death can bring on many feelings, including guilt and
sorrow. Yet anger is by far the strongest emotion to deal with.

Marty, 17, Maryland: "I felt like I was boiling inside, like a volcano. Here I am, supposed to graduate from high school in a few weeks. It's supposed to be the best time of my life, and my dad dies. Now I have to postpone going to college for a year to take care of my mom and younger brother. My whole life changed in the course of three weeks. It wasn't fair. As it turns out, I did end up going to college that fall, but the summer was pure hell. I found myself picking fights and making enemies just to blow off steam. Now I lift weights, which is a lot more healthy for everybody. Trust me on that one."

Not everyone who experiences the death of a loved one acts like Marty. Some people tend to hold things in. For teens who experience the divorce of their parents, it means the end of the stable family structure, and this can be very stressful.

Sarah, 15, Michigan: "When my parents got divorced, I was kinda glad at first. I was ten, and I thought there would be less fighting. I was wrong; they just fight over the phone now. I didn't realize that I was going to be a Ping-Pong ball back and forth between apartments. I didn't see it at first, but I can tell they use me to get back at each other. I am not the kind of person to bang pots and pans like my mother. I tend to hold things in, but there is a cost to doing this. My dentist says I have TMJ—I grind my teeth at night. I know it started after the divorce. I still have TMJ occasionally, but I found a great release—expression of my feelings through painting and sculpture, and of course, I dump my emotions on my friends a lot, but that's what friends are for."

Anger Is a Healthy Emotion— In Tiny, Tiny Amounts!

If you were to ask the best experts in the world what their definition of emotional health is, most likely they would say this: *"It's the ability to feel and express the entire range of human emotions—everything from anger to love—and to control them, not be controlled by them."* There is a big reason why anger and fear are part of the package of human emotions. First and foremost, they are survival emotions. Both anger and fear offer protection from physical danger. The problem is that we tend to use anger for nonphysical threats, like annoying brothers and sisters, school tests, stupid drivers, and money issues. That's where we get into problems.

anger, fear, guilt, grief   joy, happiness, love

▲

Diagram 5.1: The Range of Human Emotions

The good news is that anger is a healthy emotion—IN TINY AMOUNTS! Why healthy, you ask? Well, because it's part of the fight-or-flight response. But episodes of anger are only meant to last seconds—long enough to get out of harm's way. The problem is that most people don't move on after a few seconds. Whether it's a grudge or resentment, they hang on to their anger for weeks, months and years after the fact, and that's where trouble begins. Another reason why anger is thought to be healthy is because it helps create boundaries.

By communicating diplomatically that you are angry ("I am angry!"), you let people know how you feel if you have been violated. You're telling them they need to keep a respectful distance. A good example of justified anger is as a response to inappropriate sexual advances. There are many other good examples.

Unlike fear that tends to be draining, anger is energizing. Many sports such as soccer, lacrosse and football, to name a few, actually use the concept of "controlled aggression" as a means to compete, particularly when trying to score a goal or sprint across the finish line. A *burst of anger* is a reaction (like "flipping the bird"), whereas controlled aggression is a calculated response (going for a shot or thinking before you speak). The key is to use the energy from anger for a good, constructive purpose rather than a destructive purpose. Like any skill, this takes practice. Once again, anger is healthy in tiny amounts, and you want to respond, not react. So the bottom line is when you get angry about something, recognize it, maintain your composure and respond accordingly. In the adult world, it's called appropriate behavior, which, in essence, means not acting like a baby. These emotional responses are only meant to last a very short time. Anything more than a few seconds makes anger very unhealthy.

Thoughts and Reflections

Is there somebody against whom you are holding a grudge? What Hot Stone would you call this? How long have you been carrying this emotional load? What did this person do to annoy you?

_____
_____
_____
_____
_____

Make a list of all your thoughts and feelings when you hear or read the word anger. Try to come up with at least ten.

a. _____   f. _____
b. _____   g. _____
c. _____   h. _____
d. _____   i. _____
e. _____   j. _____

Unmet Expectations

Every time Jason gets mad, without fail, he says, "It's not fair!" Most recently, he explained that life wasn't fair because his family moved from Los Angeles to Denver while he was in the ninth grade, leaving all his friends behind. After a few months in his new setting, Jason changed his attitude and decided he likes Denver better than Los Angeles. after all. It took him a while to adapt to his new surroundings, but he did it!

Jose, 15, Texas: "When life throws you a curve ball and things don't go the way you thought they were supposed to go, it's like someone has hit you in the stomach and knocked the wind out of you. Your first response is to want to hit back, but you can't always do that. Unmet expectations are like something dying inside you. The greater the loss, the greater the pain, but you get over it. That's what growing pains are all about. My new coach

Reprinted with special permission of King Features Syndicate.

has this slogan about growing pains. It goes like this: Pain is inevitable; suffering is optional."

When was the last time you got angry? Think about what exactly caused the feelings of anger. Most likely, you got angry because some expectation didn't get met. You thought you were going to ace a quiz and you didn't, or you thought a friend was going to call last night and she didn't. In the course of a typical day, we have hundreds of expectations. Every time you get angry it is because of an unmet expectation. Now, this doesn't mean we shouldn't have expectations—that would be unrealistic. Developing good anger coping skills means learning to fine-tune your expectations to match your circumstances. Wherever possible, learn from the experience and then move on.

Expectations are like the mind's sonar. We send thoughts and perceptions into the future to navigate where we are going. But even the best sonar has to be calibrated every now and then for accuracy. The same can be said about expectations. Without any expectations, we would be like a ship bashing against the rocks all day long. Refining our expectations allows us to navigate the rough waters of life.

Thoughts and Reflections

List five things you are angry or frustrated about. Next to each one write down the expectation that wasn't met and what your first Hot Stone reaction typically is.

Frustration	Expectation	Initial Hot Stone Reaction
a. _____	_____	_____
b. _____	_____	_____
c. _____	_____	_____
d. _____	_____	_____
e. _____	_____	_____

The Many Faces of Anger

Most every teen who shares their thoughts about stress and anger talks about two kinds of anger: anger towards yourself, and anger towards others.

Katie, 15, Florida: "I think everyone gets mad at their parents at times, because they seem to have all the control and we seem to have none! I also get mad at some of my friends for doing stupid things, like borrowing money and not paying it back. But I also get mad at myself for saying or doing stupid things. Getting mad at yourself doesn't really help, 'cause no matter where you go, you still have to live with yourself. When I get mad at myself, I can get down on myself for several days. It's easier to get mad at someone else than at yourself. I think that's because it's harder to forgive yourself."

Indeed, anger has many faces. The most obvious ones, rage and hostility, make CNN headlines: "Postal Worker Goes Ballistic!" But anger has many more faces, such as impatience, guilt, resentment, sarcasm, envy, hatred, arrogance, cynicism, prejudice, wrath, frustration, bitterness, animosity, indignation, arrogance, jealousy and revenge. Most of these expressions don't make the headlines.

How often do you get angry? If you are like most people, the number is about twenty times a day. For some, this might seem rather low (the Silent but Deadly Stone), yet for others, this seems rather high (the Volcanic Stone). However, given all the ways that anger can show up—from impatience and jealousy to mild irritations to full-blown rage—perhaps twenty times a day doesn't really seem that high.

Take a moment to think about it, then ask yourself, "How many times do I get angry?" Once you have this answer, ask how your anger surfaces. Is it impatience or guilt? How about sarcasm or just plain frustration? Finally, ask yourself what expectation wasn't met. Ten times out of ten, you will see that every anger episode is the result of an unmet expectation.

Thoughts and Reflections

How has your day been so far? Did you get angry or frustrated? How many times? What Hot Stones were/are you carrying around today (Razor, Revenge, Volcanic, or Silent but Deadly)? Can you identify what emotion occurs most often when you get angry (such as guilt, impatience or cynicism)? Try to be specific about how anger shows up in your mind (impatience, guilt or frustration).

_____

_____

_____

Good Ways to Deal with Anger

The best way to deal with anger is to resolve it, which means letting it go, and the sooner the better. If you hang on to your anger feelings too long, not only does it drain your energy, but you end up giving your power away. This, in turn, can make you more angry. The best ways to deal with anger involve working toward some sense of resolution. Based on conversations with hundreds of teenagers, these are the most effective ways to deal with anger.

1. Talk with friends. One of the best ways to deal with anger is to release it, and one of the best ways to release anger is to talk about it with your friends, a brother or sister, or even your parents. (If none of these choices are available, there is always a special teacher you can pull to the side, or perhaps even a school counselor.) This kind of talk is called "venting," and it means letting off steam. Anger is often compared to toxic waste, which corrodes and destroys everything in its path if ignored. Sharing your thoughts with a friend is a great way to get the toxic thoughts out of your system.

Girls seem to have an easier time than boys when it comes to venting anger with their friends, but this doesn't mean that guys shouldn't do it.

Tom, 15, Colorado: "The best way to deal with anger is to talk to friends. Having just moved from Illinois, I talk to my best friends on-line, so I go on the computer often. For me, that's one way to release my anger. Everyone needs an outlet. This is mine."

Jesse, 18, Florida: "Talk to someone, like a friend—someone you can trust. I also talk to the secretary at school about a lot of stuff on my mind. I talked to the school interventionist once when I was upset. It really helped. Personally, I don't think students use the school counselors here as a resource. I think many students think that it looks bad if they see you go and talk to the interventionist. I don't really care."

Eric, 15, Colorado: "Guys don't talk to other guys about feelings because you look weak, which is the last way you want to look. So they tend to save that stuff for when they talk to girls."

Chelsea, 16, Ohio: "If you have a friend who you can really talk to and relate to, it helps to talk to them because they can understand. They may have gone through something that you're going through right now, and they offer advice on what to do."

Eric, 16, Arizona: "Just talking about it works really well. I tell my friends what happened, and sometimes they can relate and sometimes they can't. But it doesn't matter if they can relate because they are just there to listen. It makes me feel so much better. They may not understand a word you're saying, but it makes you feel so much better."

Thoughts and Reflections

Name three people you can turn to when you need an objective ear to listen to your problems.

a. _____

b. _____

c. _____

Venting about your problems to a friend can get old, even to your best friend. Can you think of two ways to discuss problems without making it sound like a daily "whine session"?

a. _____

b. _____

2. Get a clear perspective on the problem. Being thrown in the middle of a stressful situation can catch you off guard. Instead of responding with a level head, the tendency is to react, either by saying or doing something you might regret later on. So rather than react, step outside the situation to see the bigger picture and what really matters. Once you have a clear perspective, come back to the situation and do your best to resolve it.

Harris, 15, Florida: "Go have some time to yourself and think about what the problem really is. Try to figure out why you are angry, and let it go. To deal with frustrations, you need a clear head."

Alana, 15, Colorado: "Think about what frustrates you in a bigger picture. You think maybe you're really mad at your friend now, but if you think about it in two years or even a month later, is that really going to matter? Just think about it in the long run, because you don't always know how things are going to work out."

3. Express your feelings. It is perfectly natural to feel angry. Everybody does. And whether you're a girl or a guy, everyone feels anger the same way, although women have been cultured not to express it like men. (If they do, they are often called a name that rhymes with witch.) It's a myth to think that only guys can feel angry because they have testosterone. Remember that guys do not have a monopoly on anger.

Because anger has been considered such a cultural taboo subject over the past few centuries, to even suggest a sense of anger publicly was thought to be dangerous. Now experts agree that holding back your feelings is actually worse than not expressing them at all. The key is to do it diplomatically and appropriately so that you keep friends rather than making worse enemies!

To acknowledge and express your anger, all it takes is the ability to say the words "I feel angry!" or "I am angry!" Sometimes merely saying these words releases the frustration that has been bottled up inside. How you express your feelings is important, especially the wording. For instance, if you say "YOU make me angry," you cast blame on somebody else who might become defensive. This could make matters much worse. Once again, diplomacy is essential.

Sometimes we assume other people can read our minds when we act a certain way or say certain words. Men may be from Mars, and women may be from Venus, but right now, we're all living together on Earth. When expressing your anger creatively and diplomatically, it is essential to use words that everyone understands, leaving nothing open for interpretation.

Kirby, 15, Colorado: "Good ways to deal with anger? I definitely suggest reflection; there are so many times I have been really mad about something, and then I've sat down and thought about it and realized I was wrong and that I was really being mean to whoever I thought was being mean to me. Think about it logically—try to talk to yourself about it. I know that sounds kind of weird, but if you are like me, it's not a big deal. You begin to realize that you shouldn't be angry, and it's not the end of the world. So I think that before you do anything else, you need to sit down and think about the problem to calm yourself down. Another good way is to have a simple, honest conversation with whomever you're angry with. It's almost like therapy in itself. When you do this, you feel like you are bonding with that person by having a conversation with them and it works out your problem. Those are the two things I do."

Heather, 16, Vermont: "One good way I let off steam is writing in my journal. Writing helps me get anger and stress out. I sometimes write parts of poems or lyrics and then reread them to myself, allowing myself to see what I am going through in a different perspective and realize that being angry isn't healthy."

Kathleen, 14, Colorado: "I deal with my anger best through some physical force, not hurting anything, but I play my cello as hard or loud as I possibly can, or sing as loud as I can in the shower just to get rid of all this tension."

4. Hang out with your friends. There is an expression that says "misery loves company." Although the expression may sound rather negative, what it really means is that hanging out with friends tends to take the sting out of a bad situation.

Friends act like a buffer zone for stress. Friends are like a bunch of pillows; they tend to soften the impact when you get knocked over. In some cases, you might not even talk about what's on your mind. Just being together is enough. Hanging out with friends to reduce stress is not the same thing as hanging out with friends to form a critical mass of misery, and it's important to know the difference.

Alonso, 17, New York: "My parents are alcoholics, so I try to get out of the house as much as possible and hang out with my friends. I don't tell my friends, mostly because I don't want them to know. But just getting out of the house is a big help."

Marcie, 13, California: "The first thing I do when I go to school is gather around my friends. Since I am an only child, they're like my sisters. We talk about everything. When I am having a bad day, they are always there for me. That's what a family is: people who are there for you."

Sara, 14, Texas: "Good ways to deal with anger include being with your friends. Talk face to face with someone about whatever is on your mind, because if you have a really good friend and you talk to them about it, I believe that helps. Your friends can help you with the problem, and if you're close to your parents, talk to them, too."

5. Keep a journal. Many teenagers who were interviewed, both girls and guys, mentioned keeping a journal. They said there are many things they don't feel comfortable sharing with others, but they can write it down and let it go away.

Girls said they tend to write in their journals as if they are writing a letter, whereas guys not only write essays but also write song lyrics, poetry or create some other form of artwork.

Brad, 17, Texas: "If you listen to music, like Pearl Jam, Eminem, Rage Against the Machine or even the Beatles, the lyrics are an expression of their emotions. These are like the lyrics I write. It's a way of expressing myself. I hope to be a musician, which is why I use this as an outlet. I know other guys who write lyrics or poems or rap songs as an expression, too. This really helps."

Darcy, 18, North Carolina: "I think a good way to let off steam is to go in your room, lock the door and start crying. When you are done, get some paper and a pen, because I also find that writing poetry lessens the pain."

Ali, 14, Colorado: "To deal with anger in a good way, I write in my journal. I start writing really fast. When I get angry, it's like all of these thoughts are spinning in my head, and I'm getting angrier and angrier. So these would be running through my head, and I would be so mad, and I would start journaling. Keeping a journal is a great way to get these thoughts sorted out, and at the same time, writing about the problem helps let off steam. My writing starts out as angry words, but then it tones down to a strategy; what I'm going to do, this is why I'm so sad, that it will get better tomorrow or next week, and I'll get through it. When you're journaling, it doesn't have to have a theme—just write whatever is on your mind."

Thoughts and Reflections

Journaling is a great way to get toxic thoughts out of your head and down on paper. Journaling is different than keeping a diary in that, with journaling, you take the time to express and process your emotions. At the end of this chapter there is a journaling exercise. Please read it and write down what thoughts come to mind.

If journaling is not your thing, perhaps drawing is! Art therapy is also a wonderful way to get toxic thoughts and feelings out of your head and down on paper. (Several of the art pieces in this book are examples of art therapy!) So if the spirit moves you, pull out a pen, or better yet, a box of pastels and express your feelings about one of the following:

a. Draw how you feel when you're angry or afraid (use lots of different colors if possible)

b. Draw your house

c. Draw a picture of yourself

d. Draw an expression of your regrets or desires

e. Draw a vision of your future

f. Draw anything you want

6. Diversions: sports, music, etc. Sometimes what you really need is a good way to vent your anger; a harmless way to let off some steam. There are no shortage of ways to do this: Sports and physical exercise are a great way. Hobbies are another. By placing your focus on other things, such as sports, singing and hobbies, you begin to get a better perspective on your life, and with this perspective, anger dissipates.

Chris, 14, Colorado: "When I get frustrated, I go out in the front yard and shoot pucks. I'm a forward on my hockey team, and this is one way I relieve the tension. I've broken some garage windows. It really feels good when you break the window, until your parents say, 'Chris, how dare you?' Now I'm helping my dad install Plexiglas in the windows. Sometimes when I am really pissed, I play with my dog. He's a golden retriever. It takes my mind off the problem. Animals do that."

Aaron, 13, Colorado: "One way I deal with anger is by being alone, spending time by myself. I can read or play music. I like listening to the emotions in the music. If I'm happy, it will be light and cheerful. If I'm angry, it will be fast. I might even practice my instruments. I play violin, viola, cello, bass and piano. Whatever I'm practicing always sounds different if I'm in a different mood."

Eric, 14, Illinois: "Well, for me, it's music, and if you ask me what kind of music I like, I'll tell you I like everything. If it's on the charts, I probably like it. Anything that's popular, anything that I just personally like, I'll listen to. And that's another thing when I'm mad, I'll go up to my room and turn on my radio. Then it kind of cools me down, and I get my mind off whatever I'm mad about and start thinking about good things. Sometimes, not thinking about my problem helps; it gives me some distance. I also think that friends help a lot. Whenever I'm real mad about something, I'll call my friends about this issue or that issue; tell them about it and get their opinion. Often, my friends are right, and I'm like, 'Okay, thanks! That's cool.'"

Brittany, 14, Illinois: "Some of the good ways I let off steam are walking or singing. When I sing, I think of a song that makes me happy, or lyrics of a song that make me happy, and I sing them (sometimes to myself, sometimes out loud). I find that when I sing like this, I won't say anything I might later regret, or that will get me into trouble or hurt somebody else."

Thoughts and Reflections

There is an expression, "Don't put all your eggs in one basket." What are your baskets? List three areas of interest outside of school that give balance to your life. (If you don't have healthy diversions, what are some areas of interest to create some?)

a. _____

b. _____

c. _____

Music holds the capacity for emotions, ranging from anger to love. Can you list three songs that allow you to optimally vent and release your frustration?

a. _____

b. _____

c. _____

7. Fine-tune your expectations. Remember that every time you get mad, frustrated or impatient, it is the result of an unmet expectation. Expectations aren't bad; they just need to be fine-tuned, especially when things don't go as planned. What can you do to fine-tune expectations? First, try to see what the problem really is. Second, ask yourself if you have all the information you need. Many times, unmet expectations involve misinformation. Third, create some options so when you get tossed a curveball, you can move in a new direction.

Finally, fine-tuning expectations means accepting that which you cannot control. Acceptance is not impossible; it just takes practice.

Kevin, 16, Maryland: "When I was about twelve years old, I really wanted my dad to take me to see *Star Wars: The Phantom Menace.* He kept promising he would, but something always came up with work, and I believed him. Well, the movie came and went, and I never saw it till it came out on video. My dad breaks a lot of promises, so I just learned to lower my expectations, especially if he cancels the first time around. I have also learned to make back-up plans so that I am not disappointed."

Xavier, 17, New York: "There is a fine line between lowering your expectations and lowering your self-esteem. You've got to make sure you don't do the latter. Walk into each situation with a game plan, a strategy. If things turn out differently, adjust your attitude. It's all about attitude. Of course, this is easier said than done. I sat down for a test the other day thinking it was multiple choice, but it was fill-in-the-blank. Boy, was I surprised (and pissed!), but I refocused my thoughts and pulled off a B. Lowering your expectations doesn't mean lowering your standards. Don't compromise your integrity."

8. Acceptance. Let's face it, there are some things you can never change, like your parents' divorce, the death of a close friend or the latest test scores. The best strategy is to acknowledge what you cannot change and move on. It's easy to want to change everything that meets with your dissatisfaction, but you'll go nuts trying. As the expression goes, "Pick your battles," and this means letting go of (accepting) the things you cannot change. What are things you cannot change? For starters, other people like your parents or stepparents, brothers and sisters, teachers and coaches, and traffic are things that are impossible to change.

> **Donna, 15, Vermont:** "Trying to change something over which you have no control is like banging your head against the wall. What good is that? This doesn't mean you should accept everything at face value, either. The real message is not to get stuck in the past, but keep moving."
>
> **Philip, 18, Florida:** "I got my driver's license at sixteen. I'm eighteen now, and I drive to my part-time job after school. Traffic is one thing that used to really piss me off; there are so many dumb drivers who don't use their turn signals, it baffles me. At first I fought it, until I realized there is no way I can control this. Given the situation, now I just accept it, and I play loud music to pass the time in the car."

9. Volunteer for others. Several kids suggested that if you want to feel better about yourself, lend a helping hand to someone who really needs it. Examples include hospitals, soup kitchens, Goodwill, tutoring at school or helping your local church. By doing this, you take the attention off yourself and place it on someone else who is usually a lot worse off. Unresolved anger can turn into a self-pity party where you become consumed with how bad off you think you are. When you take the time to serve others, you begin to realize that perhaps you don't have it so bad after all. Volunteering lends perspective to a very foggy situation.

Eric, 15, Colorado: "I did some volunteer work with my church last year. When you start working with people who have serious life problems, it really puts your own life in perspective. I walked away from that experience with a lighter heart. It really allowed me to let go of some things that were bothering me."

Thoughts and Reflections

Have you ever volunteered for an organization? If so, which one(s)?

_____

_____

_____

Describe how you feel when you are done helping others. Does this help relieve tension and frustration?

_____

_____

_____

One of the most commonly heard criticisms of teens is that they are self-centered and simply not aware of their actions toward others. Here is a suggestion: Go out of your way to do something nice for someone, someone you don't know and who could really use a helping hand. Practice a random act of kindness. Remember, when you do this, don't expect anything in return.

10. Count to ten. Thomas Jefferson once said, "If you get mad, count to ten. If you get really angry, count to one hundred." The idea behind counting to ten is that it gives you a chance to chill out. By and large, anger is an immediate reaction. "Flipping the bird" or swearing when you feel threatened is the ego talking, which will most likely get you in trouble. Counting to ten is a conscious response. When you take time to chill out, you gain a sense of perspective that is clearly missing when you first lose your temper.

> **Josh, 18, Texas:** "I used to have a really bad temper, and there are many times I wish I had counted to ten. I do this now, and it works. Rather than speak my mind and say something I might regret later, I close my eyes or get a drink of water to clear my mind. If it is someone else who has angered me, I explain to him or her why I feel angry. My mom taught me this. She also said that if you're going to get mad, be sure to attack issues, not people. If you attack people, they just put up their defenses, and nothing is resolved."

Thoughts and Reflections

This reflection exercise is designed to help you see the issues behind the situation. Next time you get angry, turn to this page and write down (1) what the situation was that got you mad, (2) what the issue is behind the situation, (3) the Hot Stone associated with this situation, and (4) (this is the hard part) separate your ego and get some perspective on the problem, perhaps even through someone else's eyes. Here's an example:

Anger Situation:	Parent's won't allow me to go to concert.
Issue:	Trust—they don't trust me, and I don't trust them!
Initial Hot Stone Reaction:	I want to hit something!

Provide Some   There could be drugs or alcohol at the
Perspective: concert. Someone could get into a serious
                    car accident from a drunk driver and
                    possibly die. It could be me.

Now it's your turn:

Anger Situation: _____
                        _____
                        _____.

Issue: _____
                        _____
                        _____.

Initial Hot Stone   _____
Reaction: _____
                        _____.

Provide Some   _____
Perspective: _____
                        _____
                        _____.

11. Sweet forgiveness. Many teenagers, when asked about
dealing with anger, mentioned the importance of forgiveness.
Everyone who mentioned forgiveness said it is perhaps the
hardest thing to do. Holding a grudge against someone only
hurts you in the long run. More often than not, they don't even
know they have done something to offend you, so holding a
grudge is like drilling a hole in the bottom of a boat and spending the rest of your time bailing water. Here are some pointers
on acts of forgiveness:

1. When you forgive someone, whether it's face to face or simply in your heart, don't expect an apology. You could be waiting a very long time.
2. When you forgive someone, do it for yourself, not for the other person.
3. Forgiveness does not mean to forget. It means you can move on from the situation without feeling victimized.
4. Forgiveness frees you up from the bitterness of sarcasm, cynicism and resentment.
5. Forgiveness of someone else also means forgiving yourself for similar wrongdoings or mean comments.

Kessel, 17, California: "There are many times when the best, and perhaps only, way to deal with anger is forgiveness. You really have to learn to forgive people or else you end up being mad at so many people that you won't even remember who you are mad at anymore."

Thoughts and Reflections

Can you name anyone you have been holding a grudge against who you need to forgive?

_____

_____

_____

_____

Based on the information in this chapter, what are three things you can do to start the forgiveness process?

a. _____

b. _____

c. _____

Feeling Good About Myself: Boosting My Self-Esteem

*Don't think of your bad qualities.
Instead, think of the positive
and good in yourself.*

KRISTIN D., 15

*C*hances are good that if you were to ask your friends what's really important to them, you would most likely hear them talk about their image or some aspect of identity. It might be the clothes they wear, the music they listen to, the grades they are studying for, the person they want to date or the ideal car they want to drive. So much of what we talk about directly involves our identity. And with our identity comes self-esteem. In fact, self-esteem is the cornerstone upon which our identity is built.

Self-esteem is a topic that is rarely talked about or addressed by parents. Nor is it a topic of study in school. Yet for as important as self-esteem is, it should be, because most everything you do in your life is directly related to it. So why don't people talk about self-esteem? Perhaps it's because in American culture high self-esteem is often confused with conceit and self-righteousness. As it turns out, people who have high self-esteem are never considered to be conceited. Yet the myth lives on.

Without a doubt, self-esteem is essential to dealing effectively with stress. If you have high self-esteem, things that might normally bother you tend to roll off your back. But when self-esteem is low, it's like you are a target, and every stressor in the world is coming your way.

High Self-Esteem

What is high self-esteem? Perhaps it can best be described as an overall sense of confidence. Confidence is the belief that you can do almost anything you set your mind to, even if it means it may take a few tries. High self-esteem also includes self-worth, meaning how you value yourself. People with high self-esteem see themselves as having great value, meaning they have much to give the world, including being there for a friend, being part of a team, helping out with chores at home, or simply making the world a better place to live through their talents and abilities.

People who have high self-esteem aren't cocky or arrogant—that's low self-esteem. Instead, they are really nice people to be around. They feel comfortable about themselves, even when they are trying, like everyone else, to figure out where they fit in this world. We all have the potential to have high self-esteem, but it takes work. There are many people, like beautiful models or sports heroes, who can start knocking down our self-esteem if we let them. The key to maintaining high self-esteem is to know that it comes from within, not from some external force.

Amanda, 14, Colorado: "My self-esteem varies. Sometimes I feel like I have high self-esteem when I play the piano because I know I'm good at it, but I have low self-esteem when doing something else. School can give me low self-esteem because my sister is always doing well, and I'm always trailing behind her and not getting perfect grades. So it's kind of stressful, but I'm pretty sure I have gotten over most of it. Overall, I just feel I should be myself and look the way I do and act the way I do."

Harris, 15, Florida: "I think that if you have high self-esteem, your stress will be lower because things don't hurt you as much. If someone says something bad about you in class, and you're feeling good about yourself, you're not going to be too uptight about it. You are just going to let it go."

Julie, 16, Colorado: "There are different types of self-esteem, at least for me, like how one looks and how one does in school. It's easy to compare yourself to other people. I think the best way to stop that is to get your priorities straight and try to work on school because you want to get your work done. Hard work pays off."

Michelle, 14, Colorado: "When people are happy, it's not because everything in their life is perfect. It's because they are brushing past the imperfections. I guess that's something I've thought about often because when people have really low self-esteem, they think they are the only ones who have problems. Yet everyone has problems and imperfections. Some people just brush past it, but other people dwell on it. Focus on the positive. You should not adjust to people's whims. Allow them to adjust to you."

Low Self-Esteem

We all have bad-hair days. These are the days when, after you wake up, shower, get dressed and take one look in the mirror, all you want to do is go back to bed and hide. If you have ever had one of these days, you are in great company. Low self-esteem is more than one or two bad-hair days; it's an endless string of bad-hair days. In simplest terms, low self-esteem is the sense that you're simply not good enough. Not just with one thing, like sports, school or friends, but with everything! Our self-esteem is constantly under attack as we build our identities. It's fair to say that low self-esteem is very common among teenagers. Not only do we have our egos telling us that we aren't good enough, we are barraged with all kinds of marketing from corporations that if we don't buy their products, we are not good enough.

Darren, 15, Texas: "The whole issue of self-worth is one I'm struggling with because I've always had low self-esteem. Ever since seventh grade, all I've heard is bad things about myself from people, like those kids who have a lot of money. All they've ever done is make fun of me. When people say things to me now, I stick up for myself. I'm going to counseling because I'm trying to learn how to raise my self-esteem and be more confident. I've learned that one way to have good self-esteem is to have some good friends. When I'm with other people, I don't necessarily feel bad about myself. But when I'm with people I don't know, it's hard. For example, if I have a friend over and he happens to bring another friend along, I don't necessarily feel all that great. It's kind of weird. I guess I worry about myself. I know that kind of sounds selfish and everything, but I do."

Brittany, 15, Illinois: "If you have low self-esteem, you might take the wrong route for dealing with stress and do something you might regret. You are more susceptible to peer pressure when you have low self-esteem. Take a look at the magazines today. They contain the all-American girl (super-thin, etc.). You see this, and you begin to doubt yourself. If you see too much of this, you might even think of committing suicide or fall back into the peer pressure trap again—doing things with others that you would *never* do on your own."

Keegan, 15, Colorado: "I think that having bad self-esteem can promote more stress. If you have bad self-esteem, you might say to yourself, 'Oh, I'm not smart enough. I can't do this.' So you don't do your homework and you start failing in school. Then you'll never get a good job; you'll never get the house you want, the car or the family. It's a downward spiral. Without self-esteem, you also don't care what you look like, thinking, 'Oh, I don't care if I don't take a shower for the next three days, have wax in my ears or forget to brush my teeth.' If you start acting like you don't care, people in school will rip on you even more."

Chelsea, 16, Ohio: "I used to have really low self-esteem. I wasn't really good about dealing with stress. I was really sad. All my friends could tell, and my parents could tell, but once I started feeling better about myself, everything has become a lot better. My grades have improved. My attitude has improved. I just feel a lot better. Self-esteem can take a nosedive if you let other people's opinions about you rule your life. What makes it hard is that we try so hard to be accepted, but if we're not accepted by everybody, it feels like we're being dragged down and we start feeling bad about ourselves. Now I'm only insecure about some things."

Thoughts and Reflections

How would you rate your overall self-esteem (on a scale of one to ten, with ten being the highest)? _____

What are four areas in your life where you would rate your self-esteem high (sports, school, etc.)?

a. _____

b. _____

c. _____

d. _____

What, if any, things deflate your self-esteem?

_____

_____

_____

_____

How does the Hot Stone you tend to carry most often deflate your self-esteem?

_____

_____

_____

Success and failure

We live in a society in which success is greatly rewarded. Movie stars and professional athletes earning multimillion-dollar contracts are the most extreme examples of how society rewards success, but these are the exceptions. Typically, success is judged by our achievements. For some people, success seems easy. They seem to have natural talent in whatever they do. These are the people who can succeed just by showing up. Yet for most everyone else, success takes work. As the expression goes, "It takes ten years to be an overnight success," meaning that true success takes a lot of effort. Talent will only get you so far. Repeated success requires effort, ambition, inspiration, discipline and motivation. What do successful people have in common? They are not motivated by fear. They believe that over time, they can accomplish just about anything.

Rob, 14, California: "Confidence means believing you can do anything. It can be something specific or more general, like believing in what you want to do with your life. I didn't believe that I could take on what I have with my life (the death of my mom), but I have—that's confidence. I've gone out for the wrestling team and made some friends on the team. I'm in Knowledge Bowl. I'm in the Future Business Leaders of America and Foreign Language

Club. I'm taking French and Spanish, and I am involved with MESA—Odyssey of the Mind, where we take on a different problem each year and try to solve it. I couldn't do all these things if I didn't believe I could do them."

How does success differ from failure? For the most part, failure is the absence of effort, just not trying. Failure isn't making mistakes; that's just the end result of not giving it your best effort. Of course, there are people who try and fail, but they learn from this experience and use the failure to succeed later. Not all failure is bad. Sometimes we need to fail once or twice to finally succeed. Some of the greatest inventions came about as a result of failure. Thomas Edison tried several hundred filaments before he found one that would work to make a lightbulb. Author Mario Puzo had his *Godfather* manuscript rejected nearly one hundred times before someone published his famous book. Michael Jordan misses hundreds of baskets, Brad Pitt has made some bad movies, and Janet Jackson has had a few songs that flopped. Failure isn't the lack of success. It's the lack of trying to succeed.

Thoughts and Reflections

Make a list of five areas in which you are truly successful. It can include anything from sports to designing Web pages. (It could even include making something for dinner without burning it.) Next to each item, give a brief explanation reminding you how you got to this level of success.

	My successes	Steps that led toward this success
a.	_____	_____
b.	_____	_____
c.	_____	_____
d.	_____	_____
e.	_____	_____

There is a story of a teacher who taught a class called FAIL-URE 101. He taught his students how to fail gracefully. He gave each student an assignment to create a product that nobody would buy. Then they had to try to sell it. What amazed the students was that failing took some work, because some products actually sold. Try this: Pick an impossible task and purposely fail at it (please, schoolwork not included). Write a letter to your favorite singer and ask for a response, write a poem that no one likes, or cook a meal straight from a cookbook and see how it turns out. You might find that failing is not as easy as it seems.

Nurturing a Healthy Ego

You may think that having an ego is a bad thing, but in truth, we all need egos because that's the part of us that keeps an eye out for threats to our physical existence. The problem is when the ego gets out of control and decides to run all other aspects of your life. You may know people like this. We often say, "He's got a big ego." People who have big egos really have low self-esteem, which is why they have to prove to the world how great they are. If they really knew it, they wouldn't have to prove it.

A healthy ego actually supports high self-esteem because it promotes confidence, not cockiness. There is a fine balance between confidence and cockiness! Believing in yourself doesn't mean that you have to brag about how great you are. Your actions will speak for themselves. A healthy ego is a humble ego. A healthy ego is someone who prefers to share the limelight with others rather than steal it all for him- or herself. The teen years are when the ego goes through its greatest growing pains: forming an identity, sorting likes from dislikes, admiring your parents but wanting to be different from them, and perhaps most of all, wishing to be accepted as yourself. A healthy ego is a person who is accepting and open-minded. A healthy ego is someone who is discerning but not judgmental. A healthy ego is a balancing act, and it takes work to tame.

Thoughts and Reflections

What does ego mean to you? Do you feel like you have a healthy ego? Why?

_____

_____

_____

_____

_____

Being accepted by friends is crucial to self-esteem, but so is accepting yourself. Try to list three things you can do to accept all aspects of yourself.

a. _____

b. _____

c. _____

List three things you can do to create a more healthy ego.

a. _____

b. _____

c. _____

The five Pillars of Strong Self-Esteem

People who have high self-esteem have a number of things in common, and these have nothing to do with genetics or how much money their parents make. The beauty of self-esteem is that we all have the potential to achieve it, but like everything worth having in life, it requires some effort. The following are factors that contribute to high self-esteem.

1. Uniqueness. Uniqueness is a combination of attributes and qualities that make you feel special (sense of humor, athletic ability, music ability or a sense of creativity). Some people call these gifts. Typically, people focus on what they feel are their negative aspects. Uniqueness suggests that you focus on your special attributes and gifts and use them to your greatest advantage.

> **Keegan, 15, Colorado:** "If you have good self-esteem, you smile inside, you like what you wear and you feel good about yourself. I think what makes me unique is my sense of humor and loyalty to my friends."
>
> **Francesca, 14, North Carolina:** "What makes me feel special is doing all my activities. I do so much, and that makes me feel good because I'm able to do all of these things. I'm in the band, and I'm in a few school plays and musicals."

Kaitlyn, 14, Colorado: "I don't care what people think about me anymore. I have pink hair, and although somebody might make fun of me, I don't care. This is my way of being unique. I really don't care what people think about me. Either they like me or they don't; that really helps my self-esteem. Being more confident has helped me make new friends, too. I've got a better reputation now, and it helps my self-esteem a lot."

Thoughts and Reflections

Everyone has various attributes and qualities that make them special and unique. Take some time to complete this list. Please write down five talents, gifts or resources you have that make you feel special and unique. Then note how you recognize these talents in yourself.

a. _____

b. _____

c. _____

d. _____

e. _____

2. Role models and heroes. Do you have someone you look up to? Role models and heroes are people we view as successful. To have a role model doesn't mean you want to be just like them. Rather, it means you wish to develop the traits that make them successful. Role models and heroes act like a compass because they often guide us to our highest human potential. Even heroes have heroes. Role models and heroes are an essential part of building our own character. There is a difference between a role model and an idol. What do you think the difference is?

Brittany, 16, Illinois: "My mom is my role model because she works hard to support me and my siblings. She's also my mentor because she is intelligent and independent. I also consider Mariah Carey a role model because she doesn't care what anyone says about her."

Heather, 16, Vermont: "One of my role models is my mom. I look up to her in so many ways, and I always go to her when I have problems. She knows what to say to make me feel good, and she deals with problems and life really well. I couldn't ask for a better mother. My boyfriend is also a role model and even a hero to me. I look up to him because of the way he treats me. He is so kind and loving, funny and even stupid sometimes. He doesn't really care what other people think of him, and he does what he wants because it makes him happy. Yet if he knows something bothers me, he'll tend not to do it. I look up to him, because he is so thoughtful about people, and he deals with stress in a good way."

Tom, 15, Colorado: "Michael J. Fox is a hero because of his illness. He seems like a great guy, one of those people you wish you could get to know better. To be honest, today's movie stars and politicians aren't exactly people you want to look up to. A hero is someone who is willing to give up something for something else. Whatever that something might be, heroes give it up for the sake of someone or something they believe in."

Thoughts and Reflections

Everyone has someone they look up to. A role model or hero is someone we admire; specifically, we admire certain traits in him or her that we see in ourselves. Who are your role models? See if you can list three people who inspire you.

a. _____

b. _____

c. _____

Sometimes we outgrow our role models. These are people we might have admired when we were younger, but with age, we have moved on. Is there anyone who used to be your role model?

_____

_____

_____

_____

3. Friends. Without a doubt, friends can help boost self-esteem. Friends who are really sincere and can give you honest feedback are more valuable than all the world's treasures. Friends act like a mirror to reflect things you cannot always see in yourself. Friends can also cheer you up when you need a lift.

> **Caitlin, 14, Colorado:** "Friends are essential for self-esteem. Have your friends reassure you that you are important to them, and do the same for them. Also, try to make new friends."
>
> **Seth, 15, Virginia:** "Probably the biggest booster of self-esteem is good friends. When life pulls you down, receiving compliments from friends can really lift your spirits. It's not

like you go fishing for compliments, but just listen to what your friends say about you. Basically, it will boost your self-esteem. It does for me."

Lacey, 14, Colorado: "Boosting your self-esteem should come from your peers—it's that whole 'what goes around, comes around' thing. Say things to your friends that are encouraging, like, 'Wow, you look good in that! I like that shirt. You did a really good job on the math test. Congratulations! Maybe you could help me out.' These people look on you as a friendly person, and they want to hang out with you. They will give you encouragement, too. They want you to be around because you help boost their self-esteem, thereby boosting your self-esteem because you feel a sense of being needed."

Aden, 14, Colorado: "I'm the kind of person who sometimes feels bad about myself and sometimes feels good about myself. It really depends on who I'm hanging out with. If I'm hanging out with my best friend, she makes me feel great about myself. We really understand each other and have a good time together. I think if you do the things you like to do, hang out with people who won't judge you and accept you as you are, you're going to feel a lot better about yourself."

Thoughts and Reflections

As best as you can in a few words, describe what it means to be a friend.

_____

_____

_____

_____

The number of friends you have isn't as important as the quality of friends you have. Who are your closest friends, and what makes these people so special?

_____

_____

_____

As the expression goes, "A friend in need is a friend indeed." Who are three people you can count on in times of trouble?

a. _____

b. _____

c. _____

4. Empowerment. Empowerment is best described as a feeling that makes you feel confident. Empowerment is not about trying to control others. Instead, it is about being empowered to make the right choices in life, as well as learning from your poor choices. There is a big difference between empowerment and control. Empowerment comes from a sense of inspiration, and it makes you feel good inside. Control, on the other hand, deals with manipulating others.

> **Kirby, 15, Colorado:** "I feel empowered by traits that I'm proud of, I guess. One of them is that I consider myself a pretty perceptive person, and that is something I hold very high in value. Also, I'm compassionate. I've been trying to help people in a great many ways ever since I was little. I went to Mexico last Thanksgiving break on a mission trip with my church. We built a house for a family there. It was amazing to watch their faces when we gave them the new house. It was great, and they were crying. It was wonderful and very empowering!"

Pablo, 13, Colorado: "My confidence empowers me. Whenever I am playing a game or anything and I win, it really boosts my self-esteem and makes me feel good. Yet when I lose I think, 'Hey, it's just a game.' But winning gives you a whole different attitude toward it. Any sort of game—card game, soccer game or whatever—really boosts your self-esteem. Getting a good grade also boosts your self-esteem. It's confidence that gets you there."

Jason, 15, Colorado: "I think artistic expression feeds your self-esteem, and this is empowering for me. I discovered poetry as a means of self-expression, and it's very cathartic. I think I first started poetry in creative-writing class and never stopped."

Thoughts and Reflections

What makes you feel empowered? These are usually intangible things, such as love, creativity, faith or humor. Empowerment comes from a special knowledge inside that things will work out. So what makes you feel empowered? Where do you draw your inspiration?

_____

_____

_____

_____

Here is an exercise you can do alone or together with some friends at a sleepover. Get a big piece of paper and draw a circle on it. Divide the circle into four equal areas (for uniqueness, role models, friends and empowerment). Then collect a stack of old magazines, some scissors and a glue stick. Start going through the magazines and cutting out pictures and words that remind you of these four areas (you can also add personal photos). Then hang the collage someplace where you can see it often.

5. Calculated risks. A fifth aspect of self-esteem deals with risks and challenges. Life is full of risks. Avoiding all risk is dangerous, but taking foolish risks is equally dangerous. Taking calculated risks means carefully looking at all your options before you make your next move and then making the best choice possible. Taking calculated risks means making educated decisions about everything, from how many colleges to apply to for admission to whom to ride home with after a school function. Risks and goals have something in common. Calculated risks get the goal accomplished safely.

> **Kyle, 18, Tennessee:** "Here is my suggestion. Try different things till you find something you're good at and you feel good about doing. Even if you're not good at it at first, give it a shot and keep with it, and you'll improve because whenever you are good at something it makes you feel really good."
>
> **Peter, 17, Maryland:** "Life is full of risks. There are good risks and bad risks. Here's my advice, and it comes from experience: Think things through before you do them. Good risks have benefits; bad risks have consequences. How each affects self-esteem is rather obvious."

Thoughts and Reflections

What does taking calculated risks mean to you? Give it some thought and share your thoughts in a few words.

_____

_____

_____

We have all made some bad decisions. Experience is a good teacher—if we can learn the lessons from previous mistakes. What are some experiences of yours in which a risk wasn't well-calculated?

_____

_____

_____

_____

What are some challenges you face as a teen that you would consider risky? Select one and come up with as many consequences (positive and negative) that you can think of. What options do you have with this challenge?

_____

_____

_____

_____

Eight Great Ways to Boost Your Self-Esteem

When it comes to boosting self-esteem, there is no shortage of ways to make yourself feel better. Boosting self-esteem starts with a belief that you are worthy and valuable. It continues with a sense of assertiveness. Finally, boosting self-esteem includes action to put your belief of value into play. The following are some ideas and suggestions on ways to boost or maintain your level of self-esteem.

1. Positive self-talk. It is easy to fall victim to the critic that constantly reminds us we have flaws. But that voice is just like a radio station that can be changed to a better, positive voice. Positive self-talk means tuning in to the voice that says you are good and valuable. This is the voice that successful people listen to.

Alison, 14, California: "Just think you're the best; keep giving yourself positive feedback. Forget about what other people think of you (people will always try to cut you down, but that just means they are jealous). Don't let other people's thoughts affect the way you act, because that can totally kill your self-esteem."

Sean, 18, Michigan: "To boost your self-esteem I have only one tip: Don't worry about what others say and think about you. Be yourself, and be happy with yourself (provide yourself with lots of positive thoughts). Unlike happiness generated from outside sources, when this happiness occurs, no one can take it away from you."

Thoughts and Reflections

Stop and listen to the voice of the critic in your head (it gets really loud when you look in the mirror). Perhaps you are well aware of this voice. What does it say and how does this make you feel?

_____

_____

_____

_____

_____

Positive self-talk uses affirmations to steer you off the cliff of low self-esteem and back to smooth waters. Affirmation statements usually begin with the words "I am" (e.g., "I am a successful lacrosse player," "I am a good poet," or "I am calm and relaxed"). Think of four affirmations that are personal and empower you.

a. _____

b. _____

c. _____

d. _____

Having an affirmation is a good start, but once you have it, you are going to need to use it. This means saying it to yourself (and drowning out the negative self-talk) in times of stress. Name three places that you can repeat one or more of these phrases to yourself when you need it most.

a. _____

b. _____

c. _____

2. Build a strong support group. A strong support group includes friends who are supportive in both good times and bad. This isn't a big group, but a small core of best friends who are there when you really need a friend.

Eric, 14, Illinois: "Well, I think that interaction with good friends is a great way to build self-esteem. I think you need to stay around people who really appreciate and know you. That's why I was heartbroken when my friend, Tom, moved away. Whenever we were together, nothing was wrong. I think that when you're with people who understand and really know you, the way Tom and I know each other, it's a good self-esteem boost. Being in sports, groups and various activities helps build your self-esteem. Be proud (but not arrogant) of yourself. A couple of years ago, I was so worried about pleasing everybody else I got nowhere. Now, I'm just worried about being myself. Everybody accepts you because you're yourself, and people would rather see that. It took me awhile to figure out that people would rather see that."

Pam, 15, Virginia: "I kind of look to other people to boost my self-esteem. Whenever I'm feeling like, 'Oh, should I wear this' or 'I'm not good enough,' I turn to my friends and say, 'I'm having a down day; remind me of my best features.' And then I'll feel better. It's not like I want pity or sympathy. I don't. A good friend knows to cheer you up when you're down."

Thoughts and Reflections

There is an expression that says, "You can never have too many friends." In our transient society, where people can move overnight to another state, good friends are hard to come by and harder to keep. This exercise suggests that you go out and make one new friend this month. Pick someone you don't know or don't know very well, and invite this person over to get to know him or her better. Note: Friendships cannot be forced. It may take talking to several people before you find one you can really call a friend.

3. Lift your head up when you walk. People who are down on themselves show it in the way they walk. Their posture is slumped, and they drop their heads. People who are confident walk with their chin up. If you want to start feeling better about yourself, observe how you walk and how you carry your head.

4. Make eye contact when you speak to somebody. We all have moments of being shy and tend to dart our eyes down or to the sides. Strong eye contact, especially when you are speaking to someone, conveys a sense of confidence. Try practicing this with your friends.

5. Do something good for yourself. Treat yourself to something special. It doesn't have to cost lots of money. It could be making pancakes for dinner, burning a CD of your favorite songs, going for a walk in the park or having a few friends sleep over.

Julia, 16, Colorado: "To make myself feel better I take a 'me night' or a 'me day'. It's not a selfish thing—actually, it's just the opposite. Being down on yourself is a drain on other people. Taking a 'me day' is recharging. You are saying to yourself, 'I am worth it.' It could be a bubble bath, putting on your facial goop and watching sappy movies and eating popcorn—it doesn't matter!"

Thoughts and Reflections

Make a list of five things you can do for your personal "Me Day."

a. _____

b. _____

c. _____

d. _____

e. _____

6. Sing a song in your head that makes you feel good. If you are having a bad-hair day, and you cannot hide in bed, start thinking of a song that makes you feel good. Listening to music, whether it's on the radio, or an MP3 or in your head, helps drown out the inner critic.

Heather, 16, Vermont: "Some of the songs I hear on the radio make me feel better about myself, and I love to listen to music."

7. Don't lose your esteem to the media. People who create advertising and marketing thrive on your insecurities. Models and movie stars make up less than 1 percent of the population, yet they set the standard for how to look. This whole Hollywood mirage is an illusion. You don't have to buy into it. In fact, doing so is a sure-fire way to not only lower your self-esteem, but to stomp the remains of it into the ground.

Stacy, 17, Pennsylvania: "The media is an interesting analogy— the way it stereotypes everything, it all seems like one big high school to me. The media portrays everybody in one way. Take the beautiful models—they think everybody should look and dress like that. All women should be models, and all guys should be star football players. It's nonsense, yet people buy into this mentality. It puts the message into your head that you need to be like that, and that you will make everybody really happy if you look and act the way the media says you should. It's a sad reflection on society."

Michelle, 14, Colorado: "Television portrays the perfect person, and it makes you feel really insignificant about who you are and what you look like. Sometimes I still have days when I feel very insignificant compared to Britney Spears or anybody like that because they have all the publicity and everything that everyone wants. They might be able to sing really good, or act really well, but I'll always know that I completed school. I like to do all kinds of things they didn't get to do. I get to lead a normal life, but they can't even go outside because of paparazzi (photographers) and everything."

Heather, 16, Vermont: "Things on television are kind of fake. All you see today are makeup ads and all these skinny, beautiful people. I don't have a huge problem with myself, but when I see that on TV, it makes me feel that I should look and feel that way. I know some people see that on TV and then look at themselves, and all of a sudden their self-esteem totally drops because they feel they are not pretty enough or skinny enough to be beautiful."

Thoughts and Reflections

What are your thoughts on how the media (television, magazines and radio) manipulate our desire to look and act a certain way? Do you ever feel pulled to look or dress a certain way? Why do you suppose this is?

_____

_____

_____

_____

Can you think of any ways to filter the negative impact of the media and advertisers so it doesn't deflate your sense of self-worth? Try to come up with five ideas.

a. _____

b. _____

c. _____

d. _____

e. _____

8. Make goals for yourself. Self-esteem isn't just the accomplishment of personal goals, but when you do accomplish something significant, it makes you feel special. Accomplishing goals gives a person a sense of meaning, a sense of purpose, and this definitely contributes to self-esteem. Having goals is always a good idea.

> **Darcy, 18, North Carolina:** "Here is what I do to keep my self-esteem up: I eat healthy foods, and I get enough sleep at night. I recommend that everyone plan to graduate from high school. Make a goal and create steps to reach it."

Thoughts and Reflections

Getting a good grade in English is a goal, but you can have several goals that are not school-related. List three short-term goals you wish to accomplish in the next few months. Follow this with three lifetime goals—things you really have your heart set on accomplishing.

Short-Term Goals (for the next several weeks)

a. _____

b. _____

c. _____

Lifetime Goals

a. _____

b. _____

c. _____

7

Chilling Out: Great Ways to Reduce Stress and Thrive in a Crazy World

How do I relax?
I watch great movies and eat popcorn.
I take bubble baths. I go hiking in the mountains
and smell the pines. I love to exercise and dance.
All of these things are very relaxing to me.

JAMIE L., 18

This is something your parents most likely have forgotten, but teens thrive on sensory stimulation: loud music, spicy food, new clothes, you name it. Your parents are trying to minimize their sensory stimulation (they get enough of this at work) while you are increasing yours. Their idea of relaxing is soft background music (it's a sedative), but yours is cranking up the volume on the boom box or stereo. Adults relax by having their private time, whereas teens would much rather chill out with friends. So remember this: One person's chill can be another person's hell. Knowing this little fact may help explain why you and your parents do not chill out the same way. It also explains why they keep asking you to turn down the stereo, even if they say it's the same music they like.

Chilling out means taking time to step out of a stressful moment and regain your composure. It also means backing away from the heat of a stressful situation and cooling off long enough to get a better perspective on everything in your life. Chilling out isn't avoiding your problems. It's merely a break from what you consider "too much information." Chilling out is a minivacation, a time-out from life's troubles and problems, enough to catch your breath before you head back into the game of life. Today, teens are literally wired for sound, from cell phones and MP3 to the Internet. You need to remind yourself to unplug every now and then.

The Art of Calm

No matter how you choose to chill out, finding balance is essential to having a life. Even though the mind of a teenager is like a sponge, soaking up every bit of information it can, there still comes a point at which the mind and body have got to relax. What happens when you don't find that place of relaxation? Continually being off-balance and never taking the time to calm down can set the stage for a series of health problems ranging from the common cold to mono. The art of calm suggests going back to your happy place to chill out and relax.

Remember, Sleep Is Not the Same Thing as Relaxation

Sleep is one of the great pleasures of life. Sleep is so important that we spend nearly a third of our lives doing it. At first glance, sleep might seem like the best way to relax. After all, curling up with a pillow feels so good. But research shows that while you sleep, your mind is anything but relaxed. It is racing with all kinds of thoughts and emotions (even when you're not dreaming). The body isn't fully relaxed either because your heart rate and blood pressure can go through big swings in the course of a good night's sleep. Stiff necks and muscle soreness can also occur, and perhaps the worst problem is when teens grind their teeth at night, a condition known as temporomandibular joint (TMJ) dysfunction. What makes relaxation different than sleeping is that you are consciously relaxing the mind and body to provide a greater sense of balance.

Thoughts and Reflections

Although sleep isn't the same thing as relaxation, it is very important. How much sleep do you get each night? How would you rate the quality of your sleep? Do you sleep straight through the night, or do you wake up a lot?

_____

_____

_____

_____

Relaxation Through the Five Senses

There is an art to being calm. The art comes through six different styles of processing information, including sight, sound, taste, touch and smell. The sixth category includes anything not listed in the first five, such as friends. When it comes to relaxing, there is no shortage of ways to chill out. Let's take a closer look.

Sight. In the course of a normal day, we take in the majority of information (about 70 to 80 percent) through our eyes. Math, English, French, social studies, you name it, much of the information gained on these topics enters the mind through the eyes. Closing your eyes every now and then is a good way to chill, but you can also refocus your eyes on visual sensations that bring a sense of calm to the body. What are some examples? Movies, videos, computer games, comic books or the next sequel to Harry Potter.

Virginia, 14, Georgia: "I read a lot. Sometimes I stay up till midnight with a good book. I can read for hours. Sometimes in the morning I pretend that I'm sleeping, because if my mom knows I'm awake, she will make me work. Then I read 'til 11 because I know she is going to come in to wake me up. I read a lot, and I like to draw; those are the two best things I can do. Talking to friends is kind of relaxing, but it's kind of work sometimes. I like to be myself when I'm relaxing."

Kyle, 15, Colorado: "My first choice is to sleep. I have like seven Nintendo systems in my room, and I like sit and play a lot. It's fun. It takes me away from all the problems I have, kinda like a temporary escape, a diversion from the mundane."

Meghan, 13, Wisconsin: "I like to read. The book I am reading now is *Night John* by Gary Paulson. It's about a slave girl and all she goes through. I like to read because it's fun, and I learn things. Of course it's educational, but it's also a nice escape."

Tom, 15, Colorado: "I like going on the computer to get away from it all. That's what I do a lot. I may spend somewhere between one to two hours a day, and one time I think I spent three and a half hours because I was really, really bored. I do Web pages, and you know, over the summer I was working on learning how to do Web pages, building them and stuff. You know, basically trying to find hobbies you can do."

Jennifer, 13, Colorado: "To take my mind off stress, I curl up with a good book. For me, it's like a vacation; some people might say an escape. I can enter another world."

Thoughts and Reflections

What do you do to take a mini-vacation from stress?

_____

_____

_____

_____

If you get bored some day, collect some old magazines and cut out pictures of relaxing scenes (beaches, gardens, mountains, etc.) and make a poster collage. Hang this in your room as a gentle reminder to chill out when you get really stressed. Guys, if you're not into this, try surfing on the Internet and downloading some Web pages that offer the same effect: chilling out!

Sound. What is your favorite music group? Limp Bizkit, Lifehouse, Linkin Park, Train, House Nations, Pink, the Beatles? Music, as a means to calm down, is about as old as the first tune ever whistled by a cave man. People from every culture use music to both arouse and calm the senses. Back in the cave days, all those folks had were drums. Today, we've got electric guitars, synthesizers, amps, an orchestra of instruments, and of course, drums. With the exception of Fred Flintstone, cave people merely grunted and groaned along with their Stone Age music. Today, we have rock (soft and hard), pop, be-bop, classical, jazz, blues, folk, rap, world beat and New Age. We've got (and the popularity of these musicians is going to vary from region to region and middle school to high school) Eminem, Jewel, Alanis Morissette, Shakira, Enya, Justin Timberlake, Jennifer Lopez and N'Sync. The good vibrations of music come not only from listening to your favorite music, but playing an instrument as well.

Jason, 15, Colorado: "I love to listen to music. I love The Cure, Smashing Pumpkins and Pink Floyd. I like some metal stuff, like MTV kind of stuff. I like old stuff, too, like Led Zeppelin and the Beatles."

Pam, 16, Virginia: "Music is my life—I love listening to music. Anytime I have my CD player and music I'm happy. I like Linkin

Park; they're kind of like an alternative rap group. Over my freshman and sophomore years, I've totally changed my taste in music. I don't listen to pop music anymore. I listen to all kinds of rock and alternative music. I also love techno music. I think it's really cool, and it gets me into this zone. I also play guitar. I have a Fender flyer. I've been playing for maybe a year."

Jesse, 18, Colorado: "I like playing guitar and listening to music or playing video games. I have an electric guitar. My parents got it for me. It was kind of a bribe. I got a drinking ticket last spring, and we made a contract that I wouldn't smoke or drink anything for three months. I talked my parents into getting me a guitar package—that was like a reward. And my mom wanted something good for me to do. I like it."

Katherine, 14, Colorado: "I'm really into film. I want to become a film critic or a director. I love watching movies. It's my favorite thing to do. I liked *The Exorcist* because it's very intriguing and controversial. I also like *Psycho* and *Taxi Driver.* My all-time favorite is *The Nightmare Before Christmas.* Tim Burton is my all-time favorite. He's my hero. He's awesome. I love Johnny Depp. He's so cool. *The Matrix* was good, too. I listen to music. Music is my life! If I didn't have my music I don't know what I would be. (I love the Smashing Pumpkins.) I also love the computer and the Internet. Sometimes it's easier talking to your friends on-line, because you're not face-to-face, and you can say more. It's fun and entertaining. I like TV also, but I'm not into sports at all. I don't see the point in sports. I go for walks sometimes; that's fun, but lots of times it's just to clear my head. Walking helps me think. I've been playing drums for about six years, and it's a great way to release tension. I like hanging out with my friends and just talking or going out for walks or going to the park and playing on the swing sets and stuff."

Thoughts and Reflections

Who are your favorite groups to listen to when you want to chill out? What kind of music do you find to be the most relaxing? Is this the same kind of music your parents like? Is it the same kind of music your brothers or sisters like?

_____

_____

_____

Here is an idea: If you have the means to burn a CD or make a cassette tape, make a mix of your favorite songs to promote relaxation. This is also a great idea for when you have friends sleep over—invite them to bring some of their music, too!

Taste. Food is a natural pacifier. Eating is a great way to relax. Food doesn't just nourish the body; it also nourishes the mind and spirit. You might think that ice cream is the best food for chilling out, and you're probably right, but there are many, many more. The most important aspect of relaxing through the sense of taste is personal preference. It's hard to believe, but some people chill out by chewing on jalapeno peppers, while others eat a bowl of cereal. We should also point out that although eating is a great way to relax, some people get it all wrong and use food as a Hot Stone. Eating disorders, such as anorexia, bulimia and overeating, are anything but relaxing.

Ali, 14, Colorado: "Chips and southwest-style salsa with corn in it. When I come home from school and I'm stressed, I can eat a whole bag of chips and a whole bottle of salsa."

Amy, 16, New York: "Sushi! Since the third grade, my girl-friends and I have had a plan—after the first one of us gets a car, we are going to ditch orchestra, take a long lunch and go out for sushi because it's really healthy. We think it's the best thing you can eat because it is healthy and it tastes really good. I also recommend ice cream or cookies once in a while."

Harris, 15, Florida: "I have a sweet tooth, so I like to eat candy. I like gummy candy. I also like Ben & Jerry's Phishfood ice cream. And I like rainbow sherbet with sprinkles. My stepmom is kind of a naturalist and we don't have that much junk food at our house, so whenever I can get candy, I get candy. Food is a major part of our lives, so I believe if you eat bad stuff, you can have a bad day. I have a friend who eats pizza every night, and he is getting kind of fat. Not good! When I eat dinner every night, we have vegetables, meat and some sort of rice or pasta. I eat pretty well! I'm still pretty strong and lean and have a lot of energy. My friend just doesn't have much ambition."

Jamie, 18, Colorado: "I drink cappuccino and stuff like that. I work at a coffee shop, so I'm real bad about coffee. I eat healthy things when I want to relax because it feels good. For me, if I eat junk food I feel a lot worse than if I eat a pear. It sits better in your stomach and makes you more relaxed than junk food."

Kirby, 15, Colorado: "My favorite things to eat are grapes and tomato soup. I also love hot chocolate. And I really like fried calamari—whenever my dad is willing to take me out to an Italian restaurant. I also like home-baked bread!"

Pam, 16, Virginia: "I love good food. I like pizza, soda and buf-falo wings. I don't eat much ice cream, but when I eat it, I eat a lot of it. I like mint chocolate ice cream. It's sooooo good. I don't really like chocolate. I like sour candy, like sour berries and Skittles."

Kyle, 15, Colorado: "I always order mozzarella sticks. When my girlfriend and I go out to dinner, that's what she picks for me. They have those at Applebee's, you know. That's why I always go to Applebee's. That's what I get every time, and that's why we go to places like Old Chicago and all these other restau-rants in Boulder that have mozzarella sticks. I also eat weird things, like this pretty good stuff that I make from frozen straw-berries and it has Jell-O and lemon juice and some other things. Eating food is a great way to relax. I never eat anything I don't like. I'm really picky. My parents make dinner; if I eat dinner with them and they make something I don't like, I don't even bother putting it on my plate. I'm just going to waste it, and I don't like it anyway."

Thoughts and Reflections

What foods do you eat to soothe your soul? Try to come up with ten different foods, five of which are NOT fast food or junk food.

a. _____   f. _____
b. _____   g. _____
c. _____   h. _____
d. _____   i. _____
e. _____   j. _____

When you have some free time (like when you are really bored), comb through a few cookbooks and see if you can find two recipes for something absolutely delicious. You might need to collaborate with your mom or dad to have them get the ingredients, but chances are they will want to help you out with this. If you cannot find a cookbook in the house, try the local library. You'll be amazed at all the great possibilities awaiting your discovery.

Food is wonderful, but it can also become a stressor, particularly when it is used to control emotions like anger and guilt. Some people (bulimics) never let food stay long enough in their stomach to digest, and the return trip back out the mouth is not pleasant. Yuck! Have you ever used food as a means to control your emotions? If you or someone you know uses food as a Hot Stone rather than a means to relax, and you don't feel comfortable talking to your parents, try calling the eating disorders hot line at 1-800-841-1515.

Touch. If you have ever snuggled up with your pet cat or dog, you know how great the touch of fur is to relax. But the sense of touch goes beyond pet therapy. It includes everything from fresh, clean sheets and T-shirts to holding your girlfriend or boyfriend's hand at a football game. It includes a warm hug from your mom or dad, the feeling of sun on your face on a spring day, or the gentle autumn wind combing through your hair. Dancing might seem like it's not in the category of touch, but moving your body to the beat of a good rhythm is definitely relaxing.

Michelle, 14, Colorado: "I take a bubble bath to veg out. This is very relaxing, and it's kind of symbolic of washing your cares away."

Heather, 16, Vermont: "I like to rent a movie or find a movie on television and watch it by myself. Maybe pop some popcorn or find some chocolate and cuddle up on the couch. Another way that I relax is to invite my boyfriend over so we can sit and talk, and he holds me. Sometimes when he is over, he takes naps, and I watch him sleep. That seems to relax me, too. But usually I like to be alone to relax. When I want to chill out, I might hang out with my girlfriends, rent a movie, go shopping or do some Tae Bo. I tend to 'chill out' with my girlfriends a lot."

Chip, 16, Massachusetts: "I love dancing. I feel the beat in my chest coming up through the dance floor, and I move with the rhythm. I am in a trance. It is so cool. It's a whole different type of energy, and it's energizing."

Rachel, 14, Colorado: "I like to go riding. I've been doing that since I was seven. I have two horses. One is named Cloud, and I ride her in shows. My other horse is Poco. There is something special about horses, and there is something even more special about riding."

Katy, 13, Maine: "When I want to relax, I go over to my friend's house and sit in the hot tub. I like sitting in the hot water and feeling the jets blast water around my body; it's so relaxing. I also like going with my friends to dances at school. You just dance, and you don't think about school."

Sandy, 17, Florida: "For my birthday, my mom buys me a massage. It is the best thing. My muscles get so tight from sports, and I just melt on the table. I wish I could afford to get them more often. I think everyone needs to get a massage."

Thoughts and Reflections

List five things you can do to relax through the sense of touch.

a. _____

b. _____

c. _____

d. _____

e. _____

Smell. Our sense of smell is at its greatest when we are born. It continually weakens over time. At first glance, it would seem that most teens don't spend a lot of time using this sense to relax. But a closer look reveals that the sense of smell should not be forgotten. About the time teens start getting into lipstick and eye shadow (females) and shaving (guys), your nose starts sniffing around the bathroom to experiment with perfumes, colognes and aftershave lotions. A small drop can smell really good. Don't forget, there are other good fragrances, most notably in the kitchen, such as the smell of fresh-baked chocolate-chip cookies, apple or blueberry pie, and last but not least, cinnamon rolls.

Julia, 16, Colorado: "Sometimes I like staying inside and baking. I like to bake a lot, actually. I like baking cookies and banana bread. The smell of cookies is wonderful. It's like a magnet in the house."

Seana, 15, California: "My mom is really into this thing called aromatherapy. It's where you smell lots of different fragrances. I think she calls them essential oils: lavender, mint, chamomile and lots of others. She places them around the house. Our house always smells so good. My friends come over, and they never want to leave. I think my favorite scent is lavender."

Ryan, 16, Maine: "This may sound kind of crazy, but I like going outside. I love the smell of salt air; I never get tired of it. I also like the smell of pine needles in the woods, especially after it rains."

Thoughts and Reflections

What are five food smells that make you feel relaxed?

a. _____

b. _____

c. _____

d. _____

e. _____

Next, come up with five scents (non-food-related) that make you feel relaxed.

a. _____

b. _____

c. _____

d. _____

e. _____

Additional Ways to Relax

As you can tell, there is no shortage of ways to relax. Using the five senses is a great way to begin the relaxation response, but there are hundreds of other ways. These include combinations of the five senses, or even activities that go well beyond the five senses. Many of these are done by yourself, but nearly every teen interviewed for this book mentioned how important it was to relax with friends.

Sean, 18, Michigan: "When I want to chill out or relax, many times it is just helpful to be with close friends, people you can truly trust and connect with. That can be a very comforting feeling. However, many times when I want to relax, it is nice to be alone with my own thoughts and do things the way I want to do them."

Lauren, 14, Colorado: "My favorite way to relax is to hang out with my friends and have sleepovers. We stay up and watch scary movies. Sometimes we just go to the mall and go shopping, but everyone's been low on money lately."

Kyle, 17, Tennessee: "I like to go over to my friends' houses and hang out. Friends are different from parents and teachers because they're the same age as you, and they're growing up at the same time, so they can relate to how you feel about things and the experiences you have. Parents can't relate to your problems."

Mareko, 13, Colorado: "I learned this in Health Quest. It's called a crisis kit. You place things in this kit to calm through the five senses, like a favorite CD (sound), a tumble stone (touch) and candy (taste). When I am having a bad day, or something brings me down, I pull out the crisis kit. It's great, and I highly recommend everyone make one for themselves."

Peter, 14, New Jersey: "My friends and I are not in the popular group of kids, but we just do our own thing. We do stupid stuff, like hang out at the movies or the mall, or go to the beach. It may seem lame, but it's fun for us. I think I've discovered it's not so much what you do, but that you enjoy the company you're with."

Anjulie, 14, Colorado: "I really like doing things with my friends, like going to movies or to their houses. I like doing things for the heck of it, rather than for a purpose. I also like to clean my room. It gives me thinking time; I can see things clearer. I also like having friends sleep over. We have the best time! It's like bonding. We talk about anything and everything. Everyone has to have a sleepover once in his or her life. You get to know your friends better this way."

Julie, 17, Arizona: "Sometimes my friends and I go out to dinner. Sometimes we go clubbing—to dance clubs. Sometimes we play putt-putt golf, and sometimes we go bowling. I also have friends sleep over, so if there is a friend who I haven't been spending enough time with, I call her up and say, 'Hey, come over to my house and we'll order a pizza.' We'll paint each other's nails, do each other's hair and talk about boys."

Kelly, 15, Texas: "I hang out with my friends to relax. We veg out in front of the TV and sit and talk. I like hanging out with them because my best friend is closer to me than most of my sisters. We can talk about anything. The only problem I have with her is that we have the same opinion on just about everything. So a lot of the time when we talk about things it's not very interesting. There's no real debate or anything."

Morgan, 14, Tennessee: "I like shopping with my friends. We usually go to the mall, and what I buy depends on how much money I have. We also go to the movies. We see whatever we think looks good. I like scary movies. I liked *What Lies Beneath* and *The Others.*"

Thoughts and Reflections

Start planning your next sleepover. Come up with a theme or activity you and your friends can do when you're together. An example is cooking a meal from scratch. Of course, ask your parents' permission, and when you get the green light, call up a few close friends and put your plan into action. Guys, you can have your own theme: sports night, air guitar night or Halloween costume night.

Make a list of five things you can do to relax that don't include your friends, or perhaps something you can do with only one friend, such as hiking or listening to music.

a. _____

b. _____

c. _____

d. _____

e. _____

It's time to make up your own "relaxation kit," a first-aid kit for stress. You need a minimum of five things, one for each of the five senses (sight, sound, smell, taste and touch). You can also throw in a few comic books, for the sense of humor, and anything else you would like (including the toll-free hotline numbers on page 371, just in case). What would you put in your relaxation kit? Find a paper bag, a purse, an old lunch box or tackle box, and do it!

The best plans in the world aren't worth a hill of beans unless you follow through. What can you do to put some of these plans to work for you?

_____

_____

_____

_____

Some Favorite Books
to Escape By

All teens interviewed were asked to recommend their favorite book to read. Here is a list of the most popular choices.

Title	Author	Publisher
Harry Potter and the Sorcerer's Stone (and other books in the Harry Potter series)	J. K. Rowling	Scholastic
Valhalla Rising	Clive Cussler	Putnam
Where the Heart Is	Bille Letts	Warner Books
Speak	Laurie Halse Anderson	Puffin Books
Gone with the Wind	Margaret Mitchell	Warner Books
The 7 Habits of Highly Effective Teens	Sean Covey	Simon & Schuster
The Giver	Lois Lowry	Laurel Leaf
Go Ask Alice	Anonymous	Pocket Books
Daddy's Little Girl	Mary Higgins Clark	Simon & Schuster
The Fellowship of the Ring (and other books in the series)	J. R. R. Tolkien	Houghton Mifflin
Red Rabbit	Tom Clancy	Putnam
The Chronicles of Narnia	C. S. Lewis	HarperCollins
To Kill a Mockingbird	Harper Lee	Little Brown & Co.
Dragonlance Chronicles	Margaret Weis, et al.	Wizards of the Coast
Chicken Soup for the Teenage Soul (and other books in the *Chicken Soup* series)	Jack Canfield, et al.	Health Communications
The Bean Trees	Barbara Kingsolver	HarperCollins

Title	Author	Publisher
The Red Tent	Anita Diamant	Picador USA
The Gift	Danielle Steele	Delacorte Press
The Four Agreements	Don Miguel Ruiz	Amber-Allen
A Cry in the Night	Mary Higgins Clark	Pocket Books
The Luckiest Girl in the World	Steven Levenkron	Penguin USA
The Best Little Girl in the World	Steven Levenkron	Warner Books
The Arabian Nights	Richard Francis Burton	Modern Library
Holes	Louis Sachar	Yearling Books
Calvin and Hobbes books	Bill Watterson	Andrews McMeel

8

Friends in Need (the Good, the Bad and the Ugly)

Friends can work for you or against you.
It seems like there is always some sort of conflict
with friends, but they're also there to help
you and be there when you need them.
That basically sums it up pretty much.

KATHERINE S., 14

The Importance of Friends

In the life of a teen, friends ARE everything! They are the greatest source of pleasure, but they can also be the biggest source of misunderstanding and strife. If you are like most teens, you live for your friends. You spend countless hours on the phone with them, and you might even send hundreds of instant messages over the Internet. Maybe you play sports with your friends or just hang out. Some of you paint each other's fingernails, shop at the mall, try on each other's clothes or go to concerts. Many teens spend countless nights sleeping over at their friends' houses, watching videos and playing games, or just eating pizza, popcorn or fruit strips 'til everyone falls asleep in the wee hours of the early morning. Your parents may have forgotten this, but as a teen you know that friends are more important than school.

As essential as your friends are to enjoying life, they are doubly important in coping with stress. Friends are like pillows that cushion the fall when stress knocks you over. Friends are the greatest means of support anybody can have, and it will be this way throughout your entire life. Unlike your parents, grandparents, brothers or sisters, your friends can relate to you better because they know how you think and how you feel because, for the most part, they think and feel the same way.

Strong friendships are based on more than just having common interests or somebody to talk to during lunch period. A true friendship is built on trust and the knowledge that things you say (your problems, your innermost thoughts and feelings) will be held in confidence. Trust is essential to a strong friendship, but admiration, acceptance and respect are also factors in this equation. It's been said that meeting peers and making friends is much like trying on clothes; everyone is looking for friends who seem like a good fit.

Friends of All Kinds

There are many different types of friends. There are friends you sit next to in class and greet in the halls, but you really don't see them outside of school. You may talk about some stuff, but for the most part, these friends are more like acquaintances. Then there are the friends you hang out with, the people in "your group." These are the friends you see after school, on weekends and during the summer. The last group of friends is special enough to be called "best friends." So rare are these friends that you would describe only one or two people as best friends. These are the friends in whom you confide nearly everything. These are the friends who know you as well as you know yourself (or better). These are the friends you wish you had as brothers or sisters—you're that close. These kinds of people are rare, so it stands to reason that you might have lots of friends, but only a few really close friends who earn the title "best friend."

Aaron, 13, Colorado: "To me, a friend is someone you can associate with, someone who understands you. Most middle-schoolers are probably in groupings. First you have the popular crowds, and then you have the troublemakers. There are a lot of different crowds, actually. Like, I have a group of friends, and we hang around with each other. You've got the science-nerd type crowd, which you know I've got friends there. My group is kind of a weird mix. I have got jock friends and skaters, yet we're all academically strong. I have got one friend, he's really smart, and he's really, really good at athletics."

Jackson, 14, Nebraska: "Friends are important for communicating with about things that happen in my life. I don't have too many friends, but it has improved lately. I'm a skater, and right now, most of my friends are skaters, too. Sometimes I feel that talking to people about serious stuff is really hard for me to do, but I'm getting better."

Heather, 16, Vermont: "I agree that friends help me cope with stress, but not all the time! There are times when you need friends for support, but all they do is tell you things you don't want to hear, and all you want is for them to listen to you without saying anything. Most of the time it is great to have a friend for support and even better to have a boyfriend or girlfriend. There are times when I'd rather talk to my boyfriend about things, because he knows me in different ways than my friends do, and my boyfriend listens and doesn't say anything until I ask for his opinion, which helps me out a lot."

Thoughts and Reflections

What kind of friends do you have? Do you have lots of acquaintances? How many close friends do you have? What group do you hang out with at school, or do you have more than one group?

_____

_____

_____

_____

It has been said that the word friend is very hard to define. How would you best define the word friend? Once you have given this some thought, ask yourself how many of your friends really match your definition.

_____

_____

_____

_____

How good a friend are you to people who see you as their best friend? Do you share the same Hot Stones in terms of anger?

_____

_____

_____

_____

Friends: The Best Stress Relief!

Anjulie, 14, Colorado: "For me, friends are bigger than family. They are bigger than anyone can possibly imagine. They are the ones I rely on because when my parents are gone or can't relate to me, I know my friends can. It doesn't make any difference if they're girls or guys. What matters is that they understand you. That is the most important thing."

Francesca, 13, North Carolina: "Oh yes, friends are extremely important in my life. You can talk to them when things in your life are going wrong. Friends help you with things you don't understand, and they're always there for you to talk to. Friends give you a pretty good reality check of what's going on."

Keegan, 14, Colorado: "Friends definitely help relieve my stress. I tell my friends things that I might not feel comfortable telling my parents. Every kid does this. You have that sense of trust with a friend. Sometimes parents take things the wrong way when you are trying to talk to them about a situation or problem. I think having good friendships and being able to talk with friends can help get a lot of stress off your back and make you feel better about things and yourself."

Reprinted with special permission of King Features Syndicate.

Ryan, 15, Florida: "Friends are crucial because teenagers need companionship. As I see it, teens think their parents don't understand them, so they gravitate toward friends in school who do. That's why teenagers rely on their friends so much. Confiding with friends really helps to deal with stress when you need someone to talk to, which we all do. I guess that's just from a guy's opinion. Usually we try to keep things cool, and there are ways, like humor, that really help. Friends will make you laugh, which relieves stress."

Mandy, 17, Colorado: "If you have a friend who has gone through a similar situation, then friends are great. Sometimes they can be there to listen, and that's about it. (Not like that's a bad thing.) You can always count on your true friends to be there through a hard time."

David, 14, Illinois: "A great friend is someone you can talk to at any time. For me, you don't always want to go to your parents because you don't always feel comfortable talking to them. Instead, you can call your best friend because you feel more comfortable with him or her."

Pablo, 13: Colorado: "Yeah, friends are important. Whenever you seem mad, your friends know not to mess with you because they know you might be kind of temperamental. Some friends might butt in and ask what's wrong because they're nosy, or maybe they really care. A true friend really helps you with your stress. They'll say, 'Let's go see a movie' or something else to take your mind off your troubles."

Morgan, 13, Tennessee: "You can talk to your friends about almost everything. A lot of my friends have the same problems I do, and we can talk to each other about the same things. You don't have to explain how you're feeling because they already know what you're feeling—they're feeling it, too! I tell them about problems with my parents, or we talk about other friends who backstab all the time."

Gail, 15, Hawaii: "When I'm stressed, I go right to my friends to talk and process what's going on. I don't really talk to my parents much anymore, unless they ask. I usually go to my friends if I'm stressed or if I have something on my mind. I usually talk to my friends about it—and everything else for that matter. I think one reason why kids don't talk to their parents is because there's too much pressure. I mean, my parents are in their forties and I think it's kind of weird talking to a forty-year-old about problems a fourteen-year-old is having. It's hard to talk to my parents. Sometimes, I find it's easier to talk to my dad about things because he works with people my age (he's a schoolteacher), so he is easier to talk to. It's harder to talk to my mom because it seems like she has a big mouth. She'll go tell my aunt, and my aunt has a huge mouth."

Thoughts and Reflections

In your opinion, why are friends important to you? How do your friends help you cope with your stress?

_____

_____

_____

_____

How do you help your friends cope with anger? How do you get your friends to drop the Hot Stone they are holding and stop getting burned themselves?

_____

_____

_____

_____

Funny Bone Friends

Lacey, 14, Colorado: "My friends are extremely important to me, but in a strange way. I think it's important to have friends to joke with, and it's important to loosen up friends who are tense about little things. It helps all of us reduce stress. You have to really know your friends before you can start making jokes with them, because you don't ever want to offend somebody the first day you meet them. If you do this, they would never want to come back and talk to you. Everybody is so self-conscious at this age. I think that building strong relationships is one of the keys to getting a good laugh. Let's face it, there are some things that you can joke with your friends about that you can never joke with your parents about."

Thoughts and Reflections

There is a saying that you can pick your friends and you can pick your nose, but you cannot pick your friend's nose. How many of your friends can you joke around with? Who among your friends makes you laugh the most?

_____

_____

_____

_____

Sometimes we can imitate our friends' behavior, even the less-desirable traits like sarcasm. Have you ever noticed that by hanging around your friends you begin to pick up Hot Stones they were using (like the Revenge Stone or the Razor Stone) and get stuck with it?

_____

_____

_____

_____

Friends in Need!

Gabrielle, 14, New York: "Thank God for Trish! Let me explain. My parents were getting a divorce, and I was really mad. Because of my anger about this, I got in the habit of wanting to hurt myself as a means of distraction from the emotional pain. One day, my best friend saw my wrists. They were bleeding, not badly, but enough that she noticed. I had been in my room the previous night using thumbtacks because I was so desperate, and there were little cuts on my wrist. She asked, 'What's this?' I said that I'd been cutting myself. I said, 'I know I should stop. I know it's not good, but please don't tell anyone.' She said, 'Gabrielle, you and I really need to go to the counselor right now.' She made me go down to the counselor and talk about it. I told them not to tell my parents, but they told my parents anyway, and I had to go see a counselor outside of school. At first I was mad at Trish, but I quickly realized that she saved my life. If she hadn't done what she did, I probably would have done something terrible to myself. I probably wouldn't even have lived to tell you this. In the end, I found that Trish got me on the right track to recovery, because at the time I wasn't planning on stopping. So I thank Trish whenever I can, because she has been so incredible for me."

Jon, 13, Colorado: "We don't really have many bullies at my school. We just have some big kids who mess around. I don't have a problem because I have a lot of friends, and I'm not threatened by them. I just ignore them. The bullies pick more on the other groups, like the computer kids. We have a lot of groups at my school. Last year (seventh grade), it was really diverse. This year, everyone has become more friendly. I can tell just about anybody anything, and they accept me for skateboarding. I have a lot of friends, like forty or fifty. I like being friends with pretty much everyone. I try not to have any enemies."

Eric, 14, Colorado: "Friends are stress buffers; I agree with that 100 percent. You can tell a good friend anything. Good friends, if they know you really well, may not get what you are saying when you open your heart and soul, but that's not the point. The point is they are there to listen. I have an example: The other day I told my best friend what was really bugging me. After hearing me talk on and on, he said, 'Okay, wait I didn't get that. Why did you say that?' I replied, 'Never mind, you just did a great job listening.'"

Thoughts and Reflections

Some friends are just people to feel connected to, while others will do anything for you. List two or three friends who are there when you really need someone to listen, to give advice or to lend a helping hand.

a. _____

b. _____

c. _____

On Making New Friends

One of the greatest joys in life is meeting someone who seems fun, interesting and enthusiastic about the same things you find intriguing, whether it's sports, music, movies or anything else. When you meet someone new, who has similar interests and a common background, it seems like you have found a treasure.

Brandon, 13, Maryland: "My friends are so important to me. Without friends, life is really lonely. At the beginning of this school year, I didn't really have any friends because it was all new. There were some new guys who came to my school. It didn't take me too long to make friends with them. We introduced ourselves, because like me, they didn't really know anybody either. So we started hanging out together, and now they're my best friends."

Sarah, 17, Virginia: "I moved from Maine to Virginia when I was fifteen. Making friends has never been that hard for me. Perhaps I'm just a likeable person, but I also knew I had to get involved in activities before school started. I got into marching band before school began in September. I jumped right in and I made a lot of friends, so on the first day of school, I knew a lot of people and already had friends."

Thoughts and Reflections

There is a saying that you can never have too many friends. Even if you have lived in the same town or neighborhood all your life, making a new friend every now and then is considered healthy. When was the last time you made a new friend? What can you do to meet someone new?

_____

_____

_____

_____

On Losing Good Friends

Take comfort in the fact that there are some people who will be friends for life. Yet be aware that it's also a fact of life that other people come in and out of your life. It just happens! Some friends move away. Some friends die tragically. Some friends become controlling and try to manipulate or even suffocate us. More often than not, as we grow and mature, our interests change, and soon we discover we don't have as much in common with our "friends" as we used to. Peers who were once inseparable start moving in different directions. This doesn't just happen in high school; it occurs throughout life (just ask your parents). Sometimes losing a friend who is controlling can be the best thing that ever happened, but there are times when losing a friend seems like the most painful thing you can ever go through. It's fair to say that losing a good friend, for whatever reason, is one of the most stressful things you can go through as a teen. The stress from this loss can range from grief to anger.

Ryan, 14, California: "I had a friend who was trying to run my life, as well as his own life. For example, if I had something I wanted to do, he would have a whole other plan. It was kind of weird because he had everything laid out even when I wanted to do something else. I would have a different plan, and he wanted to do things his way. My parents knew about this problem, but I didn't like talking to them about it. I was afraid they would get involved. I had to figure it out for myself. I ended up talking to him (my friend) about it, and I ended up settling it, but it was hard and we are not close anymore."

Lacey, 14, Colorado: "Friends do a lot to promote stress because at this age people go through friends so fast. Sometimes it seems that within a week's time, you'll realize you don't have a lot in common anymore with someone you once considered a best friend. They'll get mad at you, or you'll get mad at them, and things just kind of end. You block each other out, and there are a lot of hurt feelings and other stuff. People are moving fast toward relationships, and there's the whole thing about becoming sexually active. Losing friends you've known for years can hurt."

Brett, 16, Florida: "My best friend is this guy from Illinois who moved here last year. He moved toward the end of eighth grade, and I met him through a tennis camp. Today, my mom was talking with his mom. My mom told me he might have to move again. (There is a good chance his dad will be transferred.) I hope he doesn't, because there are so few people you can call your best friend, and the last thing you want is to have a best friend move away. At some level, there is nothing you can do about it."

Darcy, 18, North Carolina: "I don't necessarily find friends to be support systems to deal with stress, not unless the friend is a parent or a relative. I don't think friends are meant to be a support system because it puts too much weight on their backs. In addition, it's my experience that my friends are backstabbers."

Thoughts and Reflections

Losing a friend can be extremely stressful. Have you ever lost a good friend? What was it like for you?

_____

_____

_____

_____

Metaphorically speaking, friends are like eggs. If we place all our eggs in one basket and the basket falls, we have a big mess. If we have only one best friend and the basket drops, YIKES! Some people thrive on having only one best friend. Then, when something goes wrong (like backstabbing or a crush on the same person) and the friendship crashes, they are left alone with a big scrambled mess. There is wisdom in diversity of friends. How diverse is your group of friends?

_____

_____

_____

_____

_____

Friends: A Mixed Blessing?

Sara, 14, California: "Your best friends are basically a sounding board. If you're stressed out and you talk to them, they'll listen. But sometimes, if they aren't stressed out and feel the same way you do, they really don't care. They'll hear you, but they won't listen, and they won't give you any advice. It's hard because they don't always listen, and they're not always in the mood to be there for you. It's hard if your friends aren't willing to listen because who else are you going to talk to? I know some of my friends talk to their parents because they have a really strong connection and can honestly tell them what is going on in their lives. But not all my friends have this connection. My mom is really shy, so I can't talk to her about anything. I can't tell her more than the basic minimum she needs to know. I can't go into how I feel and what's going on because she's not that type of person."

Cassandra, 18, Maryland: "I definitely agree that friends are a great support system. If you can't talk to your parents, you always have your friends. You don't have to worry about the various comments your parents might have if they just don't like the situation you're in. In my case, there is such a wide age gap in age between my parents and myself, thirty-four years I think. They don't often understand where I'm coming from, so I find myself having to explain what is upsetting me to my friends because my friends can better relate. But friends can be a stressor, too, because when I'm faced with a certain situation where my friends are talking amongst themselves, I realize that they are talking behind my back."

Michelle, 14, Colorado: "Friends as a means to cope with stress? Definitely! Friends can lift the stress right off you. If you've had a really bad day, you can go home and call them, talk to them, cry with them, whatever. Good friends hold your confidence. If I didn't have my friends to lean on, I would probably be in an asylum right now. Seriously, I rely on my friends so much, and not just to talk to them. Rather, it's knowing they are there and think of me as a friend as well. But don't get me wrong, some friends can heap stress on you, too. Why? Because there is this underlying pressure to keep your friends happy."

Caitlin, 14, Colorado: "Yes, friends certainly help you cope with problems; if you are really, really upset, they'll ask you what's wrong. They try to get to the problem, and they try to help you cope with it. Friends are everything. You can't replace them, but I can honestly say they can be stressors, like when they lie to you."

Alice, 14, Colorado: "For me, friends are not a great means of support, perhaps because I am not a very good friend-maker. I have this stubborn thing about me. When I was young, making friends was harder for me than it should have been. When I moved here from California, I didn't have any friends. I don't depend on them that much for support, and now I have no classes with the friends I had in eighth grade and middle school, so I'm making friends all over again. It's kind of hard for me. I don't depend on friends. I have one friend I'm really close to and I tell her most everything, but overall, my friends at school are just people I have lunch with. They are not people I share my deepest secrets with."

Chelsea, 16, Ohio: "I've been with most of my closest friends since at least fourth grade. I had a big fight with one of my closest friends a while ago, but now we are closer than ever and talk all the time. We try to spend quality time together. I have some new friends also. I try to talk to them and spend time with them as well, trying to get to know them better, but I feel closest to my oldest friends."

Rachel, 14, Colorado: "Friendships can work for you or against you. It depends on what kind of friends you have. Good friends you can trust need to be aware of themselves (be really grounded) in order to help you. Otherwise they just make things worse. A trusted friend needs to really know your situation to be able to help you. It also helps if they have been through a similar situation to really know about it. Some friends aren't as good to help you through a situation because they cannot relate to the problem, or they can't help you because they think everything is fine. At this age, we are very emotional, too."

Jamie, 18, Colorado: "Sometimes friends can be anything but helpful. Let's say you're dealing with something that's really important to you, and you're trying to explain it to them, but they just shrug it off as if it was nothing. It really hurts because I'm trying to tell them something and they act like they don't care. So friends help a lot if they understand where you're coming from, but if they don't, it can have a really negative effect on you."

Sean, 18, Michigan: "I think that friends are great to have around during stressful times. Friends can offer advice, listen to any problems, or just be there for you and help you get your mind off the stress. Although I also feel that, if I am really stressed out, I just want to be alone to collect my thoughts. I like to do things on my own, and I'm happiest if I can overcome a stressful situation without any outside help."

Thoughts and Reflections

Friends can be a HUGE stressor in your life. Friends can be demanding. Friends can be controlling, and sometimes, just buying a gift for a friend is stressful. Are there some friends you consider to be a source of stress? How do you deal with this? Come up with three ideas to successfully cope with your friends. Here are two ideas: Pull them aside and have a heart-to-heart talk or buy a greeting card and include a note thanking them for their friendship.

_____

_____

_____

_____

_____

Are you an introvert (sometimes shy and often quiet, and you draw your energy from being alone), or are you an extrovert (outgoing, and you draw your energy from hanging around others)? Introverts tend to have a few close friends, whereas extroverts tend to have lots and lots of friends. Neither personality type is bad, but it helps to know yours.

_____

_____

_____

_____

_____

How do you cope with friends when you discover they're talking behind your back? If you ignore it, you might feel victimized. Sometimes the best thing to do is confront it diplomatically ("I overheard a comment about . . . is that true?"). Remember, when friends are confronted about backstabbing, their first response is often denial ("I didn't say that!"). Forgiveness is a great way to drop Hot Stones. Most likely, we are all guilty of talking behind people's backs. If someone comes up to you and accuses you of it, the best thing might be to apologize.

That Special Friend!

The friend/stress factor is compounded when the door to your heart opens and that special someone walks in. Some people call it puppy love. Perhaps more accurately it's called "first love" with that guy or girl who takes your breath away and makes you walk on clouds when holding hands or experiencing the first kiss. It's a great feeling, but relationships include heartache, too! This could be a whole book by itself. Rather than include passages here about girlfriends and boyfriends, it seemed these thoughts were best expressed in poems.

Pain

I can feel your pain, coming on like a never-ending train.
Somewhere along the track, remember, stop to react.
It comes on strong. I can see it long. I have a
need to take it. I have the sense to break it.
Can you feel me, touch the wounds from my war, My Battle.
He can't go there, he can't begin to know.
He will never feel the hole I am forced to tow.
This fear I have is of you, this battle needs to end,
I pray and pray that somehow you may stray.

Darcy Von Der Gathen, 18

Look at Me

I run down the hall
Hiding my tears
I lay against the wall

Letting go of my fears
Life has been rough
I've yet to smile
It's been tough
All the while
You don't understand
It's not a bad day
Don't lend your hand
It wouldn't help anyway
This is me
Slowly dying
Away you see
I wish I were flying
Away from it all
But yet I'm stuck
Against the wall
Every day I duck
From the words told
From those who despise
I want someone to hold
This creature unwise
Not one person will
So now I've decided
To go up this hill
So now I've decided
The other side I will leap
For it ends right there
So I can be yet a heap
Or maybe right here
I'll stop breathing in

That way
I'm sure to win
Nobody will say
A single word of despair
I know I cannot
So I sit and stare
My stomach in a knot
Still I fight my tears
Just wanting to be loved.

Danielle Long, 14

You Pretend

You pretend you don't see it
You act like it hasn't been written in the stars
You and I, we go together
Better than even I am willing to admit
It scares me, too. I won't pretend it doesn't.
But I will not win
I will not bury myself in my own heart's fears
I will forget the wrongs of the past, my past
If you will forget yours.

Julia B. Ramos, 16

Best Friends Forever, Nothing More

I see you all the time, you didn't even know,
That when I see you I think to myself, "I wonder if I let it
  show?"
I tell you all the time that I love you like a brother

But deep down inside, I care for you like no other
When we were together on that very special night
I loved how your embrace felt, how you held me so very tight.
You said you didn't want a girlfriend, 'cause you didn't want to be
   held down.
But what am I to do with a guy who doesn't want to be found?
You are my true friend, not a guy who's a jerk
That's why I need you as just a friend. A relationship between
   us would never work.
I'll keep my feelings hidden so our friendship doesn't fall apart,
But I just wanted you to know, that for you, there will always
   be room in my heart.

Lisa Wingo, age 15

Thoughts and Reflections

Falling in love is one of the greatest pleasures in life. Yet
falling in love is not without its own set of stressors.
Sometimes expressing yourself in the form of a poem helps
make order out of emotional chaos. Here's an idea. Write a
poem for someone you care about (whether it's a simple crush
or the love of your life). When you are done, you may choose
to share it, but not necessarily.

_____

_____

_____

_____

_____

_____

If poetry isn't your thing, draw something to express your feelings. Or make a greeting card—don't feel as if you have to share it.

9

Inspiration and Self-Reliance: Reconnecting to the Source

*Try to think about what you're really stressing
over, and remember you're not the only one.
I think we should all remember we are never alone
and everything will be better in the end, and
if it's not better, then it's not the end.*

KRISTEN D., 14

The teen years can be some of the loneliest in your life. This sense of loneliness comes from the feeling that no one understands you and no one can relate to you. It is made worse when you are alone in the house, school cafeteria or locker room. If misery likes company, consider yourself in great company, because everyone feels like this at some point in their teens. The truth is, we are never alone—each of us is a part of something much greater in scope than can ever be put into words. Yet no matter how many times we hear this, it is something we have to figure out for ourselves. This is one of the great mysteries of life! Once you solve the mystery, the world becomes a simpler place.

What often makes teen years stressful is the challenge of transitioning from dependence on your parents, grandparents and siblings to independence and interdependence with friends and family. To put it another way, the journey of the teen years is a transition from the reliance on others to self-reliance. Feelings of loneliness often accompany this transition. Inspiration is the light that guides us through the darkness.

Self-reliance is a hard concept to define because it includes so many qualities. For starters, self-reliance includes a sense of faith in yourself, a sense of confidence, a sense of optimism, and a sense of passion or inspiration. These qualities are like muscles we all have, but like your biceps and hamstrings, they need to be flexed and exercised to be fully developed.

The Essence of Human Spirituality

It is impossible to talk about stress without talking about the human spirit. Stress and human spirituality are partners in the dance of life. When teens hear the word spirituality, the first thing that comes to mind for many is religion. However, these are not the same concepts. Although spirituality and religion overlap (like two circles in a Venn diagram), they are not the same.

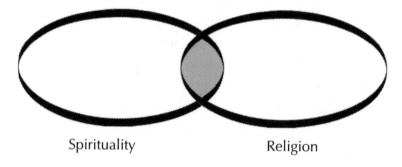

Spirituality   Religion

**Diagram 9-1: Spirituality and religion overlap,
but are not the same thing.**

Religion has a more formal structure that may include rules and regulations to guide you toward a higher level of spiritual growth. Spirituality combines divine experiences with an internal sense that you are part of something much bigger than yourself. You can be spiritual and not religious, and you can be religious and not spiritual.

Peter, 17, California: "In my way of seeing things, being spiritual means that you have a relationship with something bigger than yourself. Religion is rules, regulations and dogma—do it this way or get out. If you don't do it this way, you can't be part of our club. Some people say, 'Hey, I'm very spiritual, but I'm not religious.' I would say that I believe in God. It's kind of weird. I really don't have a good handle on it."

Kirby, 15, Colorado: "I feel that I'm a very spiritual person. I personally feel that if I am not in touch with my spirituality, I just can't deal with things. If I don't have some sort of spiritual element in my life, I get really stressed out. That's a huge factor for me."

Rachel, 15, Maryland: "I take great comfort in going to church. God is my friend and refuge. It's hard to explain, but religion is something that gives me security when things aren't going well."

Phuong, 14, Colorado: "I am spiritual when I'm stressed, and I pray. It's kind of weird because spirituality in the Vietnamese culture is totally different from spirituality in American culture. You can't come from an Asian country without being partially Buddhist. It doesn't matter if I know there is just one person, two people, or a lot of them up there controlling things, and they are helping you whenever you need it. God comes into my life when I'm stressed, especially when my mom is hurting. I also feel it at school, and when I'm stressed, I pray."

Jamie, 18, Illinois: "I'm a very spiritual person. Of course there is a God, but I don't necessarily believe in the Christian God. I think there is something else out there. When sitting outside, you can feel there's something else watching over you. The practice of yoga, in which you listen to your body, is also very spiritual. The whole concept of honoring your body, mind and spirit is very spiritual to me. I first started taking yoga videos home and practicing the postures. It got to the point where I was fairly good, so I'm taking real yoga classes now. It's really good for the mind and body. I would say I'm very spiritual in that sense."

Chris, 14, Colorado: "If I'm really stressed out, I'll try to pray. I'm trying to get through the Bible by reading a verse a night. Sometimes I'm not as disciplined as I should be. Being spiritual gives me a different kind of strength to deal with things. It makes me more mellow; it allows me to go with the flow and roll with the punches. Having faith in God makes me feel a whole lot better. I don't know why, but it just does. I don't talk about it with my friends."

Julia, 16, Colorado: "Yes, I am a spiritual person. I definitely believe there is a bigger force moving all of us. I am a Lutheran, and I go to a Christian church, but I'm not in the mind-set that Christianity is the only way. I don't believe that because you are a Buddhist that is the only way either. I think we all believe that there is only one universal power. People give this a lot of different names. It's the same concept. Love each other, and do your best while you are here. Follow your heart. Do unto others as you would have them do unto you. This is my belief."

Thoughts and Reflections

How would you best define the terms self-reliance, inspiration and spirituality?

_____

_____

_____

_____

Can you list five things that give you a sense of connecting to something bigger and more divine than yourself? Examples might include seeing a deer in the forest, watching an incredible sunset or perhaps watching the stars at night. Try to come up with five things that heighten your sense of spirituality.

a. _____

b. _____

c. _____

d. _____

e. _____

For teens who like to rebel against rules and regulations, religion may not be an important part of their lives. Since your relationship with the divine, whatever you choose to call it (God, Allah, Buddha, Gaia, etc.), is a very personal one, most people don't talk about it, even with their friends. If they do talk about it, they tend to be very general.

There are three things that comprise the core of human spirituality, as expressed through self-reliance. They include relationships, values and a meaningful purpose in life. They can be the reason for great happiness and the cause of much stress. Here is a closer look at each of these.

1. Relationships. This component of human spirituality, based on deep introspection, involves how well you know yourself and what rules you use to govern your life. Your personal relationship also involves your character, often described as what you do and say when no one else is around to watch. This internal relationship is the cornerstone to self-reliance and personal integrity. It also includes how you cultivate relationships with your friends, peers, parents and other family members. When there are problems with relationships, stress is right there alongside it.

Harris, 15, Colorado: "Yeah, I think I'm spiritual. God is part of my life. He helps me with issues that I need help on. I don't really ask him for physical help, just for help if I have a presentation and help making sure I remember all my lines. I ask for help to heal my family and keep them healthy; that really fits into my life because without them I wouldn't be anywhere. I meditate. I try to relax. I try to keep myself calm. I also try to make sure that I don't have too many things going on at once so I can keep my mind with myself all the time."

Chelsea, 16, Ohio: "I know I believe in a higher something. I'm just trying my best to be a good person. I think that if I'm a good enough person then, if there is a heaven, I should be accepted for being a good person instead of sitting down for two hours every night and praying up to the sky."

Thoughts and Reflections

There are many ways to describe an internal relationship (how you know yourself, how you deal with yourself). Some people call it a personal relationship; others call it their domestic policy (how they govern themselves). What kind of relationship do you have with yourself?

_____

_____

_____

Do you have a relationship with something higher than yourself? If so, how do you nurture this relationship?

_____

_____

_____

How does your internal relationship affect your external relationships with friends, family, teachers, etc.?

_____

_____

_____

2. Values. Values are very abstract aspects of our personalities, but they include those parts of life that are most important. Although they are hard to describe, they are more easily depicted through symbols or labels. For instance, clothes can be a symbol or an expression of freedom. Money is a symbol of wealth, a ski trip is a symbol of leisure, and a girlfriend or boyfriend can be a symbol of love. For the most part, people don't consciously think about values until some disaster like the Columbine massacre. On a more personal scale, although some values remain constant, others change, particularly in the teen years. Stress appears when values collide. The most classic example is the friction between the values of freedom and responsibility.

Michelle, 14, Colorado: "God is definitely in my life, and he has affected my life a lot, especially in the past few years. I guess it would be easier if he wasn't in my life so I wouldn't have to feel guilty about things I've done. I guess it's human nature to call people names and stuff like that. I rely on him a lot actually, because if I can't talk to somebody, I'll spend hours talking to him and myself and whatever, because, I don't know, I'm a crazy person. Morals come to mind. That's the word I was looking for. Yeah, God definitely gives me good morals."

Ali, 15, Colorado: "Yes, spirituality is a very big part of my life. I don't talk about it with my friends much because they think it's kind of [hums the *Twilight Zone* theme song]. My belief system is not very structured. It is based on values. I don't see God as a person who says, 'If you do this, you've sinned and you're going to go to hell.' I see God as something inside me, kind of like my inner self or my conscience that tells me right from wrong. If I make a mistake and offend a person, it says, 'What you did was wrong. That was really bad. But you have to learn from your mistake, and you have to not do it again.' That's what I believe. God is not a controlling thing. It ties so much into nature, and all of nature being joined. Everything has a cycle, including our lives. It's a scientific thing. I believe very much that God is within me, that I learn from my mistakes, and that nature and I are all connected. I love being outdoors, especially being up in the mountains, where I feel at peace and connected to everything. I meditate and practice the chakras, seeking balance and yin energy. It's what my dad has taught me."

Thoughts and Reflections

Everybody has a value system, even if they don't take time to think about it. Here is an invitation to start thinking about what values you deem important. Make a list of your values, and next to each value, write something that represents it. (Health is a value and exercise symbolizes health; leisure is a value and going to the movies is a symbol of leisure.)

Value	Something That Represents It

What symbols do you surround yourself with to convey your values? What do they mean to you? Your room and your locker are your personal shrines. What do you have in your room and locker (posters, clothes, jewelry, etc.) that expresses your values?

_____

_____

_____

_____

Do you have any values that tend to cause friction? An example of conflicting values would be freedom and responsibility. Take a moment to search your mind for any issues or problems and try to identify what values, if any, are associated with each problem.

_____

_____

_____

_____

Some value conflicts arise from interactions with friends. You have one value (education), but he or she has another (leisure). You want to be friends, but there is tension between you. Do you have any situations like this? How do you feel about it?

_____

_____

_____

_____

Values are not morals, but they are very similar (values are likes and dislikes; morals are knowing right from wrong). What morals do you live by? How do you distinguish between right and wrong?

_____

_____

_____

_____

3. Meaningful purpose in life. If you're like most teens, you probably don't spend too much time pondering the existence of life or your purpose in it, and that's okay. It's hard enough to sort out issues about relationships and values. Just keep in the back of your mind that meaning and purpose also play a big role in the equation of human spirituality and self-reliance. Issues of meaning and purpose tend to arise in the later teen years, when you are asked by your parents, aunts and uncles, and high-school counselors what you want to do after graduation.

Thoughts and Reflections

Sometimes it's important to write down what inspires you and what motivates you. If you are not sure what your purpose in life is, try to determine what gives your life meaning (music, books, volunteering, hobbies, etc).

_____

_____

_____

_____

There is no wrong answer to this next question, so don't get stressed. What do you see yourself doing five years from now? What do you see yourself doing ten years from now?

_____

_____

_____

_____

_____

The Mystical Side of Life

Have you ever experienced a coincidence that was almost spooky? Perhaps it was so strange your first thought was that if you tell anyone else they will think you're crazy. The word used to describe bizarre coincidences is "synchronicity." There's even a song about it on a CD by The Police. There is a mystical side of human spirituality that is very real. As a rule, people don't talk about these experiences much because they are impossible to prove (like dreams), and people don't want to look foolish. These mystical moments are simple reminders that we are never alone, and there is great comfort in knowing that we are a small, yet essential part of a much bigger picture.

Rob, 14, California: "I don't consider myself an overly religious person, because I'm still wondering if there is an afterlife or a higher power. I think there is some higher power because I've had a couple of instances, like one day, I was wondering if there was a God and we almost got killed in a car accident. We were inches away from a serious accident. This car was coming like ninety miles per hour off a turn and missed us by about six inches. So I've already kind of answered my question. I don't doubt there's a reason for that. I don't know if I'm religious, but I think there is something."

Seana, 15, California: "The night my grandfather died, I awoke to see him standing at the foot of my bed. He came to say good-bye. I looked at the clock, and it was 2:03 A.M. The next morning my mom told me he had died of a heart attack at two in the morning. I told her I already knew. A week after my grandfather died, he came to me in a dream. He looked a lot younger, but I recognized him immediately. I wouldn't normally tell this to people because they would think I was crazy, but I know this really happened. It was kind of weird, but it was really neat. I am perfectly comfortable with it."

Thoughts and Reflections

Although not everyone talks about these events, everyone has had one, if not several, mystical experiences that cannot be explained by any rational means. They range from bizarre coincidences to very supernatural phenomena. Have you had a recent experience you might classify as mystical?

_____

_____

_____

_____

The Hero's Journey

Think back to your favorite fairy tale, fable or story. Without sounding like your English teacher, take a good look at the story and you will likely see there are three parts: (1) the main character leaves home; (2) the main character runs into problems; and (3) the main character returns home, a little smarter and wiser. This three-part plot is the basis for every great story, from *Star Wars, E.T.: The Extra-Terrestrial, Pinocchio* and *Shrek* to the *Harry Potter* books and *The Wizard of Oz.* The same story line is used in TV sitcoms and good movies. Why is this plot so classic to all the greatest stories? Because the story line, often called "the hero's journey," is a template for our own lives. It's no secret there are many voyages on the hero's journey.

Each of us is on a similar journey, and each of us plays the role of the hero (although some do a better job than others). Whether you leave home to go to school, take a trip or go to college, we all leave home. We all encounter problems that challenge our integrity and help build character. Everyone is invited to learn from the experience and move on (although not everyone does), and we all return home, in some way, shape or fashion. The reason we read good books, see good movies and listen to good stories is because they offer us insight on how to deal with our own problems and return safely home.

Thoughts and Reflections

Take a moment to consider your favorite story. It could be from a book, a movie, a video or even the newspaper. Identify the hero and the three phases of the hero's journey.

_____

_____

_____

_____

One of the class exercises in Health Quest was to describe your life journey as a story. Your story, like the hero's journey, has three parts. What is your story? Can you put it into words? The third part of the story is the most important because it requires that you take some time to think about what you have learned from your current "adventure," even if the adventure is the day from hell. Now you are the hero of your life journey. What is your story?

_____

_____

_____

_____

Roadblocks and Distractions on the Human Path

Every good story requires tension. In stories, tension comes in many forms, usually personified as another character. Dorothy had the Wicked Witch of the West, Luke Skywalker had to deal with Darth Vader, and Neo *(The Matrix)* had to confront the enemies in black suits. Whether it's Jason and the Argonauts, King Arthur or Cinderella, every hero is faced with a roadblock, sometimes several. In our everyday adventures, the roadblocks we face may be our parents, stepparents, bullies at school or the assistant principal. But in truth, the real roadblocks are nothing more than unresolved anger and fear.

Remember the story of Rip Van Winkle, the guy who drank one beer and fell asleep for twenty years? Rip got distracted in a big way! In addition to roadblocks on the human journey, there are distractions as well. In every case, a distraction begins as an attraction but soon tries to pull you off the path. Today, the biggest distractions are commonly called addictions, and they range from watching television, talking on cell phones or surfing the Internet to compulsive alcohol and drug use. Distractions can be as dangerous as roadblocks. In fables, the hero musters up his or her strength to move beyond the obstacles. The same thing is done in real life, but often the hero uses different muscles.

Thoughts and Reflections

Are there any roadblocks on your life journey? Sometimes writing them down lends clarity so you can resolve them and move on with your life. Make a list of your current roadblocks and, next to each one, try to determine what emotion is associated with it (anger or fear).

_____

_____

_____

_____

Life is full of great things to explore, but there are some dangers, too (these are all the things your parents warn you about!). Remember that distractions begin as attractions! Are there any things you feel have distracted you and pulled you off "the path"?

_____

_____

_____

_____

Muscles of the Soul

There are two common ways to get through a difficult situation. The first is to complain, as if it was the worst thing that has ever happened to you (would you like some cheese with your whine?). This method tends to get sympathy from your friends at the start, but the sympathy soon turns to exasperation. Unfortunately, this is also how most people cope with stress; needless to say, it's not the best way. This method isn't useful because you tend to build up resentment and frustration, which brings more things into your life to complain about. It becomes a vicious cycle. Perhaps you know people like this.

The second way is to use your muscles of self-reliance to work through the problem. By taking this approach, you learn from the situation and move on. People who use this approach are not resentful or sarcastic. They are fun-loving people to hang around. These people are popular for all the right reasons!

What are muscles of the soul? Here is a short list.

Optimism. Optimism is a reassuring attitude about life. Optimism means you don't have a jaded perception of yourself or the people and places you know. Optimism isn't a fake smile that denies serious problems. Optimism includes a sense that everything is going to work out okay.

Confidence. This attribute reflects high self-esteem without any signs of arrogance. Confidence means having the ability to be assertive without being aggressive.

Humbleness. Humbleness is pride without the ego. To be humble means to see yourself as an equal to everyone else, not better than anyone else. It also means being modest with your talents so you don't steal the limelight.

Creativity. Have you heard the expression, "Two heads are better than one"? With creativity, the two parts of your brain (right and left) are better than one (just the left). Creativity begins with a good imagination (this is the right brain) and then the discipline to organize these ideas and make them happen (this is the left brain). Using the creative muscle is the best way to solve problems.

Humor. There is a real talent to taking yourself lightly, so when you find yourself in trouble, a sense of humor helps keep emotional balance. Humor allows you to lean on the lighter side of life so you don't get top heavy with serious issues and tip over and crash. Should you happen to fall, humor acts as a cushion to soften the blow.

Faith. Faith is a deep-seated sense that you are never alone and everything is going to work out; there is a divine force that works through you and for you. Faith combines the use of optimism, confidence and courage to get things done.

Resiliency. Just like flexing muscles, this inner resource gives you the capacity to bounce back after being knocked down to the ground.

Thoughts and Reflections

There are many, many inner resources or muscles of the soul. Make a list of as many as you can think of, and then place a star next to all the ones you feel help you to move beyond the roadblocks of your life journey.

_____

_____

_____

_____

_____

Can you think of any ways in which you can work to exercise these muscles of the soul?

_____

_____

_____

_____

_____

The Power of Prayer

This may sound ironic, but a big part of self-reliance is calling on help when you need it (the higher self). The help called upon is from a higher source (God, angels, saints, deceased relatives and others) who is with you in spirit. Prayer is the preferred call of help for many people, whether it's praying to find a lost set of car keys or something much more serious. Some people say there are two kinds of prayer: prayers of help and assistance, and prayers of gratitude. Others say that all thought is some form of prayer. Here are some comments on prayer from teens across the country, practicing a wide range of religions and spiritual practices.

Brittany, 16, Illinois: "I feel that if I come to God with my problems, he will give me some guidance on what I am supposed to do. Yes, I pray at times of stress because I know there isn't a thing that the Lord can't guide me through."

"Aren't there enough problems in the world already?"

Reprinted by permission of Randy Glasbergen. ©Randy Glasbergen, www.glasbergen.com

Tom, 14, Colorado: "I consider myself both religious and spiritual. I try to live my life by God's standards as a Christian. When I am stressed out, you know, I'll ask him to help me out. Most of the time when I'm stressed out it's because a great many things are going on in my life, and I can't make decisions. I want to be able to make good decisions and solve problems right away. Sometimes you just can't do that, so I ask God to help me with that."

Sean, 18, Michigan: "As far as spirituality goes I have had my fair share of moments that are life-changing and revolve around religion/spirituality. I was brought up in a Catholic family and attended church and Sunday school for some time. However, I got to a certain age, maybe nine, where church wasn't that important to me. That doesn't mean that I disregarded religion; I just developed my own beliefs and standards. When I was about seven, in the first grade, I was in this really hairy situation that I did not want to be in. At that time, I prayed, 'Lord, if you can get me out of this safely and unharmed, I promise to pray every night before bed, for the rest of my life.' I know. Quite a commitment for being only seven years old. Well, everything turned out okay, and I tried my best to fulfill my covenant. That experience was probably my first major religious experience, and even at that age, it had life-altering effects. I prayed every day, and everything seemed good. As I reached my teens, my promise had faded, and I found it very hard to keep it every day (naive probably). At that point, I started to make bad decisions, such as hanging out with the bad crowd, and all in all, trying to be the biggest rebel I could. I don't think it was the fact that I wasn't praying that led me down the path of rebellion. It was probably just the natural tendencies everyone has at some time to rebel against values and standards. A couple years later, I found myself in juvenile detention for shoplifting. Talk about an eye-opener. All I needed was one night in jail to change my ways. About a year or two after that, I was still missing something, and I wasn't pleased with my life. One night I was lying in bed, and I couldn't really sleep, so I began talking to God, much like I had done when I was younger. I knew I needed some type of direction, and I wanted it to be on my own. I wasn't real big on seeing a counselor or psychologist. I made another promise to God, this one a little bit more reasonable. Surprisingly, however, I still don't attend church, and I don't go around preaching what I believe in. I don't need to. I know what I believe, and in my mind, no one can change that but me."

Eric, 14, Colorado: "God plays a huge part in reducing stress in my life because sometimes I say, 'God give me comfort and compassion and love so that I don't totally go off the wall.' I turn to him most of the time that I'm stressed. It's good to know there is someone always there for you. Because he is the only person you can trust, and he'll never turn his back on you. If you do the worst thing in the world, he won't turn his back on you like some people. I just think it is really neat, and I think you need that in your life, because like I said before, everyone needs to be loved. God is the only one who will love you forever and ever. Your parents can love you, but not the way God does."

Eric, 14, Illinois: "Whenever I'm mad, there is not much you can say to me because I get pretty mad pretty quick. Sometimes I'll get so mad I won't even do anything. I won't think about anything. I'll just sit there and fret over it. I get so mad I can't do anything. Sometimes I'll pray about it, and sometimes I won't pray about it right away, but eventually I end up praying about it. Eventually, I'll end up thanking God for taking care of it or asking God to help me take care of it. In terms of stress, it's kind of hard to deal with stress in a godly perspective because you sit there and you pray and you know he's going to do something, but you don't know what. Then you pray about it again and eventually you realize he really did do something about it."

Aaron, 13, Colorado: "God fits into my life in a lot of places. I'm really, really involved with my church. I'll pray often. Even when I'm angry, I'll start praying to get rid of the frustration. As for fears, that's also something I pray about. I also pray in times of gratitude—like, if it's something I'm really thankful for, then yeah, of course I pray."

Aden, 14, Colorado: "I am a spiritual person. I am a Christian, and I used to have a really firm belief in Christianity and in God. But because of the people I hang around and the situations I've been put in, I've drifted from that somewhat. No one I know is really religious (goes to church all the time), so I haven't been doing what I should, I guess. But when I'm really stressed out or things are going wrong for me, I always go back to God and pray. If I'm in a really bad situation, and I'm really stressed out, I pray about it. I ask that things get worked out. Prayers are always answered (though not always when you want them to be), and it really helps a lot."

Thoughts and Reflections

Prayer is a lot like mental imagery. You need to have a clear mind, positive thoughts, good intentions and gratitude (even when you are putting out the distress call). See if you can list three things that allow all of these to occur (turning off the cell phone, sitting by a lake, etc.).

a. _____

b. _____

c. _____

Prayer can be a ritual, but there are other types of rituals that remind you of a divine connection. Make a list of three to five rituals that you do.

a. _____

b. _____

c. _____

d. _____

e. _____

Unamazed and Confused

This may sound ironic, but an essential stage of spiritual growth is to question everything rather than accept everything at face value. It may seem odd to say that feeling confused, questioning everything, or even calling yourself a nonbeliever or atheist is a step forward on the spiritual journey, but in truth, it is. Many teens are very skeptical about the religious practices they were raised with, and this is quite natural. If your parents are really honest, they will tell you they also questioned these things when they were your age. Keep in mind that spirituality is experiential, not theoretical. This means you have to experience something firsthand to know it, rather than just hearing about it from someone else or reading about it in a book. Real learning begins when you start asking questions to seek out the essence of truth and clear up any confusion lingering in your mind. Remember, to experience something firsthand, you have to keep an open mind.

Ginny, 14, Arizona: "I'm not religious. I don't want to say there isn't a God to people who believe there is. And for people who don't believe in God, I don't want to say he exists because they don't believe it. You never know if there is or there isn't. I don't know what to say on that subject. I'm still thinking on that one."

Kyle, 15, Colorado: "A lot of my friends are atheists, and they have caused me to question things. I believe in God, but I don't go to church. I mean, I pray to God every once in a while to help me through things, but I have doubts and lots of questions. I mean, if there was a God then I wouldn't be depressed. I pray to God to help me get through this, but it seems like it just keeps getting worse. It seems like he doesn't really listen."

Leslie, 15, Massachusetts: "I'm not a very God-loving person. I've always blamed God for my problems. But when something good happens, I'm like, 'Thank you.' When something goes wrong, I don't want to think about God. I don't want to think about him at all. It's like he's putting me on, torturing me and ruining my whole life. I heard this from someone, 'God must have a sense of humor because he made me.' I think God toys with me, so he might as well have a sense of humor."

Anne, 14, California: "My mom is Protestant, and my dad is Hindu. They didn't want to tear us apart, so I'm experiencing many different religions. I go to my friend's Jehovah's Witness church one day and my other friend's Lutheran church another day. I guess I'm looking around. It's hard for me to say that God's in my life. It's a controversial thing. There are so many different ways of praying, like going to a church and praying or just saying, 'Please help me do well at this.' I know people who pray to the trees. It's a whole hippie thing to pray to the trees. I suppose it's a way to pray without showing you're religious, but that you're spiritual."

Thoughts and Reflections

No one, including the Pope and the Dalai Lama, has all the answers to the universe. But this doesn't mean you cannot keep searching for answers. A good skeptic keeps an open mind. Some people write off the whole notion of human spirituality because unresolved anger clouds their ability to see clearly. Even so, we all have questions we'd like answered. Do you have any questions? See if you can come up with five questions to pose to the universe, answers you have been searching for.

a. _____

b. _____

c. _____

d. _____

e. _____

Reflecting Clouds

Have you ever looked at a rising sun . . .
And wondered how something could be so magnificent?
Never will you see two exactly alike.
Each sunrise is, in some way or other, different from another.
Each one is as unique as a human being
Have you ever looked at a sunrise
And felt you were floating?
Like, somehow, the beauty soaks into your body
Or that maybe, just maybe,
You'll be able to touch it if you could just reach far enough?

There is something special about a sunrise . . .
Something too great for words to describe,
Something larger than life,
Something spiritual and inspirational
Have you ever looked at a sunrise . . .
And felt this was God's reward for getting up?
It's as if the whole essence of life is reflected in these several
    minutes.

Like the sunrise, each one of us is unique,
Each one with our own special blend of personality
That makes us different from the rest,
Like the vibrant colors that make each morning special.
On some days, the sky is perfectly clear
Yet, oddly, it weakens the beauty of such a splendor.
But on those days when the fluffy clouds swallow up the sky
It's as if God's giving us a peek at heaven before we get there.

Our lives also share this queer quality.
If someone's life was to be perfect,
Untouched by sorrow, pain, anger, loss,
The human being, in fact, the life itself, would be dull and tedious.
Ironically, it's the struggles we go through on this journey
    called life
That make us so beautiful and incredible.
It's the way we struggle through these challenges
With perseverance and undying resilience
That reflects upon us and makes us so much more than just a body.

So fear not challenges, strife or loss.
For they are merely reflecting clouds

Whose purpose is to make us that much more special and strong.
And always remember . . . yesterday was the past
Tomorrow will be the future
But today is a gift, that's why it's called the present.

Phuong Nguyen, 15

Resources and References

Bolen, J. S. *The Tao of Psychology.* New York: Harper & Row, 1979.

Borysenko, J. *Fire in the Soul.* New York: Warner Books, 1990.

Frankl, V. *Man's Search for Meaning.* New York: Pocket Books, 1984.

Jampolsky, G. *Teach Only Love.* New York: Bantam Books, 1983.

Peck, M. S. *The Road Less Traveled.* New York: Touchstone Books, 1978.

Seaward, B. L. *Stressed Is Desserts Spelled Backward.* Berkeley, Calif.: Conari Press, 1999.

Seaward, B. L. *Stand Like Mountain, Flow Like Water: Reflections on Stress and Human Spirituality.* Deerfield Beach, Fla.: Health Communications, Inc., 1997.

Shield, B. and Carlson, R. (Eds.). *For the Love of God.* San Rafael, Calif.: New World Library, 1990.

Centering:
The Art of Meditation

When I meditate, everything goes
out with the breath. I concentrate on my breath,
and I concentrate on my abdomen and
how I am breathing. Breathing like
this just cools me down.

ABBY P., 15

If you have ever used the expression "too much information" when talking to a friend, you know how it feels to be continually flooded with thoughts, details and conversations, not to mention all the information from your studies. Too much information can suffocate your mind, making it nearly impossible to think straight. Too much information, whether it's studies, gossip from your friends, nagging parents, or the barrage of ads coming out of the radio and television, can be a huge distraction to clear thinking. And as we all know, clear thinking is essential to navigate the choppy waters of the teenage years.

Centering is a means to clear thinking. The technique is as old as eating; it's been practiced in every culture over the history of humanity, and in many circles it goes by the name of meditation. In simplest terms, meditation is the practice of quieting your mental chatter to gain clarity and perspective on the mounting issues you face every day.

Athletes meditate; they call this mental training. Musicians meditate (this is where they get some of their greatest song lyrics). Dancers and business executives meditate. In fact, people from all walks of life engage in the centering process to maintain a sense of balance. With the pace of life increasing dramatically every day, the art of meditation isn't just a good idea, it's essential. Athletes and actors aren't the only people practicing meditation. Since the Columbine High School incident, it has been introduced to many school programs across the country.

Kirby, 14, Colorado: "I would certainly advocate meditation for anybody who's stressed! A lot of people think meditation is sitting on top of a mountain in Nepal with scary music playing and going 'Om.' It's really not! All you have to do is lie down or sit down, relax completely and think about your breathing. For me, it is easiest to play music because it helps me to concentrate. But for some people, they just need to sit and be quiet. You have to concentrate completely on your breathing, and if your mind starts to wander off, pull it back again. Ease yourself into it. Don't expect to be really good at it at first, because you won't be. Meditation takes time. I meditate every day. I try to do it before bed to ease myself into the sleeping state. I have trouble sleeping if I don't meditate. I can't get my mind shut off. Meditation has really helped me cope with a lot in life."

Sam, 16, New York: "If I had one bit of advice for teenagers, it would be this: Learn to meditate. Meditating really helps me cope with things."

So what exactly is meditation? Meditation is the act of consciously tossing out perceptions, attitudes, opinions and fears that no longer serve you. In fact, they probably hold you back. At one time, these perceptions might have been helpful, but over time, they become outdated. By taking up space, they distort and cloud your thinking, making it hard to get things like homework done. Clouded thinking makes it hard to communicate well with your friends and parents. Centering is like deleting old e-mails on your computer that start taking up precious memory. Meditation is like erasing the chalkboard of your mind so you have a clean space for new ideas. Some people say that meditation is like using a broom to brush away crumbs on a dirty floor so it becomes nice and clean. Meditation! It's not what you think!

The word center means to enter the heart. When you take time to center, you not only calm the mind, you recharge the body and spirit as well. What are the benefits of centering? Well, there are many. First, by practicing meditation techniques, you have concentration skills and a better attention span, which is always a good thing. Meditation can also help you sleep better and feel more rested (less tired) throughout the day. Many people who meditate say they feel more emotionally balanced and have fewer health problems, including headaches, acne and stomach cramps. The benefits of centering are many.

COSMIC BREADCRUMBS

After several attempts, Jason finally
gets the hang of meditation.

©Inspiration Unlimited. Reprinted with permission.

Suggestions to Practice the Centering Process

Here are some guidelines and suggestions to help you begin a meditation practice.

1. First, find a quite place to sit, either in a comfortable chair or on the floor, with your back up against the wall. Find a place where you won't be interrupted (no cell phones, radio, television, brothers or sisters). Dedicate this spot, this corner, as your centering place.
2. Set aside a time each day so you can sit there for about five minutes (longer if you wish). Any time of day is good, but it's best if you do this on an empty stomach because a full stomach can make you drowsy. Before breakfast and dinner, or before you go to bed, are ideal times. If you have the time, mornings are great.
3. Keep a pad of paper and pen nearby. Even though you are clearing your mind, some good ideas might come up, and you might want to write them down for later.
4. Once you have a place and time, sit quietly, close your eyes and focus on your breathing. If you find that your mind becomes distracted, release the distracting thought or feeling as you exhale and bring your mind back to your breathing.

Thoughts and Reflections

List three places you can practice the art of centering:

a. _____

b. _____

c. _____

List two times in the course of your day when you can spend five to ten minutes uninterrupted.

a. _____

b. _____

List five things you can do to ensure that your centering time doesn't get interrupted.

a. _____

b. _____

c. _____

d. _____

e. _____

Here are five centering exercises* to clear your head and give you peace of mind. Read them once or twice to get the feel of what they're all about, then try them. These centering exercises are skills, and like any type of skill, the more you do it, the better you become. Try each one and see which feels the best for you.

#1 Deep, Comfortable Breathing Exercise

1. Sit comfortably with your back straight and close your eyes.
2. Place all of your attention on your breathing. Feel the air come into your nose or mouth and flow into your lungs. As

*©Inspiration Unlimited. Reprinted with permission.

you breathe, feel your stomach extend (this is why they call it belly breathing). When you begin to exhale, feel your stomach come back in and feel the air move up from the bottom of your lungs and back out your mouth or nose.

3. Repeat this several times, each time placing your full attention and concentration on the flow of air. If your mind wanders, bring it back to focus on your breathing.

4. After about ten normal breath cycles (one inhalation, one exhalation), try taking a very slow deep breath, comfortably slow and comfortably deep. As you exhale, feel a deeper sense of relaxation throughout your body. Some people like to count to themselves (1-2-3-4 when they inhale, 1-2-3-4-5 when they exhale). Repeat this two more times, comfortably slow and comfortably deep.

5. Return to normal breathing, and once again focus your attention on the flow of each breath.

6. Then take two more comfortably slow deep breaths. As you exhale with each breath, repeat this phrase to yourself, "I am calm and relaxed."

7. Return to your normal breathing cycle and continue this as many times as you like. When you complete your last cycle, feel a sense of freshness and renewal.

#2 Breathing Clouds Exercise

This centering exercise combines breathing with some visualization. As with any type of mental imagery, augment and embellish the suggested imagery to make it vivid and powerful for you. There are two images here: white clouds (inhalation) and dark clouds (exhalation). The white clouds symbolize clean fresh air; the dark clouds represent stressful thoughts, anxieties, problems, issues or concerns.

1. To begin, close your eyes and take a comfortably slow, deep breath. As you exhale, feel a sense of calm throughout your body. Repeat several more comfortably slow, deep breaths, feeling your stomach expand as you inhale, and come back as you exhale.

2. When you feel ready, imagine that the next breath you inhale (through your nose) is a cloud of pure, white air, clean and fresh. As you slowly breathe in this air, feel it circulate up to the top of your head and down your spine to reside at the base of your spine. When you are ready to exhale, feel the air move from your stomach area up into your lungs and out your mouth. Visualize that the air you exhale is dark and dirty air. As you exhale, think of a problem or issue that has occupied your mind. Allow this thought or feeling to leave as you exhale.

3. On the next inhalation, slowly breathe in through your nose a cloud of clean, fresh air, which represents a sense of calm and tranquility. Once again, feel it circulate to the top of your head and down your spine. When you are ready to exhale, feel the air come from the bottom of your lungs and move out through your mouth. As you exhale, allow yourself to release a thought or feeling that has been bothering you, a thought or feeling that is no longer serving you and holding you back. As you exhale, visualize a cloud of dark, dirty air leaving your mouth.

4. Repeat this cycle of breathing clouds ten more times. Pay close attention to the image of the clouds. Notice that as

you become more relaxed and more calm with the clean, fresh air, your mind is more calm, and the air you exhale is as clean as the air you inhale.

#3 Mountain Lake Exercise

This centering exercise also involves your imagination. As you read through this exercise, remember to embellish the details to make it as real as possible. If you simply cannot picture a mountain lake, try a swimming pool.

1. Begin by closing your eyes and focusing on your breathing. Place all your attention and concentration on your breathing. Take five comfortably slow, deep breaths, and notice how relaxed you feel as you exhale.
2. Using your imagination, visualize that you are sitting comfortably on a lawn chair at the edge of a lake in the early morning. The sun has been up for a little while, and it is very quiet. You have the whole place to yourself.
3. Take a slow, deep breath, and using your mind's eye, look at the body of water. As you look at the water, notice the ripples on the surface. These ripples are symbolic of stress in your mind and body. They represent distracting thoughts, nervous tension, frustrations or just nervous energy.
4. With each breath, recognize what these thoughts, feelings or sensations might be, and let one dissolve as you exhale. Still using your mind's eye to view the mountain lake, sense that this body of water is like your body. As you let go of these distracting thoughts, notice that the surface of the water is becoming calm.

5. Take several more slow, deep breaths, letting things go as you exhale. Notice with each slow, deep breath that the surface of the lake becomes more calm, so much so that it begins to reflect everything around it, like a big mirror.

6. Using your imagination, begin to see a mirror image on the surface of the lake, revealing the trees along the lake shore, the clear blue sky above and perhaps a snow-covered mountain in the distance.

#4 Dolphin Breath Exercise

Perhaps the most common approach to centering is closing your eyes and taking a couple of slow, deep breaths. As a rule, people tend to be thoracic breathers, only taking air into the upper region of the lungs. The most relaxing way to breathe (and the way you breathe when you sleep) is abdominal, or belly breathing. By placing the emphasis on this region of your body, you allow for a deeper, fuller breath. There is less neural tension breathing this way, hence the body relaxes more.

Breathing from the abdomen brings air deeper into the lower region of the lungs, which is closer to the center of your body. Practicing this style of breathing reinforces the idea of centering because the mind tends to follow the breath. When imagery is combined with breathing, the effect can be even more powerful. This exercise combines both breathing and imagery to clear the mind of mental chatter and center one's attention.

Using your imagination, pretend that, like a dolphin, you have a hole on the top of your head that allows you to breathe. The opening of this hole leads straight down to the core of your body (about an inch or two below your belly button).

Once you have this image in mind, take a slow, deep breath and allow the air to come into your body from the top of your head straight down to your abdominal area. When you feel ready to exhale, allow the flow of air to escape through the top of your head as well. Even though you are really inhaling and exhaling through your nose or mouth, imagine what it would be like to do this. With a little practice, it becomes quite easy.

Repeat this exercise, taking ten comfortably slow, deep breaths, pulling each breath through the top of your head and all the way to your diaphragm. Then, with each exhalation, feel a sense of calm and relaxation. Feel a sense of clarity in the core of your being as you complete this exercise. As you complete the final dolphin breath, notice a deep sense of calmness throughout your entire body.

#5 Four-Chambered Heart Exercise

Every culture speaks of the heart as a sacred space. Both the anatomical heart and the symbolic heart are intertwined. Long before medical science learned of the heart's anatomy and physiology, wisdom keepers spoke of a four-chambered heart. When four parts come together, a sacred space is formed. The mandala, a circular diagram with four quadrants, is a symbol of wholeness. Mandalas often depict the four directions, the four aspects of mind, body, spirit and emotions, or any four aspects that unite.

This meditation exercise invites us to go inward and focus on these four chambers of the symbolic heart: the full heart, the open heart, the strong heart and the clear heart. First, close your eyes and focus on your breathing. Begin by taking a slow, deep breath and feeling the flow of air through your body. As you exhale, feel a sense of relaxation in your heart space. Repeat this three times, making each breath comfortably slow and deep. With the exhalation of the fourth breath, imagine a violet circle with four quadrants. As you focus on each aspect, fill the appropriate chamber until the entire mandala is complete.

- **The Full Heart.** Taking a slow, deep breath, feel the air you breathe fill your entire heart space. As you exhale, imagine the air leaving your heart space. A full heart is an inspired heart. Ask yourself what inspires you, what makes you artistic, what makes your mind clear and focused? Imagine one thing that inspires you, and place this thought in your heart space. Take several slow, deep breaths, and with each inhalation, allow the heart space to become full with inspiration and energy. With each exhalation, bring to mind one thing that diminishes the fullness (inhibits inspiration), and let it go as you exhale. On the last exhalation, feel a sense of wonderful fullness in your heart space.
- **The Open Heart.** Take another slow, deep breath, and fill your entire heart space. Remind yourself that an open heart is one of compassion. Unresolved anger and fear close the door to an open heart. Taking five slow, deep breaths, allow the heart space to open unconditionally with each inhalation. With each exhalation, let those thoughts of anger and fear leave in a symbolic gesture of resolution. On the last exhalation, feel a sense of wonderful openness in your heart space.

• **The Strong Heart.** Once again, take a slow, deep breath, and notice how relaxed your heart space is on the exhalation. A strong heart is a courageous heart. The word courage comes from two French words meaning big heart. Take five slow, deep breaths, and reflect on courage and ways you can increase the strength of your heart. A strong heart muscle pumps continuously to circulate fresh oxygenated blood throughout the body. A strong symbolic heart is one filled with confidence. With each exhalation, feel the strength of a strong heart and the endurance to go the distance of the human journey.

• **The Clear Heart.** Placing your attention on your heart space, take a long, slow, deep breath again, and focus on your heart space. A clear heart is a heart unobstructed by negative thoughts. A clear heart is a clean heart that listens to the deep-seated wisdom of the soul. Using the breath as an imaginary broom, sweep your heart space clean with the next five breaths, releasing mental chatter with each exhalation. On the last breath, feel a sense of clarity in both heart and mind.

Pause now and take a moment to feel your heart space: full, open, strong and clear. Sit still and be at peace with the vision you hold and the feeling you have created.

Beth, 16, Hawaii: "Sometimes, if I am angry or really mad, I sit and think for as long as it takes to let the anger go. It never fails to make me a more happy, peaceful person, and in my opinion, this meditation makes me wiser in the process."

Thoughts and Reflections

After trying these various meditations, which made you feel the most relaxed? Why do you suppose this one worked the best?

_____

_____

_____

How does your body feel when you close your eyes and focus on your breath?

_____

_____

_____

Resource List

Having a daily meditation book helps focus your mind on a particular thought and set the mood for the day. Many books have a theme for each day of the year, while others have a variety of passages to reflect on.

Title	Author	Publisher
The Four Agreements	Don Miguel Ruiz	Amber-Allen
The Laws of Spirit	Dan Millman	H. J. Kramer
Attitudes of Gratitude	M. J. Ryan	Conari Press
The Seven Keys to Calm	A. M. Matthews	Pocket Books
365 Tao	Deng Ming-Dao	Harper San Francisco
Earth Prayers	Elizabeth Roberts and Elias Amidon, eds.	Harper San Francisco
The Promise of a New Day	Karen Casey and Martha Vanceburg	Hazelden

11

Tickling the Funny Bone: At Last, Some Comic Relief!

*When people laugh, that can
be the best medicine for any situation.
Laughing with friends can never be
described as an unpleasant time.*

SEAN D., 18

Sometimes, all it takes is one look at your friend to make you break out laughing. A shift in his or her eyes, a quirky smile, or a slight hand gesture at the right time can tickle the funny bone like nothing else. Friends are by far the best means to use humor to cope with stress!

If stress is a toxin to the heart and soul, humor is definitely the antidote. If issues of anger and fear are problems, laughter is a compass to steer you toward an answer. Let there be no doubt that humor takes the sting out of a bad situation. Even if it seems like there is nothing funny in the moment of chaos, humor helps you focus long enough to pull yourself together. As the saying goes, "Laughter is the best medicine."

Why is humor so important? If for no other reason, humor and laughter help give a sense of balance to a stressful day. Emotional well-being is the ability to feel and express the entire range of human emotions—from anger to love and everything in-between. It is not normal or healthy to be angry, depressed or anxious all the time. Humor is a way to bring balance to your emotional life. Considering just how stressful the teen years can be, comic relief plays a crucial role in coping with life and dealing with stress on all levels. The word humor actually means fluid; the implied message is to go with the flow.

Abby, 14, Colorado: "I'm a really giggly person. Last year I got yelled at for laughing, and just about anything makes me laugh. Like when someone says, 'Oh, look at that,' and I just start laughing. I guess my friends make me laugh, and if I am with a friend and I remember something funny that happened, that makes me laugh really hard, even though it happened a long time ago."

Ali, 15, Colorado: "I think humor is essential for me to cope with stress. I tend to hang out with my friends, watch funny movies or read a funny book. When I am acting too serious, my friends like to tickle me. They call me Squeaker because I always squeak when they tickle me. This usually pulls me out of a bad mood."

Aden, 14, California: "When I watch a TV show or read something funny, or if my friends are telling jokes, the laughing makes me feel a lot better. It's like knowing there is something out there that can still make you feel better. It really helps me. Whenever I'm upset, I watch *Friends*. I tape every episode, so I put in one of them. It makes me feel so much better."

Thoughts and Reflections

How is humor a good means to cope with your stress? What do you do to tickle your funny bone?

_____

_____

_____

_____

_____

_____

_____

Try to list three new ways to bring more laughter into your life (buy some comic books, read *MAD* magazine, or roam the greeting-card aisle at the nearest grocery store looking for the funniest cards).

a. _____

b. _____

c. _____

Good Humor

There are many different kinds of humor, all of which makes describing the topic of comic relief challenging at best. Parody, satire, slapstick, irony and puns are just a few ways the funny bone gets exercised. What's the best kind of humor? There is really no one answer, but good humor is the kind that makes you feel good inside. It doesn't decrease your self-esteem, nor does it harm others.

How many times a day do you laugh? Three? Seven? Four thousand eighty-nine? Most teens laugh about twenty times a day, so if you're hitting that number, you're in good company. If it's more than twenty laughs a day, keep doing whatever you're doing. If you're below the magical quota, hopefully this chapter will help.

Humor can take the sting out of a really frustrating moment. Have you ever been really mad about something and said to yourself, "A year from now this will be funny, but right now, it's not funny!"? This is probably when you need humor the most! Why wait a whole year? Start cashing in on the comic relief right now.

Geographic Jokes
(Guess You Had to Be There!)

Have you ever had your parents ask, "What's so funny?" and you quickly thought that even if you tried to explain it, they just wouldn't get it? Sometimes when you do try to explain it, they still don't get it. That's when you want to say, "Gee, I guess you had to be there." About 80 percent of teen humor falls under the category of "geographic jokes." The funny part is that even when you try to explain it to your friends, sometimes even they don't get it. As Confucius says, "He who laughs last didn't get the joke!"

Geographic jokes, like all jokes, come down to perception. You tend to laugh at something because what you see or hear connects with something you saw or heard before. When these two things are combined, you either get confused or tickled. The next time someone asks you "What's so funny?" and you know that no matter what you say to explain it, they just won't get it, simply smile and answer, "Geographic joke!"

Tom, 14, Colorado: "A lot of the stuff I laugh at is basically a bunch of random stuff. At any given moment, something will just hit me as being funny. Someone will be walking down the hall, and they might trip and fall. You know, they will start laughing, and then everyone else will start laughing. So basically, just random, silly things happen that are just funny; other times, they are hilarious. The only way to explain it is that you had to be there."

To Act Goofy or Not, That Is the Question!

Most teens say that much of what makes them laugh is acting goofy. It could be dancing in the street, imitating Jim Carey, or putting straws up their nose or chopsticks in their ears—there is no limit to goofiness. The only condition for being goofy and acting a little strange is shedding some inhibitions, which means not being so uptight and stressed. Of course, there are times when being goofy isn't appropriate (like funerals—by the way, why does the word funeral start with fun?). The key to being silly is to know when to step up on the world stage and improvise. Spontaneity and creativity are the cornerstones to quality goofiness.

Soma, 15, New York: "My friends and I act stupid all the time. We'll embarrass ourselves, and that's fun. One time, my friend and I went down to the store. It was Halloween, and I'd bought myself a green mask and butterfly wings because I was going to wear a straightjacket, green mask and butterfly wings for Halloween. Once we left the store, my friend put them on and was basically dancing along the road. It was so funny."

Chris, 16, Vermont: "One day, I was with some friends and we were swimming in the river. I don't know who started it or why, but somebody started making this sound. It went like this: "*budda, budda, budda.*" We all laughed and laughed. It was stupid, but it was funny. Months later, if I'm watching TV with my friends, every now and then someone will say *'budda, budda, budda'* and we all laugh. It's kind of funny."

Thoughts and Reflections

If you had to guess, how much of your humor is comprised of geographic jokes? Why do you suppose this type of humor is so funny?

_____

_____

_____

_____

_____

Are you the kind of person who can act goofy? How about your friends? Who is the most spastic, goofy person you know?

_____

_____

_____

_____

_____

Bathroom Humor

Let's face it, the teen years can be a pretty awkward time. Your body is going through all kinds of changes. Hormones start kicking in, and one day you wake up in what seems like a whole new body. It's awkward! You feel self-conscious at times, maybe all the time. And no one really talks about it. So to lighten the load, teens joke about various body parts and body functions. Really, what else can you do? Farts, burps—you can imagine the rest! This kind of humor is so unique that it has its own name: *bathroom humor.* Things of this nature start being funny in elementary school. By the time you get to be a senior, your parents really hope you outgrow it, but the truth is, some people never do. For some strange reason, guys get more into this than girls. Hollywood has caught on to this, and it's included in a lot of comedies. And if you have ever surfed all the cable channels (with your parents, of course!), no doubt you've noticed that stand-up comedians are very fluent with bathroom humor.

> **Danielle, 14, Colorado:** "My humor is perverted. I'm a very perverted person. I laugh a lot, and I can really laugh when I'm with my friend Amy. She makes me laugh all the time. Sometimes we'll just look at each other and start laughing, and we'll laugh for hours. No lie, we laugh for hours. And then, whenever one of us is sad, we call each other, and we always say, 'Hey, it could be worse.' Then one of us cheers the other up by saying something funny."

Bad Humor?

Not all humor is healthy. Take sarcasm (please!). If you were to look this word up in a dictionary, you would see that it means to tear flesh. And while sarcastic comments about other people might seem funny, it's anything but funny when they are made about you. Unlike all other forms of humor, sarcasm doesn't reduce stress; it promotes it. Sarcasm is really an expression of anger. Some people call sarcasm verbal sabotage. When people use sarcasm, whether they realize it or not, they are really displaying anger—even if the sarcastic comment isn't related to the cause of anger. Some people harbor feelings of anger and express them as sarcasm, oftentimes without even knowing it. If you hear others using sarcasm, think to yourself that this person is really angry about something. And if you are the kind of person who uses sarcasm, ask yourself what you're really angry about.

Teasing people when they are not your friends, or laughing at other people's expense, is also considered bad humor. While it's true that we tend to poke fun at things we don't understand, the last thing you want to do is hurt somebody by ridiculing them, just as you wouldn't want to be ridiculed.

Marty, 14, Connecticut: "Definitely, joking around with my friends relieves stress. I kind of tease my friend Bob because he has a funny walk sometimes. He has a funky bounce in his step. So I goof around and imitate him by teasing him about that, and he kind of just laughs and straightens himself out. It's pretty funny, and we both laugh."

Thoughts and Reflections

Everyone has used sarcasm at one point in his or her life, yet some people are more sarcastic than others. Would you label your humor as sarcastic? If so, can you relate it to one (or perhaps more) episodes of anger?

Sarcasm can be funny—if the comments aren't about you. How do you feel when you are the target of sarcasm?

_____

_____

_____

_____

There is a fine line between teasing somebody to become close with them and teasing someone to cut them down. Even teasing with good intentions can be damaging to someone's self-esteem. (Parents are known to do this unknowingly.) Can you tell the difference between good teasing and bad teasing? How does teasing make you feel, especially when it's about you?

_____

_____

_____

_____

Embarrassing Moments: Learning to Take Yourself Lightly

Did you ever do something that seemed so stupid that you just wanted to crawl in a hole and die? If so, you are not alone. We have all had embarrassing moments like walking around with your zipper open, dropping your tray in the cafeteria or locking yourself out of your car. The sign of a healthy ego is when you can laugh at these moments—if not immediately, then soon thereafter. Even though it might feel like the spotlight is on you when things don't go as planned and humiliation is written all over your face, try to do your best to turn your embarrassment to humor. As the saying goes, "Blessed are those who can laugh at themselves, for they shall never cease to be amused!"

Sally, 16, New York: "One time, I was in an auditorium with a friend at her little sister's concert. I went to sit down, and it was really dark, and I sat in some guy's lap. As if that wasn't bad enough, he turned out to be my math teacher. It was absolutely horrible because I did not like this teacher at all. I could have died then. Actually, it's pretty funny now!"

Heather, 16, Vermont: "When I am stressed and I want to laugh, I usually call my boyfriend or talk to a certain friend who always knows how to make a person laugh. They either do stupid and funny things, or they say something to make me laugh. If I am alone and need something to laugh about, I'll read a section in my magazines, the sections that talk about embarrassing things that happened to people. That always gets me going."

Phil, 17, California: "One time, I was in the locker room, walking back from the shower to my locker. There is an emergency door right by my locker. Some friends (and I use the term loosely) pushed me out the door as I was drying off. I had to run naked down the hall, through the gym and back into the locker room without a towel. It wasn't funny then, but I can laugh now!"

Thoughts and Reflections

What was your most embarrassing moment? Can you look back on this and laugh now?

_____

_____

_____

_____

Embarrassment is a form of stress, yet humor is a way to quickly deflate it. How can you lighten up the next time an embarrassing moment arises?

_____

_____

_____

_____

_____

Lighten Up (Working to Improve Your Sense of Humor)

It's no secret that teens appreciate humor differently. What is your sense of humor like? How many times a day do you laugh? Have you ever shared your favorite joke with a friend and gotten absolutely no response? Some people like to be entertained, while others like to do the entertaining (you know, the class clown). Humor is unique because it is one of those rare emotions you can experience by both taking it in and dishing it out. There are people who are really funny and creative, but they're also shy and would rather have someone else deliver the punch line. This is the kind of person who says while you're driving, "Hey, roll down your window and ask the guy next to you if he has any Grey Poupon." A "good sport" sense of humor is displayed by people who can take a good practical joke without calling their lawyer.

Eric, 14, Illinois: "I do silly things at lunch that make everybody laugh, like putting olives in my nose or wearing an omelet toupee. I just find ways to laugh, and when I'm with my friends, I laugh even more. I'm laid-back with my friends. The littlest thing will set me off, and I'll just laugh and laugh and laugh. My friends say the way I laugh is hilarious, so they'll start laughing when they hear me laugh. Then I laugh even more. It's contagious. I just find different ways to laugh. No matter what, I just laugh."

Chris, 14, Colorado: "I try to make other people laugh with the stuff I say. I just kind of think of wisecracks when the teacher is talking. Like last year, I would get all my work done in history early, so I would start talking to other people and making them laugh. I had to sit out in the hall the last two weeks."

BIZARRO © *by Dan Piraro. Reprinted with permission of UNIVERSAL PRESS SYNDICATE. All rights reserved.*

Tickling the Funny Bone: Working to Improve Your Sense of Humor

There are some people who say that no matter what you do, you can never improve your sense of humor. Don't believe them! The funny bone is more like a muscle than a bone, and it needs to be exercised regularly. Telling jokes is only one way to work the funny bone. What is the best way to improve your sense of humor? Here are some suggestions.

1. Find one humorous thing a day. There are a zillion things to laugh at in the world; it just takes a keen eye. Humor is not so much an emotion as it is a perception. So fine-tune your mind to find one humorous thing a day. Perhaps it's the comics in the paper. Maybe it's a funny TV show. Make a habit of searching for one funny thing a day, and you will be surprised at all the funny things there are to laugh at.

> **Pablo, 13, Colorado:** "Sometimes I'll go on the Internet and type in *Ahajokes.com* for a good laugh, or I might also go online and look for commercials because the commercials can be so funny. (The Cleo Awards are the best commercials.) Or I'll turn on the TV and find a funny show, or I'll ask my parents if they want to play a game because we have some humor games that play on words and stuff."

2. Exaggerate when telling a story. Want to make your friends laugh? Exaggerate when you tell something funny. All the best comedians do this, and you can do it, too. Here is one example from Comedy Central: "My cousin's family is so ugly that when they get photos taken, they only look at the negatives."

3. Turn on some good music and dance! Music and humor have much in common; they both create a fun atmosphere. If you want to lighten up, turn on some good music and start dancing. If you're really into it, turn on MTV and lip-synch and play air guitar to the music. If you're an introvert but still like to dance, remember the famous expression: "Dance as if no one is watching."

Gabrielle, 15, New York: "Sometimes I just find some great music to dance to and crank up the volume and start dancing. When I have my friends sleep over, we do crazy dance contests. It's a riot!"

4. Find a good comedy to watch. During the Depression, people would spend entire afternoons escaping the doldrums of life by going to the movies. Back then, movies cost a nickel (which is where the name Nickelodeon comes from). They had Charlie Chaplin and Laurel and Hardy. Today, we have everything they had back then and much more. Video stores have sections just for comedies. Some libraries even have these. If you're down in the dumps, pick out a good comedy and forget your troubles for a while. If you cannot find a good comedy, watching scary movies with friends and providing a running commentary seems to also provide a few laughs!

Funny Bones Movie Comedy Suggestions

- *Waiting for Guffman*
- *Liar, Liar*
- *Dumb and Dumber*
- *Meet the Parents*
- *Zoolander*
- *Evolution*
- *Sleepless in Seattle* (girls)

- *Ferris Bueller's Day Off*
- *Airplane*
- Any movie with Freddie Prinze Jr. in it (girls)
- *Wayne's World*
- *Office Space*
- Any movie with Adam Sandler in it (guys)
- *Rat Race*
- *Trading Places*
- *Singing in the Rain*
- *Best in Show*

Aaron, 14, Colorado: "I like watching comedy movies. Watching animated movies like *Shrek* and going to movies with your friends are great ways to spend an afternoon."

5. Use some imagination and creativity. Humor and creativity go together like peanut butter and jelly. All you need to do is look at the cover of the *National Enquirer* or browse through *MAD* magazine to know this. We all have a sense of imagination. Whether you're involved in a family game of charades or some school event, put your creativity cap on and see what you come up with. Some of the funniest things are just adaptations or satires of others' work.

Chris, 14, Colorado: "I love *Saturday Night Live*. When we do presentations for school, we imitate SNL skits. When we had to do a history presentation, we did *Celebrity Jeopardy*. We got a lot of laughs. I was Alex Trebek. We had Tom Cruise, Pierce Brosnan and Sean Connery; it was a riot. We had the whole class laughing."
Javier, 16, New Jersey: "We have this talent show in school every year, and last year my friends and I did this air-music, lip-synch routine to oldies. It was hilarious, and we got first place."

6. Build a good humor library. When you're stressed and there are no friends around, having access to good humor resources is a great alternative. What can you do to start building your own humor library? Think about some books, cartoon collections, videos, DVDs, audiotapes or CDs and whatever else you can come up with.

Brent, 17, Virginia: "I have a stash of cartoon books under my bed. I just love *Calvin and Hobbes*. I also have *Bizarro* and a few other books. Sometimes I get tired of watching television, so I go up to my room and pull out one of these books and catch myself laughing out loud. It's a great thing to do before you go to sleep because you have better dreams."

7. Call a close friend. By far, friends are the best means to help put a smile on your face. If you are really down in the dumps, pick up the phone and call a friend or two. If you can invite them over, all the better. Many friends are class clowns who are always looking for an audience, so don't deny them the opportunity to share a few laughs.

Sarah, 16, New York: "Often, when I'm stressed out, I call one of my friends who I know will say the right thing to make me laugh. I'll call her just to laugh and sort of get it out. It really does help. I'm not exactly sure how, but I know it does."

Michelle, 15, Colorado: "To lift my spirits, I usually try to talk to one of my guy friends. They're the funniest guys I've ever known. They make up jokes all the time. I don't know how, but they do these really funny voices. My friends do a lot of that, and they love to watch those late-night shows so they do a lot of impressions. That's really funny. My brothers and my dad are really funny, too."

Kyle, 18, Tennessee: "For humor, I hang out with my friends. We like to sit around and joke about stuff or do something funny. That's usually the funniest time I have with them, doing something funny. Everyone jokes around, and it's like having a built-in audience."

Thoughts and Reflections

Humor is perception, which means that looking for humorous things requires having the right attitude. Make a list of all the places you can look for one humorous thing every day. Start with the newspaper comics and TV shows. Don't stop till you come up with ten places.

a. _____   f. _____
b. _____   g. _____
c. _____   h. _____
d. _____   i. _____
e. _____   j. _____

What are your favorite movies? Some people like comedies. Others like scary movies so they can provide a running humorous commentary. Make a list of your top ten favorite all-time comedies.

a. _____   f. _____
b. _____   g. _____
c. _____   h. _____
d. _____   i. _____
e. _____   j. _____

Kevin Bacon danced in the movie *Footloose,* John Travolta danced in *Saturday Night Fever,* Mariah Carey danced in *Glitter,* and Justin Timberlake and Kevin Richardson dance on MTV. Dancing to loud music is a great way to relieve frustrations, and depending on how you dance, it can be rather humorous. Try this: Find ten songs to dance to and mix a tape or burn a CD. Have this music handy when you need a good emotional lift.

Make yourself a tickler notebook. It's easy. A tickler notebook is like a scrapbook of funny stuff that makes you laugh and smile. It could contain jokes, cartoons, photos of your friends, birthday cards, or anything to bring a smile to your face.

"I tried to write my school report about
Antarctica, but the computer kept freezing.
So I changed my topic to Hawaii."

Reprinted by permission of Randy Glasbergen. ©Randy Glasbergen, www.glasbergen.com

And Now, Start Flexing Your Funny Bone: Here Come the Jokes!

Teens from all over the country were invited to submit jokes for this chapter. Unfortunately, we couldn't print the majority of them, but these are the ones that got through the censoring process. Enjoy!

A Night with Sherlock Holmes

Famed detective Sherlock Homes and his gruff assistant Dr. Watson pitch their tent while on a camping trip. In the middle of the night, Holmes nudges Watson to wake him up.

Holmes: "Watson, look up at the stars and tell me what you deduce."
Watson: "I see millions of stars. And if there are millions of stars, even if a few of those have planets, it is quite likely there are some planets like Earth. And if there are a few planets like Earth, then indeed, there might be intelligent life, much like our own, sir."
Holmes: "Watson, you idiot, someone stole the tent!"

Fortune Cookie Messages

(submitted by Tom in California)

Man who run in front of car get tired
Man who run behind car get exhausted
Man who eat many prunes get good run for money
Man who tell one too many lightbulb jokes soon burn out
Man who drive like hell bound to get there
Man who live in glass house should change clothes in
basement

Some Good (Humorous) Advice

(submitted by Brian in Arizona)

- It's always darkest before dawn. If you're going to steal your neighbor's newspaper, that's the time to do it.
- No one is listening until you make a mistake.
- Always remember you're unique, just like everyone else.
- Never test the depth of the water with both feet.
- It may be that your sole purpose in life is to serve as a warning to others.
- If you think nobody cares if you're alive, try missing a couple of car payments.
- Before you criticize someone, you should walk a mile in their shoes. That way, when you criticize them, you're a mile away and you have their shoes.
- If at first you don't succeed, skydiving is not for you.
- Give a man a fish and he will eat for a day. Teach him how to fish, and he will sit in a boat and drink beer all day.
- Good judgment comes from bad experience, which comes from bad judgment.
- The quickest way to double your money is to fold it in half and put it back in your pocket.
- A closed mouth gathers no foot.
- There are two kinds of pedestrians: the quick and the dead!
- Duct tape is like The Force. It has a light side and a dark side, and it holds the universe together.
- There are two theories to arguing with women. Neither one works!

A Small Favor?

(submitted by Maria in Iowa)

A small boy is sent to bed by his father. Five minutes later . . .

"Da-ad . . ."

"What?"

"I'm thirsty. Can you bring a drink of water?"

"No. You had your chance. Lights out."

Five minutes later: "Da-aaaad . . ."

"WHAT?"

"I'm THIRSTY. Can I have a drink of water??"

"I told you NO! If you ask again, I'll have to spank you!!"

Five minutes later . . . "Daaaa-aaaad . . ."

"WHAT!"

"When you come in to spank me, can you bring a drink of water?"

The Crystal Ball

(submitted by Stephanie in North Carolina)

In a dark and hazy room, peering into a crystal ball, the mystic delivered grave news: "There's no easy way to say this, so I'll just be blunt—prepare yourself to be a widow. Your husband will die a violent and horrible death this year." Visibly shaken, Jennifer stared at the woman's lined face, then at the single flickering candle, then down at her hands. She took a few deep breaths to compose herself. She simply had to know. She met the fortuneteller's gaze, steadied her voice and asked: "Will I be acquitted?"

Driving School: Real Answers Received on Exams Given by the California Department of Transportation's Driving School

(submitted by Roy in California)

Q: Do you yield when a blind pedestrian is crossing the road?

A: What for? He can't see my license plate.

Q: Who has the right of way when four cars approach a four-way stop at the same time?

A: The pick-up truck with the gun rack and the bumper sticker saying, "Guns don't kill people. I do."

Q: When driving through fog, what should you use?

A: Your car.

Q: What changes would occur in your lifestyle if you could no longer drive lawfully?

A: I would be forced to drive unlawfully.

Q: What are some points to remember when passing or being passed?

A: Make eye contact and wave hello if he or she is cute.

Q: What is the difference between a flashing red traffic light and a flashing yellow traffic light?

A: The color.

T-Shirt Quotes

Police station toilet stolen . . . Cops have nothing to go on.

Failure is not an option . . . It comes bundled with the software.

Quoting one is plagiarism. Quoting many is research.

Stupidity is not a handicap. Park elsewhere.

Heck is where people go who don't believe in gosh.

A picture is worth a thousand words, but on the hard drive it uses up a thousand times more memory.

A Few Zen Thoughts for Those Who Take Life Too Seriously

(submitted by Joan in Illinois)

- A day without sunshine is, like, night.
- The early bird may get the worm, but the second mouse gets the cheese.
- On the other hand, you have different fingers.
- When everything is coming your way, you're in the wrong lane.
- Everyone has a photographic memory. Some people just don't have film.
- Always try to be modest, and be proud of it!
- Hard work pays off in the future. Laziness pays off now.
- Change is inevitable, except from vending machines.
- I feel like I'm diagonally parked in a parallel universe.
- Honk if you love peace and quiet.
- Remember, half the people you know are below average.
- He who laughs last thinks slowest.
- Support bacteria. They're the only culture some people have.
- A clear conscience is usually the sign of a bad memory.
- Okay, so what's the speed of dark?
- If everything seems to be going well, you obviously overlooked something.
- Eagles may soar, but weasels don't get sucked into jet engines.
- What happens if you get scared half to death twice?

Part III

Final
Comments
from Teens

Teens' Advice to Parents

Make a habit of really listening to your kids.
Try to help them and get involved with what is
going on in their lives so you can understand
what they are really going through.

SARAH, 17, VIRGINIA

At first glance there appears to be a love-hate relationship between teens and their parents. Well, perhaps hate is too strong a word. Let's just say that it's no secret there is a looming tension between you and your parents. Teens don't understand why parents cannot relate to them; after all, they were young once (they were teens, too!). Parents, on the other hand, don't understand why their kids don't act more responsibly.

Ask any teen to explain what stresses them out, and parents always come up. There is no owner's manual given to parents. The job of parenting is pretty much a learn-as-you-go process

with a lot of trial and error. Any teen will tell you parents are
not perfect. Even with the best intentions, they still make
many mistakes. But when all is said and done, there are many
good things as well. As one teen from Illinois said, "Yes, we
understand you were once teenagers, too, but it was a long
time ago. Times are different!!!" Indeed they are! If you're
like most kids today, you might have a credit card, a cell
phone and your own Web page. When your parents were
teens, there were only three or four channels, and no one was
allowed to swear on television. Most stores were closed on

Sundays (even Mondays), and while drugs and alcohol were certainly around, it's fair to say that there is a lot more available these days. Parents just don't have a good reference point for the Millennium Generation.

Perhaps the tension between parents and their children comes down to the tug of war between freedom and responsibility. Simply stated, teens want more freedom, and parents want their kids to be responsible. Like clothes that no longer fit, the parameters of freedom in grade school and middle school are considered too tight. Some parents still see their teens as little kids. Perhaps they are in denial that their kids could leave home after high school.

The following are some comments shared by teens when asked what advice they would give to adults to become better parents, and most likely, this is one chapter your parents are going to want to read.

Tips for Parents Who Don't Listen Well

Alice, 14, California: "I would say, first of all, that parents need to listen to their kids. They really need to listen to them, because when you're fighting about whatever you're fighting about, and the kids think they're right and the parents think they're right, who's gonna win? They should really listen to what the kids have to say, even if they don't agree with it. I know when I see my friend, she and her mom fight all the time. I looked at both of their points of view. It's like her mom doesn't even listen to her, and many times when all is said and done, my friend is right about what's going on. Her mom just doesn't want to change her point of view."

Margo, 16, Massachusetts: "Just take time to listen to your kids. If they seem upset, take time to ask them what is wrong, and ask them if they'd like someone to talk to. If they want to talk, try not to say anything until, or unless, they ask for your advice or opinion. Most times they need to process whatever is bothering them. I think it's best when my parents listen and wait to talk after I'm done. I like to talk to my mother. She is my shoulder to lean on. Also, when your kids talk to you about something, tell them stories so they don't feel they are alone. That helps. My mom does it all the time, and it makes me realize that I am not the only one who has gone through this before."

Peter, 14, New York: "Listen! Don't judge or jump to conclusions. If I'm telling you something that is really serious to me, that I know you are going to yell at me for, and if you jump in the middle and say, 'What did you do that for?' I would never want to talk to you again about sensitive issues. I would go to someone else. I would go to a close friend or something because I might feel like my parents would jump down my throat. So please, if you just listen and try to understand, that would be the best thing you can do."

Kelly, 18, Florida: "About the only advice I could give to parents is to listen to your kids. I mean REALLY listen to them, not just act like you are listening or put our words in your ears before we actually say something and filter it through your perceptions. You might actually be surprised at all that we have to say. You don't necessarily have to understand everything about your kids, but try to understand them as people, and be responsive to their best wishes. Furthermore, sometimes it is best to let people learn from their own mistakes. Perhaps most importantly, be forgiving and always let your kids know how much you love them. You may think that kids get sick of hearing this, but believe me, we never hear it enough!"

Thoughts and Reflections

Most teens say their parents may hear them, but they just don't listen. If you have ever felt this way, even once, you are not alone. Do you feel your parents don't listen when you talk or try to explain something? Why do you suppose this is so?

_____

_____

_____

_____

There is an expression that says, "It takes two to tango," yet the same can be said about communication. To have a good conversation, even if it's a difficult one, there has to be a conducive setting for talking. Sitting in the living room with the TV is never a good time to talk. There are too many distractions. Some of the best conversations might occur when you're in the car, but if things get heated, be assertive and ask to continue this later. (Having a mad parent behind the wheel is never a good idea!) When you want your parents to listen, do yourself a favor and create the best conditions possible. What would those be for you?

_____

_____

_____

_____

It's possible that if parents were asked, they would say their kids don't listen either. "Things go in one ear and out the other," they often say. What can you do to be a better listener and, by example, teach your parents something?

_____

_____

_____

_____

_____

_____

CALVIN AND HOBBES

CALVIN AND HOBBES. ©Watterson. Reprinted with permission of UNIVERSAL PRESS SYNDICATE. All rights reserved.

Tips for Parents Who Yell and Scream

Jennifer, 15, North Carolina: "Don't yell! I can't stand yelling. It just makes me feel awful. I'm sure it makes other people feel awful, too. I've had friends who come from families where everyone is yelling all the time, and they don't have good relationships with their friends because all they know is anger and yelling. Also understand that we are growing up and getting older, and you have to accept that you have to let us go. You have to let us be our own people and make our own mistakes, but if we need you, please be there for us. Be kind always. Be kind and loving, and understand that we go through so much at school that we don't need to come home to an angry home where our parents are being mean to us or yelling at us or being frustrated. Just talk. Don't yell! Don't be harsh. It's so much easier, and you get so much more across to us by being gentle."

Debbie, 18, Arizona: "What advice do I have for parents? Parents, love your kids as best as you can. Look back at what mistakes your parents made. This is the time to break the cycle. Your children will make lots of bad choices. Yelling isn't going to make that choice go away. So don't yell! This doesn't solve anything! Instead, hold your kids and let them know they can always come to you. I'm kind of strange, because I tell my parents absolutely everything. I mean everything! My life is an open book, and I have made lots of bad choices, including drugs, sex and a suicide attempt. But those things don't make me a bad person. I learned from them, and I've made sure they don't happen again because that was a bad place in my life. I can only say that if my parents wouldn't have cared, or I didn't think I could tell them, I would have continued doing drugs, sex and such."

Thoughts and Reflections

Unless there is immediate danger, yelling is a sign of anger. If your parents yell, this is a clear indication they are stressed! Yelling doesn't solve problems; it usually makes them worse. Yelling back is like throwing gasoline on the fire. If your parents begin to yell at you, an appropriate response is to say you will be willing to discuss this when they calm down. You might want to first practice this with your friends to refine this behavior of assertiveness.

Tips for Parents to Be More Supportive

Aaron, 13, Pennsylvania: "Basically, be understanding. Constructive criticism is good, but it's all about timing. Be mindful when you offer criticism that will affect how your child feels. They'll take it in a different way if they are in a sensitive mood, or they'll get really defensive if they're in a bad mood. If they're sad, they'll agree with you and their self-esteem will go down. It depends on timing and what you say. Parents can push you too hard, especially if they don't understand what's going on in your life. They just push you, and kids might rebel."

Carl, 18, Wisconsin: "When their kids are young, parents should encourage a lot of different activities, including all kinds of sports, and take note of the ones they are really good at. Let them concentrate on one or two of those, and they can have something they'll be good at for the rest of their lives. My parents encouraged me to play soccer when I was really little, but I didn't really want to. Now I'm glad they did. On a different note, I highly recommend that parents set a good example, because if parents drink or smoke or something like that, I've noticed that the kids often do it as well. So set a good example."

Linda, 14, Texas: "When your children become teenagers, you need to establish a better bond of trust. Trust! First of all, you need to respect their privacy. Granted, there are some situations in which you are suspicious of something bad, and well, then that's different. But you can't go through their stuff every day because they are not going to trust you if you do. Also, you need to find some way to communicate with them and learn what is going on in their lives. That way, you show compassion and that you're not there just to tell them what to do—like clean their rooms and that they're grounded. You have to show there is another side to parenting besides ordering kids around. Parents need to spend better quality time with their kids. Most parents I know spend way too much time at work. The result is that they don't spend enough time with their kids, and those are the kids who are getting into trouble. Parents need to know what's going on, and that requires quality time."

Trevor, 17, Florida: "Parents need to listen to their children. They need to understand their children's fears and desires. They need to accept children for who they are, not who the parents want them to be. If they do sports, they should be encouraged, but not forced. They should be able to do as much as they want and are capable of. Kids need to make their own decisions. They can't be told how to do everything. Trust is a big issue, and it goes both ways. There should be reasons for things beyond the typical line, 'Because I said so!' Otherwise, the kid is going to hate his or her parents. Whether it's big or little things, kids should be able to make their own decisions. And children should have to spend their own money on stuff, not have their parents give them whatever they want. I have friends who are so spoiled because their parents say, 'Oh, you did that, now let's go buy you a new so-and-so.' My parents don't do that. I think it has made me a better person, and I know that money doesn't grow on a tree. If that's all you have, that's all you have. Some parents give their kids everything because they think it compensates for not spending quality time with them. It's like a bribe for love. I think parents need to spend more time with their kids, doing what the child likes to do. Get to know your kid as a person. If the child really likes to hike in the mountains, they should go hiking instead of watching a baseball game. If the child likes to watch baseball, parents should sit down and watch baseball with their kids.

Thoughts and Reflections

Are your parents supportive, or do they push you too hard? Are you the kind of teen who needs a lot of encouragement or an occasional gentle reminder? How do you communicate your needs to your parents?

_____

_____

_____

_____

Do your parents set a good example, or do you see things they do and quickly know there is another (perhaps better) way? Do your parents spend too much time at work? If you think so, do you tell them?

_____

_____

_____

_____

Is privacy an issue with you and your parents? If so, why? Do you get mixed messages about various issues from your parents, and if so, do you tell them about it?

_____

_____

_____

_____

Tips for Coping with Stepparents

Ryan, 17, Florida: "Stepparents need to work with the child on what the kid likes to do. They shouldn't say, 'I'm your step-parent, and now I'm your parent.' You have to be a friend, not a parent, because the blood parents are the real parents. Think of it from our viewpoint—now we're answering to four people, not two. Start by building trust; it all begins with trust. So if you're a stepparent, you need to try to be a friend and interact with your stepson or stepdaughter in a way you like to do stuff."

Amy, 14, Michigan: "I have some advice for stepparents: Please don't try to be the actual parent. Don't try to work so hard to get the kids to like you. It bothers us when stepparents try too hard. They say, 'I'm not trying to replace your mom or dad' (whichever it is), but of course we already know that. You don't have to tell me. I wouldn't let you replace them anyway."

Jennifer, 13, Oregon: "Stepparents walk a fine line when it comes to doing any disciplining. One step over the line, and I think you'll make the kid hate you forever or at least lose their trust. The best thing you can do is give your stepchildren advice, talk to them and be more of a friend."

Thoughts and Reflections

If you have a stepparent, you know the stress involved with a new parental figure. Stepparents can range from a trusted friend to your mom or dad's bossy roommate. What's your relationship like with your stepparent? Can you think of any ways to improve this relationship?

_____

_____

_____

_____

_____

Tips for Being Compared to Your Siblings

Brian, 16, Hawaii: "Don't compare your children to each other. My father always compares me to my older brother. It has made me resent my brother and get mad at my dad. I am not the same person as my brother. I never will be! I think the cruelest thing you can do to your child is make them feel inferior by comparing them to someone else. DON'T DO IT!"

Thoughts and Reflections

If you have ever been compared to one of your brothers or sisters (or even stepbrother or stepsister), you know how frustrating this can be. If this happens to you, the action plan once again calls for assertiveness. Plan what you would like to say to your parents (diplomatically, of course) and rehearse it a few times before you sit them down for a talk.

_____

_____

_____

_____

_____

There is an unwritten rule that parents shouldn't pick favorites among their children, but it does happen. Do you ever feel like your siblings are favored over you? (It's okay to feel this way.) How do you communicate these feelings to your parents?

_____

_____

_____

_____

_____

_____

Tips for Narrow-Minded Parents

Derek, 16, Maine: "Try to be more open-minded. Try to remember how difficult it was when you were kids and trying to be accepted, trying to live up to what society thinks a man or woman is supposed to be. It's not easy, and it surely isn't the same now as when you were teenagers."

Jesse, 18, Alaska: "Remember what it was like when you were a teenager! Try to relate to your kids and understand their likes and dislikes. Most importantly, LISTEN! Try to understand where your kids are coming from. Don't just tell them not to listen to a certain kind of music. Listen to it for yourself and see what it's like. Don't be so restricting. If you're going to be restricting, your kids are going to do this stuff behind your back anyway. So be cool with your kids. Teach them the consequences; that's the best thing you can do."

Renee, 14, Ohio: "Parents need to sharpen their listening skills. Parents don't listen. They think that what happened in 1970 is happening now. It's not! It's different, and it changes every generation. Parents should also learn not to make assumptions. My mom does this, and even when she's wrong, she won't admit it. Parents also need to learn to apologize when they make mistakes; that really helps earn respect from their children. Another thing, don't try to get gossip from other kids' parents. My mom does that, and half of what she hears is propaganda!"

Thoughts and Reflections

Sure your parents were teens once, but they may have forgotten what it was like. Not only do you need to gently remind them, but you might also need to diplomatically educate them exactly how the world has changed. It might take some work, but if your parents keep talking about how it was when they were teens, pull out a copy of their high-school yearbook and learn what it was really like. When you're done with that, bring them up-to-date on how things have changed. Remember, do this diplomatically.

Tips for Immigrant Parents

Jennifer, 15, California: "It's really hard when you're the first-generation American. Parents aren't going to change. I think that when it comes to their kids and stuff, parents need to understand that it's a lot different compared to when and where they were growing up. Parents need to understand that things are speeding up. My mom often says, 'I didn't do this until I was like twenty or twenty-five.' It's different times now, and they need to move into the twenty-first century."

Virginia, 14, Georgia: "Kids really want their parents to listen. But parents probably had their own set of rules forced on them when they were growing up. So they say things like, 'This is the way my life was, and this is the way your life is going to be. This is what I lived by, and this is what you're going to live by!' Parents should be more opened-minded because with every generation, almost everything changes. Kids, especially those brought in from other countries and other cultures like me, have to adapt, and sometimes you can't use the old rules anymore. It's a new game every generation. The old rules don't work, and parents need to realize that. It's different here."

Thoughts and Reflections

Are you a first-generation American? Are you an immigrant? If the answer is yes, not only are you experiencing the stress of the teenage years, you are most likely living in two worlds and this translates to culture shock. Your friends who are fifth-, sixth- or even tenth-generation Americans have no idea what you are going through, and your parents have no reference point for your experiences either. One way to cope is to find people in school who are going through a similar situation—this will become your support group. Also, being bilingual doesn't just mean speaking two languages. It means walking gracefully in two worlds: the world your family left behind and the world you are now living in.

Tips for Letting Teens Learn from Their Mistakes

Jennifer, 15, Maryland: "I think my parents try to stop me from making mistakes, but that's an important part of growing up—making mistakes and learning from them. They're not even letting me make the mistakes. I think they need to back off a little bit and give me some space to do my thing. I know they are concerned and they want the best for me, but they're not going about it the right way. What are some ways they do it the right way? I think they need to let me learn from my mistakes, instead of trying to keep me from making them. Let me lose a little bit. Let me have a little bit more freedom when it comes to going out."

Alice, 14, California: "Give your child some space. Don't always try to be the helpful person. Don't always be, 'Oh, what's going on? Are you having problems?' If you're too noisy and you're stressed out, you are not going to say, 'Oh, Mom, I have this and this and this.' You're just going to want to say, 'Go away! I need some time.' Give your child some space and acknowledge that your kid is changing."

Thoughts and Reflections

It's natural for parents to want to help their kids as much as possible, but too much help can be a hindrance. Your parents are never going to know if they are in the way unless you tell them (diplomatically, of course). If and when this happens, the action plan is to be assertive. Tell them how much help and support you need. At first, they are not going to understand this, so you might have to tell them a few times. Remember: Be careful not to burn any bridges. You may never know when a situation arises where, indeed, you will need their assistance.

Tips on Balancing Freedom and Responsibility

Sarah, 14, New Jersey: "Parents should keep an eye on their kids at this age because, obviously, they are going to want to try new things. I know people in my classes who go out and smoke every day at passing periods, and I think parents should keep an eye on that. If their kids smell like smoke, parents should question them, or if they come home from a friend's and they smell like alcohol, parents should keep an eye on that, too."

Sally, 14, Kansas: "I think a good parent is someone—no matter how much their kids don't like it—who really wants to know exactly what their kids are doing and where they are at all times. Demand to know where your kids are going, who they are with, and when and how they are getting home. I think the parents who say, 'Oh, I don't care. Do whatever you want' are the parents who end up with kids who have teen pregnancies and get involved with drugs and gangs and that sort of thing."

Lucy, 17, California: "Parents need to not pressure their kids into so much. Give your kids a little more freedom, but not way too much. I know that with my mom, if she hadn't been keeping such a close eye on me, I probably would have tried smoking or drugs. I don't know. Definitely ask your kids, like the commercials say. Ask your kids where they are going, who they are going with and what they are doing. Don't be scared to ask your kids stuff. And more importantly, don't be scared what the answer might be."

Thoughts and Reflections

Freedom and responsibility go hand in hand. For every action there is a consequence. Not only are you responsible for your freedoms, but until age eighteen, so are your parents. This is one topic that definitely requires good communication between you and your parents. Needless to say, trust is an inherent part of freedom. If you wish to have your parents extend your circle of freedom, it will require a series of negotiations and some quality conversations. Good luck!

"Hi, this is Mom! If you haven't done your homework yet, press 1. If you forgot to take the dog out after school, press 2. If you've been picking on your sister again, press 3. . . ."

Reprinted by permission of Randy Glasbergen. ©Randy Glasbergen,
www.glasbergen.com

Tips on Stress-Prone Parents

Beth, 13, Connecticut: "First and foremost, parents need to listen better. If you tell them something, anything, you don't want them to go ballistic or freak out. Today, I told my mom I was going to get a D if I didn't bring this folder to school, and then I said it would be okay because I would just buy one at school. Then she started freaking out, saying, 'What if you can't get one?' Parents should learn to relax and not freak about that kind of stuff. They just pass their stress to their kids. Overall, it's my experience that parents don't listen well at all. It makes me wonder what goes on at the office if it's like this at home."

Thoughts and Reflections

Do your parents cope well with stress? Unknowingly, we pick up a lot of behaviors (good and bad) from our parents. This is a good time to look at how your parents handle stress. More importantly, this is the time to observe if you have learned their coping skills. If they are not effective skills (and you will know this immediately), now is the time to toss out the old and learn new ones.

Tips on Parents with Their Own Difficult Issues

Jason, 16, Washington: "I think my parents need to listen more. My parents don't really listen, like when I told them I was depressed. I told them this in seventh grade, and they just ignored it. They can't accept that fact, so they never deal with it. They're like, 'Oh, we'll do something about it.' But they don't. I'm a kid. I'm not always going to make the best choices. Of course I'm going to mess up, every kid does, so they shouldn't get all anal-retentive about it and completely blow it out of proportion, like my dad sometimes does.

"I think parents should get counseling, too. My dad has a drinking problem. I confronted him, and he did his little fusion thing. (I don't know if that's a word.) He went ballistic! Then I told him he needs to get anger-management counseling. And he said, 'Well, I'm not ever going to do that.' I was like, 'Okay, cool.' Then we got in a fight about a month ago, and I said, 'Why are you even talking to me if you won't get any help in solving our relationship? Why are you even talking to me now?' He said, 'You're right.' But he hasn't done anything about it. I haven't even talked to him since. He wastes so much of our money on alcohol and smoking. If he stopped, we wouldn't have so many problems with money."

Thoughts and Reflections

Many parents have addictions to cigarettes, alcohol, drugs, gambling and eating to name a few. Most children aren't aware of their parents' addictions until they become teenagers. Because of the nature of addictions, if you confront your parents in an attempt to help them, they would most likely deny the problem. Try as you might, you cannot change your parents' behaviors, but you can get help yourself. Many schools have support groups for kids whose parents have addictions (Al-Anon is a group for children of alcoholics). Every school has a counselor who can help. There is no shame in having a parent who's an addict. The worst course of action is to ignore the problem, hoping it will go away.

Tips on Setting Good Boundaries

Scott, 15, Connecticut: "Listen to what your kids have to say. Parents don't listen. And if you are going to punish your kids, follow through with it. Don't make empty threats, like saying, 'I'm going to ground you if you do that,' then soften up and never ground us. Go through with what you say, and don't let your kids get away with stuff, otherwise kids lose respect."

Rich, 14, Florida: "Let us live our lives the way we want to live them. Like me and my parents, some things we agree about and some things we don't. Music is not one of them. If I like something, it basically means my dad doesn't like it. There's that stress, but I think it's good to have your own opinion. Parents need to let us live off our own life experiences, not do it for us. At the same time, we need better boundaries. In terms of discipline, I'm not saying that kids should be raised under house arrest, but parents need to have control over part of our lives, no matter how much we shut them out. They're still our parents, no matter what, and they need to let us live our lives, but they still need some level of control. It's a fine balance, and some parents are failing miserably. If we do something wrong, they've got to be firm, and they've got to take care of us."

Lynn, 15, Colorado: "As your kids get older, you need to establish boundaries, like how late we can stay out, etc. Trust is a big issue between parents and their children. You don't gain trust when you set ridiculous boundaries. I think it goes both ways.

The child has to trust the parent, as well as the parent trusting the child. If you don't have anything there, you've got a problem. I know a lot of kids who simply do not trust their parents."

Jamie, 18, Colorado: "Go easy on your kids. The teen years are a learning curve for both parents and their kids. It's not just you having a new teenager and trying to deal with it. It's us being teenagers trying to deal with you as neurotic parents. It's a mingled, messed-up relationship in a lot of ways, but you have to deal with it. And you have to realize your kids are growing up. You have to let them grow up. There are too many parents who keep their kids confined in the house, and it's not fair."

Thoughts and Reflections

No one likes to be punished, but we all crave boundaries. We need to know our limits, or life becomes one big blur of uncertainty. It's a parent's job to establish healthy boundaries, yet many parents never learned good boundaries themselves so they have little experience to go on. If boundaries are important to you, bring it up with your parents. Remember, diplomacy works better than confrontation.

Tips on Giving Your Teens Advice

Sean, 14, Illinois: "Let your kids live their own lives, but definitely offer them advice and help along the way. You know, don't grab their hands and lead them down the road of life; just walk next to them. Be there to guide them when they fall and help pick them up. I know some parents who try to live their kids' lives and push them to do things they didn't do when they were kids. But, really, it's up to the kids what they want to do, and all their parents should do is support them in their decision and help them along the way."

James, 15, California: "My advice to parents? Don't jump to conclusions about anything your kid does. At the same time, don't patronize them or be condescending—I hate that. What's the opposite of condescending? Treat them as an equal, a human being. Treat them as you would like to be treated. I think I have been hurt the most when my parents lie. Don't lie. Kids are tougher than you think. We can take the truth a lot better than we can take lies, especially when we learn the truth. It comes down to a matter of trust, and trust goes both ways! More advice, try this: Don't interrupt when we're trying to explain something that is really difficult to put into words. Please don't put words in our mouths. If we're thinking of a word, don't supply it! That makes us nervous. Remember that being a teenager is the most stressful point in our lives so far. Your stress only adds to it!"

Sharon, 15, New Jersey: "Kids aren't as immature as you think. They have more on their minds, more than people in the seventies and eighties had, because they have a lot of pressure and stress. I think the reason a lot of people don't get along with their parents is because their parents are in denial, thinking their kids have perfect lives when they really don't. My parents say they do everything they can, but sometimes I say, 'You need to back off and let me do what I can. Even if I make a mistake, some mistakes are just necessary in order to grow up.'"

Thoughts and Reflections

How are your parents at giving you advice? Are they diplomatic, or are they bossy? How do you receive the advice they give? Are you grateful, or uninterested? Sometimes your attitude will reflect their attitude as well.

_____

_____

_____

_____

Respect is a big issue for teenagers, both from your friends and parents. As the saying goes, "You cannot demand respect; you have to earn it." One way to earn respect is through communication, telling your parents how you perceive things. What are some ways to approach various topics with your parents so you can walk away with your self-esteem intact and even gain some respect?

_____

_____

_____

_____

Tips on the Parent-As-Friend Relationship

Martha, 15, New Mexico: "My parents tell me they don't want to be my friends as much as my parents. But what they really need to do is learn to communicate like friends. Why? Because teenagers have a tendency to listen to their friends, and people don't respect their parents nearly as much as they used to, so parents need to play two roles. You just need to be their friend so they trust you. Also, don't try to lay huge guilt trips on them when things don't go as expected; when the time is right, seriously tell them your reasons and how you see things."

Tom, 15, Colorado: "Parents can and should be friends. There is some awkwardness between parents and kids sometimes. Kids probably would rather tell their friends some things rather than their parents, because they feel their parents can't relate to them or they might get mad or give them a long speech or something. But it's important for parents to be friends with their kids rather than parents all the time. They need to be there for their kids, which is basically what a friend is—someone who will stand by you and help you out in times of need. What kind of stuff can parents do with their kids? Take them out to dinner sometimes, treat them to a movie, and buy them lots of new stuff (just kidding). The best thing they can do is socialize with their kids, and have a good time with them. Joke around. My dad and I are always joking around. My dad is always making corny jokes, and we are always laughing at him, teasing each other about things and, you know, faults or whatever is funny."

Thoughts and Reflections

The teenage years are an awkward time because you're not quite an adult, but you're definitely not a child anymore. This puts parents in an awkward position, too. On the one hand, they are your parents, yet as you become an adult, you can relate to them more as adults, and this can change the dynamics of your relationship. Much of this will depend on you. Including your parents in your circle of friends is not always easy. Some teenagers don't want their parents acting like their buddies. Other teenagers really enjoy this change in relationship. What are your feelings?

_____

_____

_____

_____

Tips on Overprotection and Trust Issues

Lucas, 14, foreign-exchange student: "Let your sons and daughters find their own worlds to live in. Don't be overprotective. When parents offer too much protection, their children cannot see the bad things that happen, and they have a distorted view of the world. Overprotection is not good! Someday, their kids are going to marry and have a family, and they are not going to know how to raise their kids. They will make the same mistakes. It is time to break the cycle. Parents always want the best for their children, so they push them, encourage them; they want their kids to do better. When I was living at home, I didn't understand this. Now that I am away from my parents, I can see how good they are and how much I love them. When you leave home for a while, you get a better perspective. You need to get away to see how good your parents are. Everything they do is for the best, even though it may not seem this way at the time."

Scott, 14, Indiana: "Please don't be so hard on your children. We are going through a lot these days. We're going through social and academic issues every day, and friendships, too! We have to do homework, and we want time to relax. Just don't *always* pressure us. It's okay to give us a little pressure, to show us you are behind us and you still want us to do good in our studies, but school isn't everything! Also, give us a sense of our own boundaries; we need them. And please, respect our privacy. If you sense something is wrong, ask us. If you find that asking once doesn't work, ask again and again. Maybe we just need some time to understand ourselves before we can explain it to you. Some parents just need to relax. They get too stressed with their own issues, and they pass the stress on to us, then they wonder why we are so stressed. Go figure! On the other hand, some parents shouldn't be so nice. They let their kids walk all over them. It's obscene. Trust me, those kids are going to need years of therapy when they become adults."

Mandy, 16, New York: "Here is my advice to parents: Don't expect your children to be perfect because you'll be expecting too much. Parents say, 'You better get all A's in school or you're grounded.' I really hear this from some parents. This is very stressful to their children. And when your children don't achieve these grades, they are grounded. That makes the kids feel really bad, like they have to try even harder than they were before. And if they were trying really hard, they just have to try harder to please their parents. You can't win! If your children look like something is wrong, or they are really stressed out, you should try to talk to them about it. Kids should be able to turn to their parents in times of need. There are teenagers who feel they can't trust their parents with anything, and there are parents who don't feel they can trust their kids with anything. It's a mess! It's really confusing when something is wrong and you don't want to approach your child because you don't trust them or they don't trust you. I think communication is the biggest area that parents and kids need to work on."

Chelsea, 16, Ohio: "Parents, no matter how hard it is, should always give a certain amount of trust to their kids. Don't lock them down completely because the kids will retaliate and make it that much worse. Have trust in your kids. You have to trust they will make the right decisions, if not at first, but they will learn and then make the right decisions. Always talk to your children, not at them—there is a big difference—and hope they listen."

Ken, 13, Minnesota: "I wish my family was closer. If I had one wish, it is that we eat dinner together. We never do."

Thoughts and Reflections

Do you feel your parents are overprotective? How does this make you feel? Is this something you can talk about with them? How would you approach the subject?

_____

_____

_____

_____

_____

Trust is a big issue to a teenager. How can you deepen the bonds of trust between you and your parents?

_____

_____

_____

_____

_____

There is a big difference between perfection and excellence. Many parents demand perfection from their kids. What about your parents? Do you demand perfection from yourself?

_____

_____

_____

_____

No matter how close a family is, stress and tension can easily pull a family apart. What are some things you can do to keep your family together?

_____

_____

_____

_____

A Funny Bone Moment:
What Parents Really Teach . . .

Sometimes we need to remind ourselves to laugh about things we once found stressful. Here is a tongue-in-cheek response to our parents' best intentions (submitted by Sarah, 17, Texas):

My mother taught me TO APPRECIATE A JOB WELL DONE: "If you're going to kill each other, do it outside—I just finished cleaning!"

My mother taught me RELIGION: "You better pray that will come out of the carpet."

My father taught me about TIME TRAVEL: "If you don't straighten up, I'm going to knock you into the middle of next week!"

My father taught me LOGIC: "Because I said so, that's why!!!!"

My mother taught me FORESIGHT: "Make sure you wear clean underwear in case you're in an accident."

My father taught me IRONY: "Keep laughing, and I'll give you something to cry about."

My mother taught me about OSMOSIS: "Shut your mouth and eat your supper!"

My mother taught me about CONTORTIONISM: "Will you look at the dirt on the back of your neck?"

My father taught me about STAMINA: "You'll sit there till all that spinach is finished."

My mother taught me about WEATHER: "It looks as if a tornado swept through your room."

My mother taught me how to solve PHYSICS PROBLEMS: "If I yelled because I saw a meteor coming toward you, would you listen then?"

My mother taught me about HYPOCRISY: "If I've told you once, I've told you a million times—don't exaggerate!!!"

My mother taught me THE CIRCLE OF LIFE: "I brought you into this world, and I can take you out."

My mother taught me about BEHAVIOR MODIFICATION: "Stop acting like your father!"

My father taught me about ENVY: "There are millions of less-fortunate children in this world who don't have wonderful parents like you do!"

13

Teens' Advice to Other Teens

*Stress shows up in my life whenever
I think something is not fair. I have to remember
that life is not about being fair or unfair; it's
about how you approach each situation.*

CASSANDRA M., 18

When it comes to taking advice, you are more likely to listen to your friends and peers than adults because people your own age have more experience with today's issues. There is no doubt that experience is the best teacher. Every teenager has had to deal with some huge, stressful situations and many smaller ones. This makes your voice of experience worth listening to. Every teenager who was interviewed was asked to impart their advice and wisdom about coping with the challenges of the teenage years. Here are some excerpts from their advice.

Tips on Being Authentically You

Alice, 14, Colorado: "When you feel like you've come to a dead end, just keep going, don't give up. People might think about suicide and other stuff, but I don't think it's worth it. Keep going and don't let other people's thoughts affect you. Be open-minded, but continue to think your own way. Be your own person. It's okay to have heroes, but don't be someone you're not. Consider Michael Jordan. Everyone wants to have his physique and be able to make blind free throws. It's good if you have someone to look up to and think, 'Oh, I want to be like that.' But you have got to be yourself, too! Otherwise, it actually lowers your self-esteem, which is not a good thing. I have friends who take role models like celebrities way too seriously. Don't take role models so seriously. They are human, just like you. Believe me, they can't be that much better than you."

Joe, 13, Colorado: "I really don't know what to say except focus on what you really like to do. If you like to skateboard, and you're stressed, go do that for a little while. Do something to take your mind off the problem. Get out of the house; that helps me a lot. Let's assume that some kid who picks up this book is going through some tough times. He or she is having an acceptance issue, or body issue or family issue. This is what I would say: Be true to yourself and don't let other people try to change you, 'cause who you are is what you are. Too many kids are caught up in the popularity thing. There's life after high school. It's like a gold fish jumping into the ocean—so don't drown in the fish tank!"

Thoughts and Reflections

Everybody wants to be accepted, respected and well-liked; this is human nature. The issue of who's popular and who's not takes center stage in middle school and stays there right through high school. Unfortunately, who's popular in school is often based on physical appearance. What are your thoughts on the popularity issue at your school?

_____

_____

_____

_____

Do you do certain things to be popular? If so, what?

_____

_____

_____

_____

Tips on Your Friends As Support for Stress

Morgan, 13, Tennessee: "I think teenagers really need to talk to people when they're stressed. My best friend has a lot of problems with stress, but she won't say anything about it. She doesn't cry. She doesn't let people help her, even when I know she's hurting inside. I think it would be better for her to talk about it with someone."

Lauren, 15, Colorado: "I suggest that everyone definitely get regular exercise because it works off stress so much better than doing nothing. I would also recommend having lots of friends. Try to be nice to everyone so you'll have lots of friends. Most importantly, try not to get too wrapped up in the popularity thing. In the long run, it's not that big of a deal. If you have an older brother or sister, talk to them if you don't feel comfortable talking to your parents. They have been there, and they can help. For instance, my sister tells me who to stay away from at school—the guys who are weird. That's what she calls them. She'll tell me to stay away from them. This one guy she told me to stay away from, I ended up liking, and I found out later he was not that nice of a person. She was right!"

Chelsea, 16, Ohio: "I recommend that you find someone you really trust and can talk to. Talking always makes someone feel better. It also makes you feel nice if you have a friend who comes to you with problems. It makes you feel really important because they chose you to talk to. Always have a friend you can talk to about anything."

Thoughts and Reflections

Talking to friends is essential to navigate the rough waters of the teenage years. Friends act as a sounding board as you process your thoughts and feelings. Friends can also offer support and, at times, advice. Which friends do you turn to in times of need? Are there some friends you cannot really share your innermost thoughts and feelings with? How good a friend are you when your friends come to you with problems? Are you a good listener?

_____

_____

_____

_____

_____

_____

Tips on Learning to Confide in Your Parents

Darcy, 18, North Carolina: "Talk to your parents. If you don't trust them, or don't think they will understand, talk to an adult you know really well and who understands you, perhaps a teacher, guidance counselor at school, a neighbor, or an older friend like a youth leader or pastor. Don't let hate and stress consume your body."

Michelle, 14, Colorado: "Parents are really good to talk to. You don't have to tell them every detail of your life, but you can start with something like, 'Yeah, this is what happened today.' Sometimes you don't realize your parents are not with you all day. So unless you want to start videotaping your life, you need to tell them something to satisfy them. They raised you, so they want to know how you're doing. It's their job. Regarding teenage stress, learn not to take other people too seriously. You're the one who makes the final decisions about everything in your heart. If you place more value on what others think about you rather than what you think about yourself, you're letting all these people stress you out. Then your decisions are not your decisions anymore."

Thoughts and Reflections

Do you feel you can talk to your parents about your problems? What issues can you talk to them about, and what are some stressors you don't feel comfortable sharing with them?

_____

_____

_____

_____

_____

_____

Trust is the door through which you walk to share your problems with parents. Is this door open between you and your parents? If not, what situation closed the door? Is there any way you can open the door again if you really need their help?

_____

_____

_____

_____

_____

_____

Tips on Being Optimistic

Keegan, 14, Colorado: "My advice is this: No matter what the problem, stick it out no matter how tough things appear to be. Try to find the best in every situation. Ultimately, finding the good is a lot easier than focusing on the bad, so you won't get so stressed out. If you take this approach, you won't get sick, and you won't want to commit suicide. Look for the good in things. You'll have the balance we all crave. For example, my parents are divorced, but it's best for them, and I realize that now. Try to find the good in every situation. If you can't work out the problem right away, hang in there. The answer will come eventually, because there is no sense in taking drugs or alcohol or committing suicide, no matter how big a problem might seem. That's not the best way, and in the long run, it doesn't solve anything. It just creates more problems."

Anjulie, 14, Colorado: "Look at things in a good way. Make the best out of what you've got. Even in the worst-case scenario, there will always be a silver lining. If you are having a bad week or getting bad grades, try not to focus on it. Don't become obsessed with it. When you dwell on things like that, more bad things can happen. You start thinking it's the end of the world when it's not! The worse thing you can do is dwell, because when you dwell you just make a bigger hole for yourself. You dig your own grave. Here is what I say about stress: Cry me a river, build me a bridge, and get over it!!!!!"

Sandy, 17, New Jersey: "Relax! Sometimes things are going to go bad, and you can't do anything about it. Some things will never get fixed, but you need to relax anyway. There's a quote I absolutely adore. It goes like this: 'Sometimes we stare so long at the door that's closed on us that we don't notice the one's that open.' That's happiness! It's horrible when you're sad and you look at something and keep thinking, 'Gosh this is so horrible. I can't handle this.' If you really think about it, you begin to realize that a lot of people have problems far worse than yours. Sometimes people take tiny things and make them humungous. Here is an example: If your boyfriend breaks up with you, you have like forty years to find somebody else. Even if you don't, which I am sure you will, you may walk this Earth alone, but you can still have fun because you can have millions of friends."

Thoughts and Reflections

Each of us has a critic inside our head who loves to criticize everything, including ourselves. Stress only makes the internal critic stronger. But like a radio station that's blaring bad music, you can turn the critic down and even change the channel to a positive voice—the voice of optimism. An optimistic outlook is essential for coping with stress, and it's also very effective in quieting the voice of the internal critic. List five things you can do to shift your attention from the negative to the positive side.

a. _____

b. _____

c. _____

d. _____

e. _____

Tips on Self-Discovery

Lance, 17, Kansas: "Just be yourself. Don't try to fit into a group you don't belong with. Just be you! If people don't accept you for who you are, they're not somebody you want for a friend, believe me! Learn from your mistakes so you don't make them again."

Jamie, 18, Colorado: "Try not to judge people. There are a lot of good people out there, and they're not always the ones with the beautiful faces and nice hair. Life is not about being popular. It's about being genuine, even if you're a diamond in the rough. You can't point to a person and say, 'Oh, you're ugly, and therefore you're not cool.' It's not fair! Everyone is equal, and in high school everyone has an equal chance to have friends and stuff like that. You've also got to grow up. High school is supposed to be fun, but there is a time and place for everything. In your senior year, you can't just be like, 'Oh, I'm going to throw eggs at your house.' You're seniors now, and what you do reflects on you for the rest of your life. You need to grow up! A lot of teenagers take life for granted. They don't sit back and look at the good things in life. They just keep going around with blinders on. My advice: Sit back and breathe. Most teenagers run at full speed; they don't know how to relax. You've got to go with the flow. You've got to take a look at everything around because it's the little things that count most in life."

Pam, 16, Virginia: "You should have a venting place for your anger and all your emotions. When it comes to being angry, you need to vent so you don't drive yourself crazy or kill yourself. I'm at this point where I've dealt with some stuff, and I'm like, 'Oh, I don't care. It's no big deal.' I think people shouldn't take everything so seriously and, you know, chill out when it comes to other people. I think teenage girls care way too much. They're all so ditzy. I see this and I'm like, 'Oh, you're going to give teenage girls a bad name.' I can't stand girls who flirt around the guys. I'm like, 'Uhh, shut up!' I think people need to be themselves and not try to impress other people. If someone is going to like you, they are going to like you for who you are, not for someone you pretend to be."

Lucas, 14, foreign-exchange student: "Don't be fake, and don't care about what other people say about you. Try to be nice and don't make fun of other people when they do something. That comes back to you—three times worse."

Thoughts and Reflections

The teenage years are for self-discovery. It is a period for inventing yourself. You do this by having many different experiences to determine your likes and dislikes, such as changing the clothes you wear, the music you listen to and the foods you eat. Being genuine means taking time to figure out who you are, what your values are and why you are the way you are. Before you can really be yourself, you have to know who you are. Take some time to ponder this profound question, and write down what comes to mind.

_____

_____

_____

_____

_____

The beauty of inventing yourself is that you can always reinvent yourself if you decide your current image doesn't fit with your values and beliefs. Our beliefs, values and attitudes will certainly change over time (just consider the music you used to listen to in grade school!).

Tips on Being More Genuine and Sincere

Eric, 14, Colorado: "Here's my advice: Don't let stress control your life. Stress can really build up and change who you are and how you act, and that's not really you. You don't want to be like that. Know who you are and stick with it! Never let go of who you are (we're talking confidence here, okay?). Who you are is who you are. You can never change that. You can try, but it will always turn out for the worse. You will end up trying to please other people, and that's not good. You are just making it harder on yourself. Usually, your friends say you're like this or you're like that. This helps you find out who you are, and you can go from there. If you change to meet other people's desires, you aren't being true to yourself. You are ruining yourself. Don't do it!"

Jennifer, 18, Ohio: "What advice do I have? Go with the flow! I've been stressed out all through high school, doing a lot of things. Now that I look back, it wasn't worth worrying about. I've experienced a lot more things than most teenagers have. I have learned to go with the flow. If you get stressed out about something, it's eventually going to go away—it's not just going to sit there. If it does, it's because you're stressing out too much. If you don't stress, it's going to go away. Also, it's not important what other people think about you. It's what you think about yourself. If you think you're a bad person, then maybe you need to say to yourself, 'Wow, maybe I really am. I need to change that.' You know? In the big picture, it's how you feel about yourself, not about the shoes you're wearing or the haircut you have. What really matters is what you think, not other people. This is so important."

Julia, 16, Colorado: "The most important thing as a teenager is knowing who you are! Know how you feel about things. Take a day or a weekend to be alone and do some soul searching. Find out what you believe. It's okay to have things you are uncertain about. Set aside room for those thoughts and feelings, too. You'll find yourself saying, 'I know this. I know I don't want to do that. Maybe now I think such-and-such a way on a certain subject, but

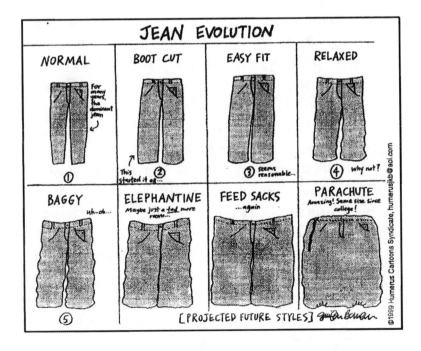

that can change.' Know what feels right and pay attention to it—that's your moral compass. Try just for a little while to shut out that outside world and discover who you really are. Be honest and truthful with yourself. In terms of relationships, I know a lot of people who try to be with people they think they can change. I think of a girlfriend-boyfriend commentary that goes like this: 'Oh, I'll go out with him, and then I'll change him.' That doesn't work with people, and that doesn't work with things in life. A lot of people try to fix other people. Fix yourself first. Make sure things are okay with you, and they will just seem to go smoother, though nothing is 100 percent sure or perfect—ever."

Rachel, 15, Colorado: "First and foremost, get to know yourself really well, and have good friends, but don't be dependent on them completely. Rely on them for some things, but you have to be able to take care of yourself. This is the most important thing! Learn to take care of yourself."

Thoughts and Reflections

Being authentic takes time. This means that you need to take time—quality time—to really find out who you are, what you believe, what you like and dislike, and why you think and feel about things the way you do. Here is a challenge: Spend a few hours alone with a journal. Make a list of ten things that are really important to you right now. Next to each item, write down why they matter. Then ask yourself when these became important to you. Keep writing, even if it seems hard at first. As you think through these issues, you will find that your mind becomes better at knowing who you really are.

Important Things	Why They Matter	When They Became Important
_____	_____	_____
_____	_____	_____
_____	_____	_____
_____	_____	_____
_____	_____	_____
_____	_____	_____
_____	_____	_____
_____	_____	_____
_____	_____	_____

Tips on Facing Your Fears

Phuong, 14, Colorado: "My advice to other teenagers? Jump into your struggles and challenges. Take them head-on. Get your entire self involved in the challenge, whether it is a death in your family, a class assignment, popularity issues, or a problem with your mom or dad. Just move on and get through it. When you do get through it, look back and say, 'I was a better person for it. Life feels better, or maybe I became stronger, understood life more or became more forgiving.' It is a great feeling when you come out of something, and you know you've learned something, and you've become a better person because of it. That's the best feeling in the world! A lot of people never learn from the lessons of life. People should take advantage of that and use these opportunities to learn."

Thoughts and Reflections

Avoidance is the most common coping technique for dealing with problems and stress. It is also the number-one most *ineffective* coping technique for dealing with stress. Conversely, confronting your problems head-on is recommended, but there are a few precautions to take. First, you always want to confront issues and problems diplomatically so you don't end up causing more problems. Second, you always want to walk away having learned from the situation. This not only helps you become a better person, but it helps ensure that you won't be caught off-guard by this problem again, and you will know how to deal with it should you encounter it down the road of life.

Here is a challenge: Make a list of your top three stressors (problems, concerns, issues). Then pick one of these and confront it (no blood, no bruises and no emotional damage). Finally, when all is said and done, ask yourself, What was the lesson? What did I learn that I can use to make my life better?

_____

_____

_____

_____

_____

_____

_____

_____

_____

_____

_____

Tips on Creating Options for Stress

Peter, 17, Florida: "If you're having problems with your parents, like if they drink too much and take it out on you, my advice is to spend as little time as possible at home. Play sports, join a team and get involved in as many school activities as possible—this is going to save your life! It saved mine. You've got to learn to rely on yourself. Otherwise you're going to see yourself as a permanent victim. So get out and get involved. You'll be glad you did."

Rob, 14, California: "If you're feeling stressed about life, go to school. There's a club at school for people who are stressed; it's called 'Everybody Else.' Everybody has stress—just different levels—so you're in good company. The bottom line is you've got to find a good way to deal with it. Do sports—any physical sport to let out your emotions—join a club or after-school group, find a friend. If these ideas don't work, maybe buy a punching bag and put it in your room. I did it and it helps!"

Thoughts and Reflections

Having lots of options is crucial to your sense of empowerment. As we all know, placing all your eggs in one basket can lead to a scrambled mess. In terms of dealing with stress, you have a great many options, such as sports, various clubs and a wide array of activities. Take inventory of your options. Make a list of five of your outside interests (outside of schoolwork). If you don't have five, what are some interests you can pursue?

a. _____

b. _____

c. _____

d. _____

e. _____

Sometimes we have a bias against activities we have never even tried. Years later, we discover it was quite good, and wonder why we waited so long. Here is a challenge: Pick one activity, either at school or in your community, that you have never done before (tai chi, photography, volunteer work or the yearbook) and force yourself to get involved. Go at least three times to give it a fair shot.

Tips on Focusing for the Future

Sarah, 16, New York: "I think you need to look toward your future; don't live in the past. So you may have a few bad relationships or serious family issues (we all do!), but don't hold it against the people who are part of it and don't hold it against yourself. Forgive and move on. We need to realize there is so much to look forward to. You're just a teenager; not even a quarter of your life is over. You have so much more to do, so much more to explore. And with modern medicine, we're going to be living a lot longer. You may as well make the best of it. I don't think stress should be such a major issue. It shouldn't be as big as it is. I think it takes a personal commitment to keep things from getting out of hand, and you need to work on it."

Chris, 16, Vermont: "Set your goals in life and make sure you do well in school. To motivate yourself, think about your future. What do you want to do, and where do you want to be five years from now? I want to go to college for a couple of years, then go down to North Carolina with some friends and learn how to blow glass at a college there. Then I'll see how things work out with that. These are my goals."

Thoughts and Reflections

Good stress management means living in the present moment while keeping one eye on the future. Goals are the bridge between today and tomorrow. Goals help make the transition from the present to the future a smooth one, rather than riding on a rocky road. Without goals, we tend to get swept along on the tides of change. The result is feeling victimized, which leads to more stress. Goals begin with personal interests. Before you make a list of goals, make a list of three personal interests (such as basketball, poetry, college or foreign cultures).

a. _____

b. _____

c. _____

Now that you have identified some deep-seated interests, it's time to make goals. The purpose of a goal is to help you accomplish your dreams, and at the same time, deepen your interests. Pick one of your areas of interest and list three to five goals that will move you in the direction of your dreams.

a. _____

b. _____

c. _____

d. _____

e. _____

Tips on Keeping a Good
Perspective on Life

Shelly, 16, Kentucky: "You have to let life's little problems go by, because if you don't, you're going to get wrapped up in them, and you really can't afford to be upset with little things. War is a big thing! And let's face it, when you're upset because your hair doesn't look right, it doesn't even compare to something like war! People are very uptight today; everyone is uptight about something. If you're uptight, you might not notice something really good. So just relax. Breathe through it. Let the rough times go by."

Harris, 15, Colorado: "My advice is to look at the big picture. What happens now (the petty things) is not going to matter in ten years, or even five years. Whatever you do is just what you do! Make a goal for yourself and work toward your goal. Keep focused on your goal. If people want you to do something that might sidetrack your ambitions, tell them you've got other plans. When that's done, you can experience other things. I would also suggest that teenagers spend more time with their grandparents. You should get to know them because you're not going to see them for much longer. I have only one grandparent left, and I try to talk to her as much as I can. Try not to get mad at your parents that much (although it's easy to get mad at times). Teenagers want to rebel, but try not to rebel against your parents. They love you a lot, and they want to help you out."

Thoughts and Reflections

Are you the kind of person who makes mountains out of molehills? Do you tend to exaggerate your problems to make a point (or even get sympathy from friends)?

_____

_____

_____

_____

Sometimes we are so consumed by our problems that we cannot see the bigger picture. Getting a perspective on any issue helps shrink it down to size. Once it's shrunken, it becomes more manageable.

Tips on Relocating to a New Town

Tom, 14, Colorado: "If you end up moving to a new school in a different state (I moved from Illinois to Colorado), don't be afraid to get out there and participate. Since I knew most of the stuff they were teaching at the new school, I always raised my hand and gave answers. The kids were like, 'Gee, how does this kid know so much?' That was one reason people wanted to get to know me. You have to provide reasons for people to want to get to know you. Be eccentric and crazy sometimes, and people will probably want to get to know you more—at least the other people who are eccentric and crazy will."

Tim, 13, Colorado: "When you move to a new town, try to find friends instead of keeping to yourself. For me, I just tried to find somebody who I liked and was nice. When I came here, I met a kid who was really nice, and he led me to my other two best friends. If you move to a new place, don't stay away from everybody. Invite some kids over to your house."

Thoughts and Reflections

In today's economy, people change jobs as quickly as they change socks. This means you might come home from school one day to learn that the whole family is moving across the country. Perhaps this has already happened to you. Moving to a new school can be very stressful. The stress comes from making new friends and feeling accepted by your peers. Can you come up with five ways to make new friends and build a greater sense of acceptance among your peers?

a. _____

b. _____

c. _____

d. _____

e. _____

Tips on the Importance of Resolving Anger

Kirby, 15, Colorado: "To cope well with stress, you need to be in touch with your entire self, not just your mind or your body, but mind and body together. You need to be in touch with your emotions and your spirituality, too. Those are two aspects a lot of kids seem to avoid because it makes them feel vulnerable. The truth is that we are more vulnerable when we don't pull it together. Teenagers need to learn to trust other people and themselves, and they need to to know what they are doing with things. Neglecting this leaves you with an identity crisis. You need to think about your own morals and values, and that should lead you to who you want to be. Also, communication is extremely valuable. If you don't talk to people, stress is going to stay inside you forever, and it's just going to keep building up more stress. You need to learn to get things out. I think it's important not only to speak but to find another way to get out the aggressive part of it. If you are only speaking aggressively, it's not good. You need to find some way to release your aggression."

Meghan, 13, Wisconsin: "Don't get grumpy with your parents because you'll probably get in trouble. The same goes with your teachers and friends. If you feel sad or angry, it's okay. Just don't take it out on other people. You'll only regret it later. So be nice to everyone, and that's how you'll be treated."

Amanda, 14, Colorado: "There are ways to deal with stress that don't involve inflicting pain on yourself like I did. You can hurt something else, not another person but an inanimate object like a pillow or stuffed animal. You shouldn't stress out too much because it is really bad for your health."

Abby, 14, Colorado: "Teenagers should deal with stress in their own ways, but not by cutting themselves. And they should not take stress out on someone else and shoot them, like the Columbine thing. I think those guys were really stressed out and had a lot of stuff on their minds that they couldn't get out because they didn't have anybody to talk to. I think they took it out on everyone else. I was in sixth grade then, and I was even more of a wimp than I am now. I was terrified! I totally understand why we do evacuation drills. A couple of weeks ago, we had an evacuation drill where we took buses over to the fair grounds. I didn't understand why we did that one, why we had to leave so quickly, but I understand why we do lockdowns and have to get up against the wall as close as we can so they won't see us. I understand that now."

Heather, 16, Vermont: "I think it's best to talk to someone when you are stressed or angry. Try not to take your anger out on other people who don't deserve it. Don't be afraid to talk to your parents, friends or someone else. You often feel great after discussing your problems with someone else. Find a hobby that makes you happy, and when you are stressed, use that hobby to help relieve yourself. Another idea: ASK someone for a MASSAGE!!! That is a great way to get rid of some stress."

Thoughts and Reflections

Dealing with anger is an ongoing process. Effectively coping with anger can prove challenging without some direction. Can you come up with five ways to deal with anger so you are headed toward resolution?

a. _____

b. _____

c. _____

d. _____

e. _____

Tips on the Cost of Worrying

Brittany, 16, Illinois: "I would say not to let stress get the best of you, because no matter what the problem is, it will be over soon—if you don't let it get the best of you."

Eric, 14, Illinois: "I would say this: Live your life! I live it the way I live it, and I know God has a plan and he's going to carry it out. Pray about it and live it. Even though you might fret about it sometimes (that's natural), don't make a habit of fretting because it's in the past, and you can't do anything about it now. Life is all about the present moment and the future. Don't live in the past. I'll be honest with you. I tend to worry a lot. I am a big worrier, so I am talking from experience."

Kyle, 18, Tennessee: "Don't worry too much about things you cannot control. Concentrate on doing your work and doing the things you really enjoy, like sports. Don't concentrate too much on stress and the things that worry you. You can get caught in all of that stuff, and it pulls you down."

Chris, 14, Colorado: "Try not to take life too seriously. It's not very fun when you have to take life seriously. Life should be fun!"

Thoughts and Reflections

Chris is right—life should be fun. What are some ways to bring more joy and happiness into your life to balance out the days when life hands you trouble?

a. _____

b. _____

c. _____

Are you a worrier? Worrying can be a huge waste of energy. It tends to immobilize you. Can you think of three ways to transform worrying into action so your stress can be resolved?

a. _____

b. _____

c. _____

Tips on Patience and Tolerance

Aaron, 13, Colorado: "You've got to learn to have patience. I will admit that I'm really, really impatient at times (so this is advice I need to take myself). I'll let things bother me and get me angry or sad, and really ruin my day. It's all about patience. This is my biggest suggestion to help other kids. Learning patience will get you through the rough times at this age."

Kathleen, 14, Colorado: "Try not to label people. I hate labeling because I get labeled a lot, usually falsely. They label me as a skater punk who does drugs all the time. When I had a coughing spell, my choir teacher said, 'That's what happens to you when you smoke too much.' I don't smoke! They try to make me feel guilty for things I don't even do. Be yourself, and be true to yourself. Try different things. Decide what you like and what you don't. Don't be persuaded by others. Don't let people make up your mind for you. You should be able to make up your mind."

Billy, 18, Connecticut: "I think kids my age should not care so much what other people think and just be themselves. Don't get involved in everyone else's business (romantic relationships). If you hear someone is going out with someone, just leave it alone and think, 'Hey that's cool.' If you don't like the person, don't tell the world, 'Oh, he's a loser, you shouldn't go out with him.' For freshmen, I have this advice: Get a good GPA your freshman and sophomore years and get a good base for your education. That way you can play around your junior and senior years and enjoy them. Try to make friends and do what you want to do. Don't go out for sports just because you want to be cool. Do what you really want to do."

Lacey, 14, Colorado: "Don't be afraid to express yourself. People are going to judge you whether you like it or not. So express yourself in a way that is true to you. If it's not comfortable for you, don't try it. You're only going to regret it in the end. I know there is a lot of social influence right now, but I've never heard adults say something like, 'Wow, what a freak, he's wearing this or that.' As you become an adult, you find more and more people who are a lot like you. With so many more people in the world to meet, don't think you are the only one who's different. If you are one of the more socially broadened people, there is no reason to be so snooty. Please realize that people are different and don't judge what they wear or what they do."

Thoughts and Reflections

Are you a patient person? What are some things that cause you to lose your patience? How can you be more patient, especially with your friends, your siblings and your parents?

_____

_____

_____

_____

How do you express yourself with the clothes you wear, the music you listen to, etc.? Do you ever give serious thought as to what statement you make about yourself with the way you express yourself?

_____

_____

_____

_____

Tips on Staying Grounded

Sean, 18, Michigan: "Stress is only what you make of it! Have you ever taken a stress-measurement test? If not, all they do is ask you many questions about your life and major events that have happened recently. Then, according to a number that is tallied up, it figures out your stress level. But I don't agree with that at all! Like I said, stress is only what you make of it. It is all about the way you cope with problems you're going through. There may be a person who has lost close family members and suffered terrible setbacks, but if that person can cope with stress and keep a calm head, their stress level won't be nearly as high as scientists would like to think. On the other side of the spectrum, someone who has lost an article of clothing might completely freak out, and in turn, have an extreme amount of stress. My advice is to find your own safe way to cope and deal with stress, and always remain calm."

Ali, 15, Colorado: "Don't let stress get the better of you. I have a friend who has let depression and stress just engulf him. Now he is depressed all the time, and he can't get out of it. He can't get out of this state of depression. I'll say, 'You know things will get better. Things will get better! Life goes on. No matter how crazy it gets, life will go on. There are going to be a few bumps along the way, but everybody encounters them.' He'll say, 'I've tried to make my life better. I've tried to get on with my life.' And I say, 'Obviously things are going to be rough for you right now, but things are going to get better.' And he will say, 'I don't want to wait that long.' So I tell him, 'You just have to be patient for some things in life. Life is not always going to go at your pace. You want it now, but it's going to come later. You can't let life get the better of you and get stuck in that space where you are feeling depressed and feeling like your life is over. Then you've lost; you've given up. You have no chance to enjoy life if you give up, so you have to hold strong and know that it will get better. Life goes on.'"

Thoughts and Reflections

How do you deal with stress? Are you the kind of person who freaks out at the littlest thing, or do things just tend to roll off your back?

_____

_____

_____

_____

What happens to you when stress gets the better of you? Do you ever get sick from having too much stress? Life does go on. Can you come up with three ways to train your mind to let go of the small things and keep moving?

a. _____

b. _____

c. _____

14

Teens' Concerns About the Environment

At this point, I think every little thing matters,
including throwing your cup alongside
the road or in the garbage can, or sitting there
with your car idling. If you think about it,
you should do something about it.
Even if it's a little thing, it will matter.

ALANA A., 14

Artwork by Keegan Brown

Chances are, the topic of global politics doesn't dominate your conversations with close friends or even family members. However, it's very likely that the subject of global warming comes up often, if for no other reason than there is a decreasing number of snow days each year, and in some parts of the country, the air conditioning stays on year-round. It's true that some students prefer not to think about environmental concerns because there are more personal issues to contend with. However, the environment is becoming its own Hot Stone; the living rock we call home is heating up.

When the topic of the environment is brought up, there is passion in your voices. In fact, it's no exaggeration to say that almost every teenager shows grave concern about the state of the planet these days. When the topic was brought up during these interviews, several teenagers from various parts of the country expressed a sense of helplessness, asking, "What can one person do?" Still others stood defiant in their outlook. Many teenagers mentioned that, indeed, one person can make a difference. In a stress-filled world, there is hope.

Lately, it's hard to listen to the nightly news and not hear some story about the continual decline of the planet Earth: global warming, animal extinction, ozone holes, nuclear waste, urban sprawl, water and air pollution, and closed landfills to name a few issues. Experts agree the Millennium Generation is the first generation to inherit a world that's in worse shape than all previous generations. To be perfectly honest, many of you would rather not think about what circumstances could lead to the Earth's demise, because this also means your demise. Yet, when asked about the environment, teenagers are not shy to voice their opinions, particularly older teenagers who are about to enter the real world. As one teenager from California said, "If you really stop and think about what shape the world is in today, it's depressing! If you think cleaning your room is an endless chore, imagine what cleaning up the Earth is like!"

Opinions and comments vary regarding what approach to take with the environment. Some opinions are general, some specific, some sarcastic, still others optimistic. Here are a handful of the comments from teenagers around the country.

Honoring Mother Earth

Michael, 18, Oregon: "We began this interview about issues that make me angry. Although I said I am an easygoing guy, I have to admit that one issue that pushes my buttons is the environment. There is such hypocrisy with regards to a booming economy and saving the Earth. It seems to me that these two concepts are mutually exclusive. We can't have it all. Americans make up a fraction of the world's population, but use over 25 percent of the world's natural resources. Something is wrong with this picture! I think most everyone knows we cannot keep living like this. The signs are everywhere! I don't know if all the problems can be reduced to greed, but it seems like the buck stops there. Gandhi once said, 'There is enough for everyone's need, but not for everyone's greed.' I think we need to take his words to heart with regard to natural resources and the concept of sustainability. How can we make this a better world? As the saying goes, changing the world is an inside job!"

Harris, 14, Colorado: "This is my advice: Remember, the planet Earth is your mother. It's where you live, your children are going to live and your grandchildren are going to live, so you've got to keep it in good condition. Don't destroy it. Whatever we use, we have to replace. This philosophy is called sustainability; it's a philosophy we are going to have to practice if we intend to remain alive for generations to come. When we destroy the planet, we destroy ourselves. I don't think people get this simple concept."

Alice, 14, Colorado: "I firmly believe that everyone should re-cycle. People should not be so wasteful. No offense, but I watch what people eat; at buffets, people will eat a fourth of what they pile on their plates and throw the rest away. Don't waste so much food! If we didn't waste so much, we wouldn't have such a prob-lem with landfills, which in turn, would help the Earth. My mom is really into that, and she got me hooked on it. Another idea: Maybe girls should not use as much hair spray because of the ozone and everything."

Thoughts and Reflections

Sustainable living means only using what you need and replacing what you use. It's human nature to take more than we need, whether it's food from a banquet table or clothes for school. How sustainable is your lifestyle? Give some thought to what you use and what you waste in the course of a day, including water, electricity, gas, paper, clothes and anything else you can come up with.

_____

_____

How do you think greed is related to our environmental problems? Can you come up with some examples?

_____

_____

_____

_____

Extinction Is Forever!

Amanda, 15, Colorado: "I have to admit that I am bothered by the state of the world right now. We are losing a lot of animals to extinction. I love animals. I don't want to see all of them gone in five years because their habitat is being destroyed. Also, I fear that pollution is going to be a really big problem. In fact, it already is in Colorado. We are depleting our natural resources, which are not limitless. There are more and more people with more and more cars, and more people running around, making more pollution and causing ozone problems. We already have ozone problems. Perhaps the first step is to get rid of some of the cars and find some other means of transportation."

Steven, 17, Maine: "If things keep going the way they are, our future, well, it's not going to be pretty, I can tell you that. We're tearing down the Earth and building on top of it—everywhere. Destroying our rainforests and endangering animals and all that doesn't make sense to me. I don't think it is necessary. We have enough here—look at the urban sprawl everywhere. Do we have a problem? Yes! Why do we have to keep knocking down old stuff to build new stuff? I just don't get it! It makes me mad that people don't think before they act. They say, 'Oh, we can cut down this portion of rainforest. It won't hurt anything.' They could kill how many types of animals? You're ruining God's creation. It's a beautiful place, and I don't think we need to tear it down."

Thoughts and Reflections

Some birds and animals placed on the endangered species list have made a remarkable comeback. Aside from the American bald eagle, can you think of any species that have been given a second chance?

_____

_____

_____

_____

Extinction of animals both near and far is a very real concern these days. Some estimates suggest that we are losing as many as one thousand species of plants and animals a day. Zoos, once a place to visit exotic animals, are now refuges for endangered species. If this is a topic that interests you, go online to your favorite search engine, type in "endangered and extinct species" and see what comes up.

Point of No Return?

Sean, 18, Michigan: "I feel the health and ecology of our planet is beyond repair. We have destroyed it with our own minds. We are too intelligent and need to have too much; we have total disregard for the possible side effects of our actions on our home planet. In effect, we are destroying ourselves. The planet is four billion years old, and although it may not be perfect, it is perfect for humans and all of life on it. Not a bad reputation, if you ask me. It's all the more reason to be mindful of our actions. However, I think many people don't care because they will be gone long before the end. But no one really knows when the end will come, so we better preserve all that we can—for ourselves and those to come."

Danielle, 14, Colorado: "I think that to make the physical world better, you have to make the spiritual and the mental world better. That's what it comes down to. We need to address the spiritual and mental issues of the world. Everyone is in the wrong way right now. Until everyone has it in their minds and hearts and souls that good is good and bad is bad, we are going to continue to have global crises, wars, pollution, etc. Until we have that correct in our minds, you can't make the world better."

Rob, 14, California: "What advice do I have to make the world a better place? We should all leave! No. Really, we need to act a lot more responsibly than we do. It's kind of ironic that adults tell us kids to act more responsibly, yet when it comes to the environment, adults are abysmal! I was reading the other day that the hole in the ozone is now larger than the United States. I thought it was maybe the size of Brazil—but that's huge! And it's still growing. You only get one planet! We have got to take care of it."

Anjulie, 15, Colorado: "I know this sounds selfish, but it's kind of hard to pay attention to these things at our age. I know some kids who think, 'I don't care, it's only the environment.' But they should care. These problems are going to come back and haunt us. It all comes down to the fact that we are messing ourselves up. I don't think people realize that by hurting the planet, we are hurting ourselves, and we have to start fixing things now. Even if we can't correct them right now, we can eventually figure out a right way. Here is a suggestion: Start respecting the land itself. The trees, the lakes and the animals are here for all of us. We have to show courtesy for them."

Thoughts and Reflections

Our thoughts and actions really express our attitudes and values about the environment. Take a moment to reflect on the current state of the environment. What values (leisure, freedom, privacy, health or recreation) do you associate with the ecology? Do you see any conflict in your values?

_____

_____

_____

_____

_____

Ancient wisdom suggests that everything connects, including the air we breathe, the water we drink, and the ground we walk on. Today, even the fields of physics and psychology suggest the same, both in terms of atoms of energy and global consciousness. We are connected in a great many ways. Can you come up with a few more ways we are all connected on the planet we call Earth?

_____

_____

_____

_____

_____

Please, Be Conscientious!

Rachel, 14, Colorado: "I don't think kids realize that every time they put a bubble-gum wrapper on the floor it affects the planet. They may think their town is such a small place it doesn't really add up, but it does. I know kids who are really concerned about the atmosphere and stuff, but they still smoke. That's pollution! What can we do to fix the planet? There are various things we can do. I don't know anyone who really wants anything bad to happen to his or her environment."

Lucas, 15, foreign-exchange student: "I think that here, in the States, teenagers care about the planet. My American friends tell me. This is the good part about the United States. There is awareness about the health of the planet. Americans do little things, like they don't throw garbage in the streets. Is America cleaner than Brazil? Yeah! In Brazil, water pollution is so bad you cannot drink water from the sink. You have to go buy it!"

Aaron, 13, California: "Basically, it's just being conscientious in what you are doing. I've seen a lot of things, like people throwing trash out of bus windows. That's probably my biggest pet peeve—littering. There is no excuse for this! There is no excuse for flicking cigarette butts out of car windows. Don't do it! Everyone knows energy is a big issue now. In terms of energy conservation, there are other forms of energy. I am glad to see more emphasis on wind energy, but we have a long way to go. What's my greatest suggestion to make this a better place to live in? Expand your mind and broaden your horizons. Be understanding of other cultures."

Thoughts and Reflections

Littering, trash and recycling are big themes in the effort to help clean the planet. Why do you suppose people litter? If you're like most people, you hate taking the trash out. Did you ever wonder where the trash collector dumps the trash?

_____

_____

_____

_____

_____

_____

Most people around the country participate in recycling programs, or at least they are supposed to. How active are you in the recycling of your waste?

_____

_____

_____

_____

_____

_____

See if you can list five ways to reduce trash by recycling.

a. _____

b. _____

c. _____

d. _____

e. _____

CALVIN AND HOBBES. ©*Watterson. Reprinted with permission of UNIVERSAL PRESS SYNDICATE. All rights reserved.*

Driven to Extinction?

Lauren, 14, Midwest: "Pollution is awful. We need electric cars. When you can see brown air, you know there is a problem. One solution is electric cars. I think everyone needs them. We need to start using the sun for energy. The whole ecology thing is so overwhelming. It's not just air pollution, water pollution or land-fills. Everything is connected. I don't know what the answer is, but we have got to find better ways to do things. This is a problem we are going to have to deal with; we cannot pass it off to our children, like it's been passed on to us."

Kyle, 18, Tennessee: "I think they need to invest more money in researching alternative power sources besides fossil fuels. We need to take a serious look at and invest in things that are renewable, like solar energy, fuel cells, wind and stuff like that. Then we wouldn't have to buy oil all the time, and you wouldn't have to worry about all the oil policies and beliefs that make the Middle East angry. The politics of oil will most likely be our downfall. The sad truth is there are so many other alternatives. I am coming to believe that politics is the greatest barrier to sound environmental policies. What can the average person do to make this a better environment? For starters, they can stop driving SUVs!"

Aden, 14, Colorado: "The whole environment thing has me nervous. I really think that we're ruining the world because we're cutting so many of the trees and polluting the air, the water, the ground—everything! It seems to me that if you could find a way to make a car, isn't there a way to make a car run on something other than gas? If you invented the car in the first place, you should be able to invent another type of car that doesn't run on gas. If there wasn't gas, what would you use? In California, where I am from, they have a huge air-pollution problem. I know they are working on these new hybrid electric-gas engine cars. Maybe there is hope after all."

Keegan, 14, Colorado: "Oh, gosh, where do we start? I say destroy every car. The problem, as I see it, is air pollution and global warming. So what we need are more fuel-efficient and environmentally safe cars, you know, hybrid cars. We all know this stuff, but we are not walking the talk. We need to walk the talk."

Thoughts and Reflections

There is no denying that Americans drive a lot! The average person makes three trips from home every day. As a teenager, getting your license is a right of passage, and driving a car is a symbol of freedom. What are some ways you can balance this freedom with the responsibility it carries? See if you can come up with four ways.

a. _____

b. _____

c. _____

d. _____

Have you thought about discussing hybrid cars with your parents? If this is something you might consider, be armed with information. Try going online and coming up with some good, solid evidence why owning a hybrid car would be a good idea.

One Person Can Make a Difference!

Chad, 18, Pennsylvania: "When I was younger, I didn't give much thought to the environment. I was too busy with my own life to care about things like the ozone hole or all the deformed frogs. All I could think about was getting my first car, a right of passage for every kid, I think. Now that I am leaving the nest to go to college, I see things so much differently. For instance, do you know that the ice sheet over one part of Antarctica is slowly slipping into the sea? When it goes in, the ocean level will rise several hundred feet, wiping out coastal cities everywhere, all because of global warming. This means total annihilation for millions of people, yet people go on right now ignoring this. I've stopped driving my car and instead ride my bike as much as possible."

Thoughts and Reflections

There are many alternatives to driving a car, including car-pooling. See if you can list four viable alternatives to having your parents or yourself drive.

a. _____

b. _____

c. _____

d. _____

When It Costs to Breathe the Air

Abby, 14, Colorado: "I was just talking to my parents on the way to Boulder. I was looking at the horizon. It was dark. I was like, 'Whoa, there is a lot of pollution here.' With so much pollution, I think we should car-pool. That's what we do in the morning, and that's what we do for Hebrew school. I think more people should do that. I think we should start riding bikes more, or like in the olden days, walk to school where it's possible. How can we make this a better world? That's a hard question. Maybe people should really think before acting. They should think about what the consequences will be. I don't think people do this enough."

Danny, 18, Ohio: "I think adults have given up on the environment. Sure, there are more laws and regulations about pollution and recycling and things, but we still have lots of environmental problems. If you listen to the news at all, you get barraged with sound bites about all kinds of problems, from antibiotics found in drinking water to toxic landfills. The list is nearly endless. I read *National Geographic* magazine, and in every issue, there is some article about the death of the planet. I think people are either in denial, thinking technology can fix it, or they have a sense of hopelessness about the whole thing. It's ridiculous to think one person can't make a difference. If we all have that attitude, we're really in trouble. One person can make a difference. Ride your bike one day a week. Buy food in the bulk section of the grocery store to avoid wasteful packaging. Recycle everything that's recyclable. It's not that hard to do, people! I saw a bumper sticker that is very appropriate: Clean up the Earth; it's not Uranus!"

Sandy, 17, Vermont: "In my civics class, we talk about environmental issues a lot. Vermont is an environmentally conscious state. You cannot talk about the environment without talking about politics. It would seem that environmental issues are just common sense, but politics cloud the issue. Take Nevada: The state was named the site of a national nuclear waste dump. The people there don't want it. No one does. So where do we put it? It seems that a lot of policies are created with very little thought about the future. It's also disturbing to me to learn that some corporations would rather pay fines to the Environmental Protection Agency than invest the money to fix the problem. Today's teenagers are the future. I just hope that we don't become corrupted once we get out in the real world."

Thoughts and Reflections

It's fair to say that many people live on autopilot, never really thinking about what they are doing. To be really conscious of what you do requires that you not only think of what you're doing, but what impact it will have on you (and everyone else) down the road. Reflect on what you did today. Are there any long-term implications from these actions?

_____

_____

_____

_____

_____

Seeing the World with New Eyes

Julia, 16, Colorado: "There is this saying, 'Don't ask what the world needs. Ask yourself what makes you come alive and then go and do that, because the world needs people who have come alive.' I agree with that 100 percent. There are these little things that maybe don't have to do with air pollution or water pollution, but have to do with this: 'Do I really need to have the water running while I brush my teeth?' or 'How long does my shower really need to be?' Take time to see the world, not through the little box we live in or through the tunnel vision that sometimes I get and maybe other people get, too. Try to see the world from other points of view. Look at it in a global scope. Don't have the opinion, 'I don't care about the world, because in two hundred years when this is really impacting us, I'm going to be dead anyway.'

Think about your children and your grandchildren who will have to live with the decisions that you make now. Try to see the world from different angles every day. Get a new set of eyes."

Thoughts and Reflections

What makes you come alive? What inspires you to be all you can be and reach your highest human potential?

_____

_____

_____

_____

It's been said that to solve our world problems, we need to get a new set of eyes. What this means is to change our perception of ourselves and the world we live in, which is not always easy. See if you can come up with three ways to "get a new set of eyes."

a. _____
b. _____
c. _____

Growing Pains

Alison, 14, Michigan: "As for cleaning up the pollution, it would take a lot of effort. It's not impossible, but it would be really hard to do. We would have to take the entire world and change our direction, all of our values and the priorities of our lives. We'd shift everything, which would be hard because lots of people have different views. We would have to do a major recycling effort and make major changes to everything we did. We would have to stop using cars, and we would have to stop using gasoline and oil and burning coal and all that. If we could do that, it would be great, but everyone would have to be on the same page, meaning we would all have to be at peace not at war. If we are all fighting, we can't make a worldly effort to do something. I saw this movie called *Pay It Forward,* and the message was to help other people make a better world. We could probably make peace with each other with the *Pay It Forward* thing. You would do three good things for three other people, and they pay it forward by doing three other things for three people. It could be big things, too, something they couldn't do on their own. It might just make us realize, 'Hey, it's easier to care about other people.' I think it's a good way to spread the word. The idea is similar to random acts of kindness. It's about doing things for the betterment of the world."

Thoughts and Reflections

The expression "pay it forward" is another way of saying, "Practice random acts of kindness." In this case, not just for other people (although this is a great idea) but for the planet itself. Can you come up with at least five small acts of kindness for Mother Earth?

a. _____

b. _____

c. _____

d. _____

e. _____

Getting Back to Nature

Michelle, 14, Colorado: "We've got to start now! Some people are like, 'Well, we don't have this problem now. You know, the ozone hasn't melted anything yet.' Yeah, right! Whatever! But I mean it will, so I think we need to start addressing these issues now instead of sticking our heads in the sand. We need to deal now with issues that are going to affect our future. We have to make this Earth livable for a long time. It's not like we can just pack up and go to Mars when we are done trashing this place. People are so out of touch with the natural world. I think if people spent more time in nature, they would see it's too precious to lose. People don't realize it, I guess. I don't know how to explain that nature is just a great thing. You have to go out in the woods or up in the mountains to realize this. I just don't want this to end, you know."

Artwork by Phuong Nguyen

Thoughts and Reflections

With more and more technology becoming a part of our lives, it is easy to become further and further removed from nature. There are some people who never even walk outside to get a breath of fresh air. Lack of contact with nature exaggerates this separation even more, and the consequences are not healthy. Can you come up with five ideas to "get back to nature"?

a. _____

b. _____

c. _____

d. _____

e. _____

The Cool Clean Waters Ran Here Once

The cool clean waters ran here once
Their babbling pools a refuge for the shy creatures of
   the night
The shade of the trees a quiet place for us to sleep

The warm sun shone here once
When the world was green and new
Warm rocks are beds for those who know how to find
   them

This once-green paradise is now one of bustling
Fierce animals who honk and rev in conflict with the
   changing light
Creatures still dwell here, in high-rise dens
And in places, the water still runs cool

And the sun still shines brightly
To warm an upturned face.

Haila Ashley, 16

A Passionate Place

As we look and ponder,
With our eyes gazing far,
We often wonder,
Where exactly we are.

This land so green,
Like the leaves of a tree,
What exactly does it mean,
To see what we see?

With the waters so calm,
As they extend to the unknown,
Just like the opening of my palm,
That have a unique yet beautiful tone.

We take this place for granted,
And overlook its meaning.
If only we'd realize the power we've been handed,
Instead of decieving.

Giving up on this place,
Will only cause pain.
If we value every space,
Then we'll have everything to gain.

Noah Rhodes, 16

Lessons Learned!

*I've learned that high school is not your
whole life, just a few years of it!*

BECKY S., 17

Life offers many lessons, even ones we don't want at the time. You may spend a fair amount of time in the classroom, but school is not the only place where real learning takes place. Lessons of equal or greater importance are taught through parents, friends and other people who we tend to dislike at times. Every time we are faced with a situation, we are encouraged to learn something from it. Chances are, if we missed the lesson the first time around, it will come back again and again till we get it.

At the end of each interview, everyone was asked if they had any additional comments they wished to share about what they had learned from life so far. Here are some final thoughts and reflections on life's lessons from a teenage perspective. As you read through these, ask yourself how you can learn from their experiences.

Lessons on Happiness

Phuong, 14, Colorado: "I have learned to really enjoy life. Some people say, 'Enjoy your teenage years, but you'll be glad when they're over.' I don't think that's true, not for me anyway. I like the way I am right now. I don't want to be older. I want to enjoy all there is right now because we are only young once. I want to be right here and now. You can spend so much time living in the future that you miss out on the present."

Alice, 14, Colorado: "I have learned that a teenager's life is not simple. It's very, very hectic and chaotic. If it's simple there is something wrong with your life because every teenager has his or her problems. I don't like the way the world revolves around money and how money is equated with happiness. I also don't like the TV view of how everyone has to be the model type person. If you can take a class like Health Quest, do it! It gave me a new perspective on life and other cultures. I kind of knew about the Chinese people, since I'm Asian, but it helped me understand more deeply about how to think, how to relate, and how to deal with stress and stuff."

Thought and Reflections

What is it about life that you enjoy? List three things that bring a smile to your face.

a. _____

b. _____

c. _____

Do you think money equals happiness? Name three things that bring happiness to you but require no money.

a. _____

b. _____

c. _____

Lessons on Knowing Yourself

Emily, 13, Illinois: "If I have learned one thing so far in my life it's this: Be yourself! If people don't like you, that's their problem—they don't deserve to be your friend. You deserve everything good in life, you deserve the best, because you're worth it. This is so important to remember!"

"We're at that awkward age...too old to
blame our parents for everything and too
young to blame it all on the government!"

Reprinted by permission of Randy Glasbergen. ©Randy Glasbergen, www.glasbergen.com

Colin, 15, Florida: "I have learned that you cannot please everybody all the time, including your parents. If you are always bending over backward to please other people, you will never be happy."

Julia, 16, Colorado: "If I have learned one thing, it's this: Get in touch with yourself and see what you can do, where you are going in life. A lot of people try to fix other people. Fix yourself first. Make sure things are okay with you, and then things will just seem to go smoother. Though nothing is 100 percent sure or perfect, it makes no sense to dwell on the negative."

Thoughts and Reflections

What do you think it means to be yourself? Can you give two ideas?

a. _____

b. _____

Do you try to please others at your own expense? Name two people you find yourself trying to please but end up feeling taken advantage of.

a. _____

b. _____

Sometimes, in being a friend to others, we try to control them by helping or "fixing" them. We really cannot help someone else until we fix ourselves. What are two things about yourself that need some attention and improvement (sarcasm, rudeness or selfishness), and what are two ways to work toward that improvement?

1. _____

   a. _____

   b. _____

2. _____

   a. _____

   b. _____

Lessons on Prejudice and Forgiveness

Aaron, 13, Colorado: "I have learned not to stereotype people, because if you do, you're going to miss out on meeting some really neat people. Try to meet people from different crowds, even if they are not like you, people you might think you'll not get along with. That's what I try to do. I've got other branches in my own crowd. There's a lot of ways you can meet new friends and get along with people. Stereotyping results in prejudice, which is quite limiting. Also, be patient. Patience is really important in coping with everything."

Eric, 16, Arizona: "I have learned the importance of forgiveness. I think it is important to forgive people. If you hold grudges, you are always thinking about it. Every time you see him or her in the hall, you think to yourself, 'Oh, I hate that kid.' I've learned that if you don't hold a grudge, you don't think about it, and you move on with your life. You forgive them for what they did, and they talk to you. You put the ball on their side of the court, and let them return it whenever they want to. You did everything you could do. You forgave them, and now you can move on with your life."

Thoughts and Reflections

Do you feel like you've been stereotyped? Describe how you feel when labels are attached to you that you know are *not* true.

_____

_____

_____

_____

Stereotyping begins as pattern recognition (hair color, skin color or clothing) and continues by coloring the pattern with attitudes and opinions. Stereotyping is a generalization made toward one person, usually someone we don't know very well and might feel threatened by. Who are you prone to stereotype?

_____

_____

_____

_____

Forgiveness is a powerful antidote for anger. Remember that when you forgive somebody, whether it's face-to-face or in your heart, don't expect an apology. You might be waiting a very long time. When you forgive somebody, do it for yourself and move on with your life. Are there people (former friends) who you feel have violated you? Make a list (two to three people) and set your mind to forgiving them. (Think of what you can do to let the matter go.)

a. _____

b. _____

c. _____

Here is a challenge: Sometime in the next week, identify someone at school (or work) who you have stereotyped and break the ice by introducing yourself. Get to know the person behind the image you have created for him or her.

Lessons on Friends, Change and Mistakes Made

Leslie, 14, Minnesota: "I have learned that one good friend is worth more than ten superficial ones."

Stacy, 17, Massachusetts: "I have learned that coping with the bumps in the road, no matter how big or small, is what makes a happy life. There are some things you just can't change. You have to learn to deal with it. I know that sounds sort of harsh, but you really do. You've got to figure things out for yourself sometimes, even if people are telling you to do this and do that. You've got to learn for yourself, or you won't really have learned the lesson for real."

Amy, 17, California: "I have learned that there are consequences for every action, and no matter how much you want something, shoplifting is not worth it."

Thoughts and Reflections

One of the themes of this book is how important good friends are. Do you have lots of friends, or do you have lots of acquaintances? Make a list of your three best friends (you may have more but start with three), and explain why you consider them to be such an important part of your life.

a. _____

b. _____

c. _____

It's true. Our actions do have consequences, sometimes painful ones. What are two situations you got into that had some powerful consequences? What things have you done in life that just weren't worth it?

_____

_____

_____

_____

Lessons on Expanding Your Horizons

Lucas, 14, foreign-exchange student: "I would recommend that teenagers travel and see the world. It's a good thing! They should do it so they can get a better perspective of the world (and their parents, too!). Traveling to different countries allows you to see how life is there and how it differs from your own country. Maybe travel increases tolerance, too. We need more tolerance in the world. Be true to yourself. Be very strong, focus on the good things, and the bad things won't matter as much."

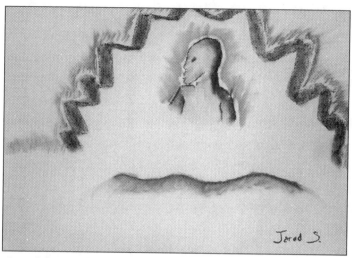

Artwork by Jarod Stewart

Thoughts and Reflections

Traveling to another country is an education all by itself. Learning from various cultures, speaking new languages, eating new food and observing how people live in other parts of the world is a very valuable experience. Everyone who travels to a foreign country comes back a changed person: more humble, more tolerant and more worldly. If time and money weren't factors, where would you like to travel? Identify three countries you have not been to, and explain why you would like to go there.

a. _____
b. _____
c. _____

Lessons on Faith, Hope and Love

Amanda, 14, Colorado: "I have learned a lot about faith. You shouldn't get discouraged if you did something wrong and feel really stressed about it. Life will get better. Remember that you can always make it up to yourself, and you shouldn't stress out about something in the past. There is always more than one way to deal with depression and stress. Remember that you should always talk to somebody about it and let it go, rather than letting it get worse."

Darcy, 18, North Carolina: "Always know you have a friend in God, and there is always someone out there you can trust. Drugs aren't worth it, and girls, sex makes you feel more empty than you already do. If you are trying to fill the emptiness in your life, God is holding your hand, and all you have to do is ask for help!!"

Kristin, 14, Missouri: "I think we should all remember that we are never alone, and that everything will be better in the end. If it's not better, then it's not the end."

Michelle, 14, Colorado: "I think we need to remember how important the concept of love is. Without love, there would be no purpose in life. I don't think God sent us here to have all this hate. So having love (compassion, tolerance, patience and joy) for everybody is important in having a good life. That's just how it is. Humans are supposed to have human relationships. If you don't love people and nature and everything, you won't have human interactions. Love is essential with everything."

Thoughts and Reflections

How would you describe your faith: a belief in yourself, or a belief in something bigger than yourself? List three things that strengthen your faith. What can you do to remind yourself of this belief?

a. _____

b. _____

c. _____

The paradox of life is that, in a world of six billion people, our own lives are rather short and insignificant, yet at the same time, precious and essential to the universe. We are part of a grand scheme, yet from any one perspective it's hard to see the entire picture. To make matters worse, stress can act like blinders and narrow our focus. What are some things to remind you that (1) you are essential, and (2) you have a contribution to make? (If you cannot think of something right now, ponder this and come back to it.)

_____

_____

_____

Ask anybody who's honest enough, and they will also mention the importance of love. What are your thoughts on love and compassion?

_____

_____

_____

Keegan, 14, Colorado: "If you can, try to get into a stress-management class. It will be the best thing that ever happened to you. It was for me. It changed my life for the better. I cannot even begin to tell you. So do it! Do it now."

Thoughts and Reflections

What lessons have you learned that are worth remembering? Think of two and share them here.

a. _____

b. _____

Finding the Heart

Each person at birth,
Is born with mind and soul.
And our search on Earth,
Begins with a goal.

This goal we seek,
Is hard to achieve.
Life can be meek,
But you have to believe.

Hope makes us strong,
With our emotions so sweet.
To know that you belong,
Makes sadness retreat.

Because inside of each body,
And inside of each mind.

Is something we cannot see,
That is one of a kind.

How do we look?
Where do we start?
What if we took?
This thing apart.

It's simple you see,
It all begins here.
There's a special place to be,
Where there is no fear.

This place contains the heart,
Which is needed so true.
It can be broken by a dart,
Or a feeling of blue.

But we need it right now,
To make our lives complete.
We must figure out how,
To do away with deceit.

Noah Rhodes, 16

Toll-Free Hotline Numbers

Having a problem and no one to talk to about it only makes you feel more alienated and troubled. Help is only a phone call away. These toll-free numbers are here to help you or someone you know who needs help. Please use them if you are in trouble or need someone to listen, help you understand your situation or find a viable solution.

AIDS Hotline 800-342-2437

Alcohol Hotline...........................800-ALCOHOL (800-252-6465)

Depressive Illness Foundation 800-248-4344

Dyslexia Hotline...800-222-3123

Eating Disorders Treatment 800-841-1515

Epilepsy Foundation of America 800-332-1000

Hill-Burton Free Hospital Care....................................800-638-0742

Juvenile Diabetes Foundation 800-533-2873

Missing and Exploited Children Hotline 800-843-5678

National Council on Compulsive Gambling...............800-522-4700

National Institute on Drug Abuse 800-662-4357

PMS Access..800-222-4767

Runaway Hotline..800-621-4000

Sexually Transmitted Diseases....................................800-227-8922

The Cast of
Hot Stones & Funny Bones II

If you would like to be part of the sequel to *Hot Stones & Funny Bones,* please send an e-mail with the words "I want to be interviewed for HS&FB 2" in the heading to *BrianlukeS @cs.com.* Thanks! We look forward to hearing from you.

Upcoming Topics

- Freedom and Responsibility
- Peer Pressure
- Managing Time Better
- More Funny Bone Moments
- Creative Outlets
- Good Vibrations: Music to Relax By
- Parental Mistakes
- Sports and Exercise
- Thoughts on Being an Adult
- More Lessons Learned
- If You Had One Wish for the World

About the Authors

Brian Luke Seaward, Ph.D., is considered a pioneer in the field of health psychology, and he is internationally recognized for his contributions in stress management, human spirituality and mind-body-spirit healing. The wisdom of Brian Luke Seaward can be found in college lectures, medical seminars, boardroom meetings, church sermons, keynote addresses and political speeches all over the world. He is respected throughout the international community as an accomplished teacher, consultant, lecturer, author and mentor. Dr. Seaward has authored more than ten books, many published in several languages. He is a faculty member of the University of Colorado at Boulder and the University of Northern Colorado, and his books, *Stand Like Mountain, Flow Like Water* and *Stressed Is Desserts Spelled Backward,* have helped tens of thousands of people overcome personal life crises. When not instructing or presenting stress-management programs, Dr. Seaward relaxes in the Rocky Mountains of Colorado. He can be reached at *www.brianlukeseaward.net.*

Linda K. Bartlett, M.A., is an eighth-grade teacher for St. Vrain Valley Schools. She has worked in the public school system for twenty-six years promoting numerous business, community and school partnership programs. She is the co-creator of the Interactive Mentor Partnership Program with Ball Aerospace and Technologies Corp. Her current creation is Health Quest, a course designed in collaboration with community health and wellness professionals to teach life skills to help teens reach optimal health.